Twentieth-Century Scottish Poetry

Douglas Dunn was born in 1942 and grew up in
Inchinnan in Renfrewshire. He worked as a librarian in
Britain and the United States until 1971, when he
became a full-time writer. He has published ten
collections of poetry. In 1991 he was appointed
Professor in the School of English at the University of
St. Andrews.

TWENTIETH-CENTURY SCOTTISH POETRY

Edited by DOUGLAS DUNN

faber and faber

First published in Great Britain in 1992
by Faber and Faber Limited
3 Queen Square London WC1N 3AU
This edition published in 2006

Printed in England by Mackays of Chatham

The publisher acknowledges a subsidy from the Scottish Arts
Council towards the publication of this volume.

A CIP record for this book
is available from the British Library

ISBN 978–0–571–22838–6
ISBN 0–571–22838–0

10 9 8 7 6 5 4 3 2 1

Contents

Language and Liberty

The first part of the history of Scottish literature is part of the history of English literature when English was several dialects; the second part is part of the history of English literature when English was two dialects – English and Scots; the third part is something quite different – it is the history of a provincial literature. And finally, there is no longer any tenable distinction to be drawn for the present day between the two literatures. (T. S. ELIOT, 'Was There a Scottish Literature?' *The Atheneum*, 1 August 1919)

Seldom can Max Weinreich's famous aphorism – 'a language is a dialect with an army and a navy' – have found such a classy illustration. Were they to appear now, Eliot's crudely potted history and questionable philology would look calculated to offend. However, in 1919, Eliot reflected the status quo of his day in politics and literature. Few Scottish readers would have felt irked, as if by a snub, while the book he was reviewing, G. Gregory Smith's *Scottish Literature: Character and Influence*,* went some way towards encouraging Eliot's decisions. Smith interpreted the vernacular Scots poetry of Ramsay, Fergusson and Burns as the last kick of a vividly indigenous Scottish poetry. Indeed, many Scottish readers would have supported Eliot's defensively British (or English) post-war anxiety before the threat of European cultural disintegration.

At almost exactly the same time as Eliot deliberated on Scottish literature as a meaningless phrase, Christopher Murray Grieve (better known as Hugh Mac-Diarmid, the pseudonym he adopted in 1922) was demobbed from the Royal Army Medical Corps when not far off his twenty-seventh birthday. Although in the kindliest of military corps, Grieve had participated in a World War, fought, or so it was believed, for the rights of small nations, and, in the process, grown aware of his own country. An articulate, political (as opposed to sentimental) Scottish nationalism still lay a few years in the future. Grieve's national awareness was first of all one of a country in a state of cultural stagnation and contented provincialism. Grieve (b. 1892) and Edwin Muir (b. 1889) were contemporaneous with modernism's early adventures. Deplorable as the local literary condition was – things were more interesting in painting and architecture – neither Grieve nor Muir was insulated from European literature and ideas.

We Moderns,† Muir's collection of aphorisms (published under the pseudonym Edward Moore), could be hailed as the first publication in modern Scottish literature after the death of Scotland's proto-modernist, John Davidson, in 1909.

---

*Macmillan, 1919.
†George Allen & Unwin, 1918.

That is, if the book deserved it in anything other than a bibliographical sense. Muir was to disown it as 'pinchbeck Nietzschean prose peppered with exclamation marks'. It is easy to see why. Equality and humility, for example, were dismissed as 'great fosterers of the mediocre'. It was to be around these and similar qualities that Muir would later form his personality and work. Grieve, however, was to cultivate Nietzschean cerebral solitude and super-élitism as a platform for the lofty intellectual superstructure of his alter ego, Hugh MacDiarmid. It is tempting to think that Muir and Grieve parted company in advance of meeting.

Weariness of immediate resources and lack of predecessors are suggested by the sort of thing Grieve was writing in April 1918:

> The ancient chorus of the rich blue flood,
>   The mystic sundance of the Middle Seas,
> What have you in your heart, Scots Borderman,
>   Prithee, that can compare with these?

If he had been reading John Davidson's later poetry (and it is almost certain he had), then it made little impact on Grieve's own until some time later.

In his 1919 review Eliot wrote that:

The historian of literature must count with as shifting and massive forces as the historian of politics. In the modern world the struggle of capitals of civilization is apparent on a large scale. A powerful literature, with a powerful capital, tends to attract and absorb all the drifting shreds of force about it. Up to a certain limit of dissimilarity, this fusion is of very great value. English and Scottish, probably English and Irish (if not prevented by political friction), are cognate enough for the union to be of value. The basis for one literature is one language.

That finely crafted detail – 'Up to a certain limit of dissimilarity' – expresses perfectly the established attitude that MacDiarmid determined to contest. Scottish culture had become provincial because a nation had allowed itself to become a province. A return to Scottish principles of poetry and thought was therefore understood by MacDiarmid to be necessary. After a few attempts at poetry in the Scots vernacular – at first, MacDiarmid thought little could come of these experiments – he realized that the language of his poetry should externalize the Scottishness of his mind and imagination. Dissimilarity was, therefore, to be cultivated in a language that would take him beyond conventional Scottish wisdom as expressed in Stevenson's phrase, 'a strong Scotch accent of the mind'. Eliot sketched Scottish literature in four phases, the last being its assimilation into English literature. For several productive years, marked with fiery self-awareness, Grieve/MacDiarmid set himself to create what, in Eliot's terms, amounts to a *fifth* phase. As well as a loathing of the provincial, an even more remarkable instinct lies at the heart of MacDiarmid's struggle. It is nothing less than the recovery of a distinctive Scottish psyche and its true objectives and concerns from the slow sundering initiated by the Union of 1707. It is hard to see how such a feat of psychological archaeology was supposed to have been feasible. Clearly, though, in MacDiarmid's poetry in Scots, and in the work of the poets he inspired, it was the ideal that mattered. The desire to reconstruct a national identity was never matched by an accurate expression of what that identity might be outside of poetry and philosophy. *Political* nationalism turned out to be a phenomenon of more recent times.

Sangschaw, MacDiarmid's first collection of lyrics, appeared in 1925. *A Drunk Man Looks at the Thistle* and *Penny Wheep* came out the following year. Other poets were also writing in Scots and had appeared in *The Scottish Chapbook*,* which Grieve founded and edited and where he began to proselytize the vernacular cause. But none of them wrote with anything like MacDiarmid's intuitive philology or campaigning critical ardour. Perhaps the most remarkable aspect of MacDiarmid's first three major books (at least, with hindsight) is that his poetry remained undamaged by the extensive prose suburbs that grew around it. The same can hardly be said of his later poetry, which was invaded by prose (some of it not even his own), purposive clamour, and political extremism – although that had existed from the beginning.

MacDiarmid's poetry in Scots is different from his contemporaries', although Lewis Spence was a forerunner, and poets like Violet Jacob and Marion Angus at least helped to keep the Scots language alive. Nor is it like Stevenson's verse in Scots, Burns's, Fergusson's, Ross's or Ramsay's; and it is unlike the poetry of the Makars, William Dunbar, Robert Henryson and Gavin Douglas, whose artistry and accomplishment MacDiarmid held up as exemplary. It was not an art of simple rediscovery so much as one of transformation in the crucible of modern sensibility. Diction and cadence combine to suggest that a lapsed phonology has been restored to the Lowland Scottish voice. In MacDiarmid's best lyrics – 'The Eemis Stane' is a good example – the poetry depends on a daring, speculative image. In that poem, it is the world seen as a loose gravestone, or an unsteady boulder on which words have been inscribed, now buried beneath the moss and fame of history. The poem seems to withhold its meaning. It could evoke a poet glimpsing posterity, perhaps his own, and the vanity of having believed this

---

*Fifteen issues were published between August 1922 and November/December 1923. William Soutar, Edwin Muir and Neil Gunn were among its contributors. In retrospect, however, it looks more like a remarkable one-man show, serving to present MacDiarmid's poetry in Scots, and C. M. Grieve's editorials.

possible. It could be the world seen as a stone book in which its written chronicles fade into the half-forgotten and incomplete. What the poet might glimpse in the sky is a vision of the human record. It is the poem's mysteriousness that is exact, not its meaning. It is a poem that persists in a state of permanent unfamiliarity.

Equally remarkable is that a stunningly modern image should be conveyed in a language that had been interrupted by history. 'The Eemis Stane' is not only a fine poem; it is a gesture through which the reader witnesses a lapsed language modifying itself in order to engage with a new aesthetic. MacDiarmid's essays and comment in Scottish Chapbook leave you in no doubt that he intended Scots (or the Vernacular, as he called it then) to serve a double function: modernity, and the reconstruction of a national identity fitted to inhabit the Scottish republic of which he dreamt – but no, he was not a dreamer: he was a visionary exclaimer, an urger of extremes and upheavals. In October 1922 he rediscovered in the Scots language 'unrealized qualities which correspond to "unconscious" elements of distinctively Scottish psychology.' In March 1923 he wrote that

we base our belief in the possibility of a great Scottish literary Renaissance, deriving its strength from the resources that lie latent and almost unsuspected in the Vernacular, upon the fact that the genius of our Vernacular enables us to secure with comparative ease the very effects and swift transitions which other literatures are for the most part unsuccessfully endeavouring to cultivate in languages that have a very different and inferior bias.

He also noticed a 'strong moral resemblance' between Jamieson's Etymological Dictionary of the Scottish Language* and James Joyce's Ulysses.

A vis comica that has not yet been liberated lies bound by desuetude and misappreciation in the recesses of the Doric [Scots]; and its potential uprising would be no less prodigious, uncontrollable, and utterly at variance with conventional morality than was Joyce's tremendous outpouring.

Passionate modernism and a low opinion of the English language and its literature were united in MacDiarmid's excitable advocacy:

The Vernacular is a vast unutilized mass of lapsed observation made by minds whose attitudes to experience and whose speculative and imaginative tendencies were quite different from any possible to Englishmen and Anglicized Scots today. It is an inchoate Marcel Proust – a Dostoevskian debris of ideas – an inexhaustible quarry of subtle and significant sound.

MacDiarmid went far beyond the customary critical risk of trying to create the taste in which a new poetry could be appreciated. He leapt from his own

---

* 1808; the revised, expanded edition of 1879–82, in four volumes, is the one on the reference shelves of most Scottish libraries. There is also an abridgement in one volume ed. W. Metcalfe, 1912.

unpredictable inspiration towards the would-be deliverance of a nation-language. His action can be seen as extraordinarily generous; or it can be seen as an attempt to externalize an interior bigotry, a great heave of will, or a charge against history's facts and fences. By 'minds', 'attitudes to experience', and 'speculative and imaginative tendencies', he meant that the poet was obliged to remake Scottish poetry on the basis of a pre-1707 mentality. That is, write *as if history had never happened*; or write in such a way that history would be rewritten, and unknitted, in the work. Both, I think, are involved. But the first is a forlorn choice, and the second, to say the least, a challenge. In terms of modernism, though, it can be seen as MacDiarmid's Scottish equivalent of Pound's eccentric scholarship, Eliot's literary erudition and concern with civilization and its values, or William Carlos Williams's belief in the American Grain.

The difference is that MacDiarmid was trying to make a nation as well as poetry. He did so with a language that through disuse had become the victim of an inbuilt preterite. Vernacular, Doric, Braid Scots, Scots, Synthetic Scots, Plastic Scots, Aggrandized Scots, or Lallans, were and are (but, by and large, they are all one) instruments with which to cleanse the Scottish psyche of generations of English influence. It was for decades, and remains, a language unexposed to actual contact with changing intellectual and domestic life. It is a language with very few, if any, new words. Indeed, it is a language in which old words are used in poetry with the force of neologisms, the shock of the unfamiliar.

Synthetic Scots is a language devised to enrich its vernacular foundation through the culling of words and expressions from the dialects of the several districts of Lowland Scotland. MacDiarmid *made a language* as he wrote – not just 'an individual voice', but a language. Spontaneity might seem hampered by principles of composition that rely clearly on the patient or inspired rediscovery of apt terms from dictionaries, old poetry, field work, and childhood memory. MacDiarmid rationalized his methods in *Lucky Poet* (1943), where he stated that the act of poetry is 'the reverse of what it is usually thought to be; not an idea gradually shaping itself in words, but deriving entirely from words.' His experience of writing in synthetic Scots could have encouraged that dogmatic overstatement. It can also be associated with his beliefs about the imagination, for these, too, run counter to the usual convictions. Here he quotes P. D. Ouspensky:

. . . one of the barriers preventing us from waking up is our imagination, which intrudes constantly into our thought. Imagination runs away with our thoughts and leads a thoroughly destructive life within us. We are only able to think beyond a certain point, and this point is very soon reached. Our thoughts are then taken over by our imagination, which runs amuck with them, without direction, aim, or control. We can only stop the wasteful chase of our imagination by being attentive. The moment we are attentive the activities of our imagination cease, and thought can come into action. Imagination is a very violent destructor of energy; mental effort on the other hand stores energy.

Later in *Lucky Poet* he discloses what he held to be the imagination's more positive function. This time he quotes Kierkegaard:

The imagination is what providence uses in order to get men into reality, into existence, to get them far enough out, or in, or down in existence. And when imagination has helped them as far out as they are meant to go – that is where reality, properly speaking, begins.

By 'reality' MacDiarmid meant the place 'where the unknowable ends'.

Although *Lucky Poet* appeared after he had given up writing in synthetic Scots, an eclectic intellectualism was always massively present in MacDiarmid's mind.* It was probably that cerebral poetic passion that enabled his work in Scots to surpass its antiquarian, lexicographical trappings, with which it was always in danger of being burdened. However, it can hardly be denied that the idiom he explored is one that asks to be absolved from the usual contingencies to which languages are tied, especially that of living, quotidian usage. It is – above all – a Scottish language; but it is also devised and artificial. On the evidence of the poetry that has been written in it, it seems to resist the forms and techniques of the modernity which it was created to exploit. In terms of psychology, MacDiarmid was probably right; in terms of form (the essential modernist wager), technique, and contemporaneity of expression, he could hardly have been more wrong so far as wider usage was concerned, if not for his own poetic practice.

MacDiarmid's poetry has tended to identify his synthesized use of Scots with his notions of nationalism and politics, some of which are curious, eccentric, cruel, wilfully extreme, or poses which exploit eccentricity, cruelty and extremism. A founder member of the first nationalist party, he was later expelled for being a communist. In due course the Communist Party found his nationalism inappropriate, and he was dismissed, re-joining after the Soviet invasion of Hungary. While these knee-jerk reactions among the political parties disclose their own pathos, they say something about MacDiarmid, too. His nationalism coexisted with hard-core Stalinism, which itself had been preceded by a brief but tantalizing affair with Nazism (in the 'Blutesgefühl' section of his essay, 'The Caledonian Antisyzygy and the Gaelic Ideal').† A decade's interest in Mussolini's fascism probably prepared MacDiarmid's own nationalism for one totalitarian

---

*Part II of George Elder Davie's *The Crisis of the Democratic Intellect*, Polygon, 1986, describes MacDiarmid's poetry in terms of philosophy, especially Scottish thought.
†Reprinted in *Selected Essays of Hugh MacDiarmid*; ed. D. Glen, Jonathan Cape, 1969.

escapade after another. Whatever its turbulence, or sheer ill will, it seems safe to conclude that his political mind had little use for democracy.

'Dissimilarity' was not enough for MacDiarmid: he wanted synthetic Scots to achieve a complete break from its near-sorority with English. 'Quite untranslatable Scots', he wrote in *Lucky Poet*, was what he aimed for when he rose to 'the height of my theme'. 'Water Music' should give some idea of the lexical density of which synthetic Scots is capable; the poem is contrived from sheer love of the language it uses, a devotion to its exuberance and peculiarity. Its word-gathering, its felt philology, is far removed from Burns's Scots. Rarely, if ever, do individual words in Burns's poems draw attention to themselves as lexical splendours. Some of them may have been unusual to Burns, but they were insured by the experience of speech, and introduced on a balanced, colloquial metre, and on a voice that insists on the demotic integrity of its idiom. 'Water Music' revels in as many words associated with streams and rivers as MacDiarmid could manage to get in. Here, too, as in his criticism, as in many of his poems, a modernist concern is announced, in this case in the opening lines:

> Wheesht, wheesht, Joyce, and let me·hear
> Nae Anna Livvy's lilt,
> But Wauchope, Esk, and Ewes again,
> Each wi' its ain rhythms till't.

Joyce's famous passage is being passed over in favour of the waters native to MacDiarmid. A Scottish assertion is undoubtedly present in the poem, but, in playfully silencing Joyce, MacDiarmid draws attention to himself as *another* modernist, albeit a lonelier one, stranded proudly in Scotland with his aboriginal, urgent concerns, and dedicated as well, to the language that he believed could solve them. But it is also a poem of remembering; it is a poem in which garnered Scottish words are made to adhere to memory. As Alan Bold suggests in his admirable biography of MacDiarmid,* it was the *personally* regressive ingredient in Scots that contributed to MacDiarmid's transition from Scots to English. It might also be suggested that he could have written one lexical rhapsody too many, or gone a 'divertissement philologique' (as he sub-titled 'Stony Limits') too far, and left himself facing the closed doors of the language that he had himself opened in the first place. If that is true, it hardly detracts from his linguistic audacity; it might even reveal it more clearly. Acumen and recklessness, an intuitive poetic scholarship, abundant energy, and national passion, could have led him to exhaust the idiom that to a large extent he invented, at least for his own

---

* *MacDiarmid. Christopher Murray Grieve. A Critical Biography*, John Murray, 1988; Paladin/ Grafton Books, 1990.

poetry. He continued to support other poets who wrote in Scots, and I doubt if he would have deplored the procedures of three contemporary poets, Raymond Vettese, Robert Crawford and W. N. Herbert, who, in their different ways, demonstrate that MacDiarmid's philological verve is far from dead.

Places and times matter in appreciating the use of Scots in poetry. William Soutar's language, for example, stems from his native Perth, and, while enriched by his reading, relies less on the synthesizing impulses necessary to MacDiarmid's conception of a new poetry in Scots. Soutar's best lyrics, like 'The Tryst', are more regular and less 'modern' than MacDiarmid's (which could be why 'The Tryst' appeared in Cecil Day Lewis's update of *The Golden Treasury*). MacDiarmid's lyrics characteristically set two or three uncommon or well-retrieved words, so as to make them appear not just out of the common way, but as having arrived from out of this world. Soutar's instinctive goal seems to have been a lyrical but local timelessness. It is the voice of an individual poet; but it is just as much the voice of a people's poetry. MacDiarmid's lyrics often create the same startling effect. Although at a higher, more intense, and more intellectual level of poetry, MacDiarmid's lyrics can sound as if they have emerged from a language and its community as much as an individual writer, a point that is worth stressing: it is, after all, unique in the poetry of modernism. In MacDiarmid's *A Drunk Man Looks at the Thistle*, however, long passages are clearly self-centred, the result of the poem's real and imaginary occasions, and of a 'thinner' Scots diction, at times little more than the notation of accent. Scots loses much of its poetic power when stripped of words and expressions rediscovered in 'the recesses of the Doric'. Its strength could lie largely in the meaningful past which it embodies, and which it thrusts, either joltingly or melismatically, against a frustrated present.

The language of Lowland Scotland was known as 'Inglis' until the late fifteenth and early sixteenth centuries, and only after that as 'Scottis'. English and Scots are both dialects of the same original language stock. Gaelic and Norse are additional etymological sources, as are Brythonic Welsh and Pictish, especially as far as place names are concerned, which form an important part of any country's linguistic atmosphere. Geographical, climatic and other domestic and historical forces contributed to its distinctive vocabulary, the extent of which is recorded in *Dictionary of the Older Scottish Tongue** and *The Scottish National Dictionary*.† Latin is another presence, intellectually more than linguistically, but powerful enough for all that, especially in the educated mind. Modern Scottish poetry is reminded of it through Robert Garioch's verse translations from the Latin of George Buchanan and Arthur Johnstone.

*In progress, 7 vols. so far: A – Sanct.
†10 vols. 1931–76.

Characteristic or traditional stanzas are associated with Scottish poetry, the best known being Standard Habbie (or Burns's Stanza). MacDiarmid left these well alone. A form like Burns's Stanza, closely identified with the eighteenth century (although it is considerably older), would have looked far from a modernist ploy. In the new climate that MacDiarmid was attempting to create it would have risked establishing the wrong loyalties and pieties. Imitated Burns provided much of the worst poetry in the century after his death (and the travesty is not yet over and done with). MacDiarmid also believed that Burns sold short the revival of the Scots language. It was left to Robert Garioch to renegotiate the terms on which the stanzaic verse of Burns, and, especially, Robert Fergusson (1750–74) could re-enter the living stream of Scottish poetry without fudging contemporary subjects and attitudes to them. In other words, the revival of writing in Scots that was instigated by MacDiarmid in the early 1920s was modified by other talents. MacDiarmid's work was important to Garioch, but he tired of the older poet's worst dogmatic habits so far as to refer to them as 'pulpit objurgations'. Garioch's poetic personality is self-consciously wry and sensible. Behind his poetry the persona is often that of an Edinburgh Everyman. Powerfully, and often wittily direct, his work is crafted on a metrical pulse and these older stanzaic shapes which pull back into Scottish poetry the eighteenth-century tempos of Fergusson and Burns (see 'To Robert Fergusson') and of earlier fifteenth- and sixteenth-century verse forms that influenced them (see 'Embro to the Ploy').

Garioch's 'The Wire' is one of the finest poems of the Second World War. Its mood, its almost panoptic view of a prisoner-of-war camp (in Silesia), and the eeriness with which tetrameter metricality enforces the poem's Scots diction, all contribute to what seems a virtually mediaeval poetic atmosphere. Time seems as displaced as those incarcerated on

> . . . this dour mechanistic muir
> wi nae land's end, and endless day,
> whaur nae thing thraws a shadow, here
> the truth is clear, and it is wae.

Garioch's poetry is almost always direct and candid, drawn from life and experience. MacDiarmid's 'Water Music' can sound like word-fantasy, and, despite its passionate evocation of streams and rivers, it seems diminished when compared with the harrowing fortitude, despair and indignant energy of Garioch's 'The Wire'. Synthetic Scots, lavishly employed for its own sake, is a creative tactic largely limited to MacDiarmid. Narrative, lyric and other pressures enforced on writers younger than him a more tactful, perhaps a more experienced distribution of wondrous or otherwise exceptional diction. Passages in Garioch's writing are often lexically massy, but usually appear on a more colloquial pulse. Some sections of *A Drunk Man Looks at the Thistle*, though, could hardly be more demotic or colloquial, or more metaphysical. Poetry in Scots can seem like a search for a convincing balance between stupendous Scots vocabulary and commoner terms in Scots and Scots-English. Garioch's poetry achieves that harmony through its spokenness, personality, humour and directness. His work diverges from MacDiarmid's example while at the same time drawing from the energy created by it. Indeed, given MacDiarmid's 'pulpit objurgations' on poetry and politics, it can seem remarkable that individual talents not only survived their friendship with his ideas, but took strength from them. On the evidence of Alan Bold's biography and the testimony of several writers, MacDiarmid's personality in print may have been considerably more severe than in his companionship. From MacDiarmid's criticism, for example, you would expect him to have had little time for Sydney Goodsir Smith's highly personalized poems, or much of their language. Again, Smith's poetic temperament is strikingly different, for his poetry courts a kind of Scottish neo-classicism infected with a late-romantic self-loathing, or a willingness to exploit bad behaviour for lyrical or humorous poetic ends. Garioch, too, dabbled in native neo-classicism, as in his Scots translation from Arthur Johnstone (1587–1641), who wrote in Latin. Garioch especially, and Smith, too (only in Smith's poetry it is more superficial) possessed a sense of the Scots language of the fifteenth, sixteenth and seventeenth centuries. Echoic resonances sound through their poetry when read in the available collected editions.

'Sorley MacLean, a Scottish poet second only to MacDiarmid, writes in our third language – Gaelic', Norman MacCaig once declared, 'and thereby restricts his intelligent audience to a mere handful. Nobody does that except for the deepest and most compulsive reasons.'

Conventional opinion invites us to believe that a poet can write in only one language – the language of a life's lengths and affections, experience, memory, and dreams. Conventional belief may well be right, but only for those born and brought up in a rigidly monoglot environment, which, in the British Isles, is likely to mean a middle-class background and notional RP from birth. Poets drawn to write in Scots do so on a basis of childhood acquaintance with its residual, colloquial forms, or what, for practical purposes, might best be described as a strong Scottish accent of one kind or another. An awareness of accent, together with curiosity directed at a few Scottish words spoken since childhood, can convince young Scottish poets that their authenticity lies in the dictionaries and poetry from which a complete native poetic idiom can be reconstructed. With Scots, it is not a case of bilingualism as it might be with French-and-English or

English-and-Russian, or English-and-Gaelic. What it shows is an urge to insist on Scots as a language worthy of the poetry that can be written in it, as a language separate and of-itself in relationship to the English language. It is when this urge is involuntary that Scots becomes the medium of poetry, as in MacDiarmid's lyrics, or in the best work of Soutar, Garioch, Goodsir Smith, Douglas Young, Tom Scott, Alexander Scott, Alasdair Mackie and the younger poets who work with the forms that Scots can take. Although applied to poetry in Gaelic, MacCaig's pointer to 'the deepest and most compulsive reasons' is very apt when directed at poetry in Scots. It is when the language of poetry arises from decision rather than instinctive need that it risks artificiality and fraudulence. By its nature, poetry in Scots risks a confrontation of real feeling with unreal or archaeological diction. Faked emotion could also be encouraged by a national overview of language and poetry. That is, priorities other than those of poetry could come higher up the list then they should.

Before attempting to discuss poetry in Gaelic (for which I have to depend on translations) this might be the moment to say something about what is a common feeling among Scottish poets and readers, no matter their preferred or necessary language. Despite the survival of poetry in three languages (and it was far from guaranteed) there seems a hunger for unity, not through a single language, but through one nationality that sanctions a tripled linguistic and poetic experience. An introduction to an anthology of poetry might seem an improper occasion on which to introduce the topic of nationalism; but it can hardly be avoided without tampering with the record. Scottish poetry has been steeped in politics ever since MacDiarmid's instigatory drum-beating back in the early 1920s. By 1943, however, in *Lucky Poet*, he could say 'The language element, the Scottish national character of my poetry, is not the most important thing about it.' A little later in the same book he expounded Scots as an anti-English stop-gap on the way to achieving a 'Gaelic Scotland', and he described poetry in Scots as 'a temporary fighting literature'. By this time his overviews of culture and politics had gone awry. They were summed up by his vision of a Celtic Union of Soviet Republics – Brittany, Cornwall, Wales, Ireland, Man and Scotland. MacDiarmid's satisfaction in that kind of make-believe map-making is difficult to detach from racism of a fairly crude sort. However, despite his extremism, and to some extent because of his kinder, personal influence, Scottish poetry has moved gradually into its liberty. For those 'deepest and most compulsive reasons' it has managed to resolve the more petty of its inner controversies; it is more and more the poetry in three languages of one nationality.

A passable attempt could be made at writing a poem in Scots after two or three days of leafing through a dictionary. Developing an ability to 'think' in Scots would take considerably longer. To learn to think in Gaelic would take a very long time indeed. Those 'deepest and most compulsive reasons' would seem to apply to writers who grew up speaking Gaelic, or whose family backgrounds included the language – perhaps not much, but some – and for whom loyalty's tug is not to be denied. Sorley MacLean's family was not only Gaelic-speaking but included bearers of traditional song, an important element in Gaelic culture, and in Scotland as a whole. Yet while Gaelic traditions are crucial to MacLean, he was able to introduce to them such ostensibly divergent influences as Yeats and Eliot. MacLean has also testified to the importance of MacDiarmid's lyrics where his earlier work is concerned, as well as to that of personal contact with MacDiarmid himself.

His first collection was *Dàin do Eimhir* (*Songs to Eimhir*) in 1943. Passionate lyrics, sometimes in an adjectival Gaelic manner, their intensity and incantatory pitch survive in the poet's own translation:

> Girl of the yellow heavy-yellow gold-yellow hair,
> the song of your mouth and Europe's shivering cry,
> fair, heavy-haired, spirited, beautiful girl,
> the disgrace of our day would not be bitter in your kiss.

'Small-scale, face-to-face rural societies, with a strong emphasis on communality, seldom set a high premium' on 'cool analysis of life', D. J. MacLeod writes in his essay 'Gaelic: the Dynamics of a Renaissance'.* Irony plays little part in the work of Gaelic poetry, the exception being Rob Donn (d. 1778). Interestingly, MacLean describes Donn's poetry as 'humanist sermo-pedestrian verse', and while he praises its 'courageous sense of honour', he asks, 'how can such relaxed poetry be great?' Large-scale urban societies, placing a strong emphasis on mass organization and individual privacy, rely on irony as a defensive, sometimes critically explosive, cultural device. In earlier Gaelic poetry, it was simply out of place, which is not to say that the ironies of history are allowed to go undetected.

MacLean's reputation was deserved long before his work was more widely distributed; a general awareness of his importance dates from the 1970s. Around 80,000 people speak Gaelic (the population of Scotland is not much more than 5 million). Within its own cultural boundaries, then, Gaelic's demographic pool is small enough to suggest its vulnerability – a language not only on the edge of Europe, but on the edge of time. Sorley MacLean accepts the threatened existence of Gaelic with a characteristic lack of passivity:

It is natural for a poet to love his own language if it is the language of his ancestors, and dying, even if it were a poor defective thing. Gaelic is not a poor language, in art at any rate. Though it had only its ineffable songs, which cannot be put in other words, it would

---

*In *Gaelic and Scotland*; ed. W. Gillies, Edinburgh University Press, 1989.

still be a priceless medium of expression. Therefore the Gaelic writer must be 'political', and in our day the teaching of the language is the prime business of its 'politics'.*

Love of a native language is a powerful force in poetry, especially in countries where it can be subjected to political pressures (for example, the Highland post-Jacobite period clearly exemplifies this, but it has happened in more subtle ways since) or frustrated, or diminished by depopulation and emigration, or the tendency of modern life with all its blandishments to change the social structures which language and poetry reflect. Against such a background Gaelic might be expected to look like a fallen language, exhausted, miniaturized, and relegated to scholarly sub-departments dedicated to pathos. It is not what has happened. Gaelic poets, who have been prominent in Scottish poetry as a whole, have contributed in a major way to halting the decline of a language poised, for more than a century, before the prospect of extinction. Derick Thomson, for instance, founded the magazine and publishing imprint, *Gairm*, and the Gaelic Books Council. His *Introduction to Gaelic Poetry*† is an indispensable guide for readers who want to know more of the subject. Gaelic poets, however, can seem surprised by their renascent surge, or coincidence of talents:

Can there have emerged from such a small area, with its declining Gaelic population, against all contemporary pressures, a modern Gaelic literature? Is it possible that such an extraordinary thing could have happened? Is it possible too that against anaemic ceilidhs, primitive breast-beating, the backward look, there should have come into existence a truly contemporary Gaelic literature? The answer to this is that strangely enough such a literature has emerged.‡

MacLean's passionate directness, his quality of spoken singing, is less pronounced in Derick Thomson's writing, or Smith's poetry in Gaelic. Much of their work is drawn from a burdened, rueful awareness of a dispiriting cultural present, and the past from which it emerges. Thomson's 'Coffins', for example, contains the line 'I did not understand that my race was dying'. Both its dilemma and directness run counter to the English poetry of Thomson's lifetime; but the point is worth making only because of the distance between English and Gaelic poetry, as well as the disregard and complacency which identify as expendable traditions which are not native to the official State. 'Gaelic poetry must be judged within the culture itself': Iain Crichton Smith's opinion is probably true, but it tends to block what might be valuable for non-Gaelic speaking readers, that dissimilarity to poetry in English which has been found fruitful and exciting over

*Sorley MacLean, *Ris a' bhruthaich: criticism and prose writings*; ed. W. Gillies, Acair, 1985
†Gollancz, 1974; Edinburgh University Press, 1989.
‡Iain Crichton Smith, 'Modern Gaelic Poetry', in *Towards the Human*, Macdonald Publishers, 1986.

the past few decades. Poetry from other languages, and other national traditions in English, have exerted a considerable influence on the poetry of the British Isles. There seems no good reason to insulate Gaelic poetry, even when it laments its own history, as in Thomson's fine poem 'Strathnaver', with its bitterly exalted portrayal of the Highland Clearances; or 'The Well', where the source of his people's culture is seen as almost-lost, hidden, but still available:

> 'Nobody goes to that well now,'
> said the old woman, 'as we once went,
> when we were young,
> though its water is lovely and white.'
> And when I looked in her eyes through the bracken
> I saw the sparkle of that water
> that makes whole every hurt
> till the hurt of the heart.

Iain Crichton Smith places a quite different emphasis on Rob Donn than does Sorley MacLean. 'One of our most important poets, in many ways our most important', Smith writes of Rob Donn in 'A Note on Gaelic Criticism', an article in which he finds Gaelic adjectival listing 'a menace to the development of good poetry', and where he praises Donn's intelligence and irony. Smith's 'Gaelic Stories'* is drawn, at least to an extent, from exactly the kind of 'relaxation' that MacLean found questionable in Donn. It is a divergence of opinion that does not prevent Smith from acknowledging MacLean as the 'Gaelic master'. That it should exist, however, suggests that Gaelic poetry's struggle with modernity is one in which traditional expectations could be resistant to ideas of 'good poetry' when these have been taken in some measure from languages other than Gaelic itself.

By the time of *Stony Limits* (1934) MacDiarmid's creative engagement with Scots began to weaken. Poems in colloquial and synthetic Scots appear in the collection, but it is his newer work in English, such as 'On a Raised Beach', which suggests that a combination of philosophical, meditative and temperamental pressures forced him into a more extensive language. While that language is English, it is hard to appreciate it as the language of English poetry. It is English in its guise of a world-auxiliary language; it is an idiom that MacDiarmid also bent to his will as part of the gesture that extended poetry into scientific and philosophical knowledge.

---

*Smith prints his Gaelic poems in translation only in his *Selected Poems*, and some other volumes, although they appear in Gaelic collections first. Accordingly, his Gaelic writing is represented by his translations without a parallel text.

Edwin Muir's *Scott and Scotland* came out two years later.* MacDiarmid promptly opened fire on arguments which seemed to undermine everything for which his Scottish Renaissance movement stood. Not only was his own poetry in Scots challenged, but so was the direction he insisted Scottish poetry should take, as well as the Scottishness of mind, character and nationhood which he had expounded, and, in the process, fantasticated. Expertly vituperative – he fingered Muir as the leader of 'the white mouse faction' in Scottish letters – MacDiarmid's counter attack is usually regarded as having won the day. However, *Scott and Scotland* can be seen as other than treasonable. Only in recent years has its insistence on English as the only authentic language of Scottish poetry been proved mistaken through developments which have brought about a healing in the controversy that used to be described as 'the language question'. Much of what Muir says is still of interest. His admittedly tentative emphasis on Sir Walter Scott highlights the very curious neglect of 'the greatest creative force in Scottish literature as well as one of the greatest in English'. Some of the reasons for avoiding Scott are social and political. Like Stevenson, or Buchan, he was born on the wrong side of the tracks. All three were Tories, and more or less High. Each has become a casualty of nationalism's rush as well as of its simplifications.

In spite of its variousness, its disproportionately high count of achievements in the arts and sciences, Scotland *is* a small country. Genuine critical debate tends to be discouraged by the intimacy of the cultural atmosphere. Back-slapping and other exaggerated forms of courtesy can turn the critical process into little more than flag-waving. On the other hand, the consequences of an opposed view can be immediate. There are some famous silences in Scottish poetry. There are also celebrated enmities. That of Muir and MacDiarmid is the most disagreeable. Not only did it separate the two most gifted writers of their generation, it introduced conspicuous side-taking and the exploitation of controversy.

Muir's extended essay provides a contrary view, a series of arguments with which poets who use either Scots or English have had to contend, just as they are obliged to come to a workable decision regarding MacDiarmid's poetry and the convictions from which it was made. I shall quote it at some length:

The riddle which confronted me in approaching Scott himself, by far the greatest creative force in Scottish literature as well as one of the greatest in English, was to account for a very curious emptiness which I felt behind the wealth of his imagination. Many critics have acknowledged this blemish in Scott's work, but have either made no attempt to account for it, or else have put it down to a defect in Scott's mind and character. Yet men of Scott's enormous genius have rarely Scott's faults; they may have others but not these particular ones; and so I was forced to account for the hiatus in Scott's endowment by considering the environment in which he lived, by invoking the fact – if the reader will agree it is one –

* George Routledge & Sons, 1936; Polygon Books, 1982.

that he spent most of his days in a hiatus, in a country, that is to say, which was neither a nation nor a province, and had, instead of a centre, a blank, an Edinburgh, in the middle of it. But this Nothing in which Scott wrote was not merely a spatial one; it was a temporal Nothing as well, dotted with a few disconnected figures arranged at abrupt intervals: Henryson, Dunbar, Allan Ramsay, Burns, with a rude buttress of ballads and folk songs to shore them up and keep them from falling. Scott, in other words, lived in a community which was not a community, and set himself to carry on a tradition which was not a tradition; and the result was that his work was an exact reflection of his predicament. His picture of life had no centre, because the environment in which he lived had no centre. What traditional virtue his work possessed was at second hand, and derived mainly from English literature, which he knew intimately but which was a semi-foreign literature to him. Scotland did not have enough life of its own to nourish a writer of his scope; it had neither a real community to foster him nor a tradition to direct him; for the anonymous ballad tradition was not sufficient for his genius. . . .

So that my inquiry into what Scotland did for Scott came down finally to what it did not do for Scott. What it did not do, or what it could not do. Considered historically these alternatives are difficult to separate.

Having traced Scott's greatest fault to his geographical and historical position as a writer, I began to wonder what he might have been, given his genius, if he had been born into a genuine organic society such as England, or even into a small self-subsistent state like Weimar. Could he possibly have left his picture of life in such a tentative state, half flesh and blood and half pasteboard, unreal where he dealt with highly civilized people, and real where he dealt with peasants, adventurers and beggars? Would he not have been forced to give it unity? or rather, would not a sociological unity at least have been there without his having to make a specific effort to achieve it? . . .

But behind this problem of the Scottish writer there is another which, if not for the individual author, for Scotland itself is of crucial importance. This is the problem of Scottish literature, and it is clearly a question for the Scottish people as a whole, not for the individual Scottish writer; for only a people can create a literature. The practical present-day problem may be put somewhat as follows: that a Scottish writer who wishes to achieve some approximation to completeness has no choice except to absorb the English tradition, and that if he thoroughly does so his work belongs not merely to Scottish literature but to English literature as well. On the other hand, if he wishes to add to an indigenous Scottish literature, and roots himself deliberately in Scotland, he will find there, no matter how long he may search, neither an organic community to round off his conceptions, nor a major literary tradition to support him, nor even a faith among the people themselves that a Scottish literature is possible or desirable, nor any opportunity, finally, of making a livelihood by his work. All these things are part of a single problem which can only be understood by considering Scottish literature historically, and the qualities in the Scottish people which have made them what they are; it cannot be solved by writing poems in Scots, or by looking forward to some hypothetical Scotland in the future . . .

Every genuine literature, in other words, requires as its condition a means of expression capable of dealing with everything the mind can think or the imagination can conceive. It must be a language for criticism as well as poetry, for abstract speculation as well as fact, and since we live in a scientific age, it must be a language for science as well. A language which can serve for one or two of those purposes but not for the others is, considered as a vehicle for literature, merely an anachronism. Scots has survived to our time as a language for simple poetry and the simpler kind of short story, such as *Thrawn Janet*; all its other uses have lapsed, and it expresses therefore only a fragment of the Scottish mind. One can go further than this, however, and assert that its very use is a proof that the Scottish consciousness is divided. For, reduced to it simplest terms, this linguistic division means that Scotsmen feel in one language and think in another; that their emotions turn to the Scottish tongue, with all its associations of local sentiment, and their minds to a standard English which for them is almost bare of associations other than those of the classroom. If Henryson and Dunbar had written prose they would have written in the same language as they used for poetry, for their minds were still whole; but Burns never thought of doing so, nor did Scott, nor did Stevenson, nor has any Scottish writer since. In an organic literature poetry is always influencing prose, and prose poetry; and their interaction energizes them both. Scottish poetry exists in a vacuum; it neither acts on the rest of literature nor reacts to it; and consequently it has shrunk to the level of anonymous folk-song. Hugh MacDiarmid has recently tried to revive it by impregnating it with all the contemporary influences of Europe one after another, and thus galvanize it into life by a series of violent shocks. In carrying out this experiment he has written some remarkable poetry; but he has left Scottish verse very much where it was before. For the major forms of poetry rise from a collision between emotion and intellect on a plane where both meet on equal terms; and it can never come into existence where the poet feels in one language and thinks in another, even though he should subsequently translate his thoughts into the language of his feelings. Scots poetry can only be revived, that is to say, when Scotsmen begin to think *naturally* in Scots. The curse of Scottish literature is the lack of a whole language, which finally means the lack of a whole mind.

    MacDiarmid's basic premiss was that discontinuity in literature and national-ity could be repaired simply by taking vigorous action. It was probably MacDiarmid whom Muir had in mind when he wrote that the problems of Scottish literature could not be solved by individual writers – 'only a people can create a literature'. Over the last two or three decades, however, Muir's major reservations have decreased in pertinence. Scotland has revealed itself to be a more 'organic community' than was suspected. Its literary traditions have become clearer as the result of scholarly and critical work. Readers, or, if you like, 'the people themselves', have demonstrated that a Scottish literature is desirable. A poet in Scotland is no more likely to make a living from his or her work than a poet anywhere else, but fellowships, bursaries, literary journalism and public performances extend a system of support – if always fragile – which is superior to anything enjoyed by Muir or MacDiarmid.

    In a letter in 1940, Muir wrote: 'It seems to me, looking at Scottish life, that discouragement is everywhere in it'. That is no longer anything like as true as it undoubtedly was, even if contemporary conditions are far from perfect in whatever sphere of life you care to investigate. Muir and MacDiarmid wrote from circumstances of near-penury. Neither MacDiarmid's productivity, which was ferocious, nor Muir's, which was considerable, could support life and family on its own. MacDiarmid's self-imposed exile on Whalsay in the Shetland Islands (where he wrote 'On a Raised Beach'), his nervous breakdown, wartime industrial conscription, and service as a crewman on an Admiralty tender in the Clyde naval anchorages suggest some of the disappointments and humiliations which he had to endure. Muir's background as a boy displaced from the Orkney Islands to industrial Glasgow created the foundations of heartbreaking inner turmoil. His work in a boneyard, in Lobnitz's shipyard in Renfrew, and, by 1940, in the Food Office in Dundee, illustrate what Muir was up against.

Scotland was neglectful of its poets and artists, chiefly, it would seem, because as a non-nation it was scarcely aware of possessing any. With a disliked status quo to react against, writers tended to be identified as outspoken and 'colourful', but embarrassing in their contrariness. National caricatures were preferred to realities, truth and aspiration. It can hardly be denied that an element of that persists. Most poetry in the twentieth century has been oppositional in its relations with society and the political scene at large. Scottish poetry, however, in some of its major figures, has been peculiarly hostile to standard assumptions. MacDiarmid, Muir (earlier in his career), MacLean, Goodsir Smith, Thomson and a number of others have been either on the Left and/or explicitly nationalist. Others have been less conspicuously political; but in their relish of language, or their directness, or breadth of outlook, they have identified their nationality in other ways.

Scottish poetry in this century has been far from a tragic scenario; but an undoubted awkwardness has been the relatively limited object lesson communicated by two of its major figures to subsequent writers for whom the available, common language is the obvious and natural one to use. MacDiarmid's English is too much of a special case, while Muir's, although appropriate to the timelessness of the stories he tells, would look archaic in any other context.

Neither was a formative influence on Norman MacCaig, for instance, whose first two collections, which he disowns, were deeply coloured by the rhetoric of the Apocalypse School, in which Scottish poets were prominent. Having rejected that – a friend, apparently, asked: 'When are you publishing the answers?' – MacCaig then began the long haul back to lucidity. A poet like Andrew Young may have been of more help than either MacDiarmid or Muir. *Riding Lights* (1955) established MacCaig as an important presence, while since MacDiarmid's death in 1978 his work has looked like the major body of poetry that it is.

Until around the mid-1960s MacCaig's poetry appeared in elegant English, often with intricate stanzas in which his metrical artfulness and rhymes surpass recent Scottish averages in those aspects of versification. Lightness of touch, intellectual playfulness, conceited figures, melismatic smoothness, a highly *polished* English – these were, and still are, unusual in Scottish poetry. But it would be mistaken to think of MacCaig's idiom as one of English-English. Muir was surely wrong to talk of 'English', pure and simple, as if English were one language. Although 1936 could have been too early for the wider ramifications of the English language to have been explored in confident detail, Muir's detailed knowledge of American and Irish writing should have led him to notice the particularity of the case with which he was dealing. Not much about Scottish poetry in English is likely to be appreciated at the highest aesthetic level without its intonations being taken into account. Muir's mistake was to ignore how accent represents the phonology of a previous way of speaking – a Scottish accent could be described as Scots stripped of its diction. Nor did MacDiarmid appear to think it worthy of consideration that the English written by Scottish poets is to varying degrees English repossessed by the voice of the Scots vernacular, or, as in MacCaig's case, modified by proximity to a Gaelic inheritance if not by Gaelic itself. No one seems to have paid much attention to the natural phenomenon of language in Scotland as dictated by history. Most of the attention swings to the glamorous, fateful and possibly luckless last-ditch stands of Scots and Gaelic. Between the three languages of Scotland, however, writers have managed to negotiate a climate of opinion which allows the freedom to write in the tongue in which a poet feels most at home. That obvious liberty was not one always to be taken for granted. Despite the excellence of the poetry that was being written, the justifications surrounding it could give the impression that a romantically inferiorist insularity was preferred. It was a failure of criticism, a flaw in the literary atmosphere, and it helped to make Scottish poetry as a whole look like a subject best left to its participants and native readers to squabble over.

One consequence of that state of affairs was the postponement of criticism in favour of the puffery that supports a 'reputation', or the malice, or silence, that destroys or prevents it. Only in recent years have MacLean, MacCaig, Edwin Morgan and W. S. Graham been written about intelligently or at any length,[*] while proper studies of Soutar, Goodsir Smith and Garioch[†] do not exist.

---

[*] Raymond J. Ross and Joy Hendry eds. *Sorley MacLean: Critical Essays*, Scottish Academic Press, 1986; Joy Hendry and Raymond J. Ross eds. *Norman MacCaig: Critical Essays*, Edinburgh University Press, 1990; Robert Crawford and Hamish Whyte, *About Edwin Morgan*, Edinburgh University Press, 1990; Tony Lopez, *The Poetry of W. S. Graham*, Edinburgh University Press, 1989.
[†] A collection of critical essays on Robert Garioch is in preparation, edited by Joy Hendry and Raymond J. Ross, for Edinburgh University Press, due 1992.

MacCaig's *Collected Poems* (1985; new edition 1990) encouraged a belated attention to his work, and more detailed examination than it had hitherto received. As a body of poetry made up for the most part of short lyrics, brief discursive narratives and satires, it can seem to resist identification as the work of a major writer. However, what finally marks it as such is the importance of its themes, and the extent to which poem after poem seeks to define and clarify the individual's relationship to existence. It is a poetry of detailed resemblances that cumulate into a glimpse of 'the whole world's shape'. 'Summer Farm' and 'Byre' should illustrate MacCaig's figurative habits of mind and feeling. Perception itself is explored and investigated in many of his poems, while others put history, topicality and politics firmly in their place (see 'No Interims in History'). Between 'Summer Farm' and 'Intruder in a Set Scene' the change in style is measurable: MacCaig has moved from precise verse to a freer idiom. As a result, his later poetry feels less 'literary'. It is also more open to achieving a direct form of address to reader or listener.

A good deal of Scottish poetry is close to its potential audience. The poet as Everyman/woman is a cherished persona, or fact of poetic identity, as might be expected in a country where Robert Burns is a figure of national importance. G. Gregory Smith's image of the grinning gargoyle beside the kneeling saint pictorializes the happy coexistence of the vulgar and the holy, the cruel and the kind, the low and the high, the demotic and the artistic, the anarchic and the ordered, the simple and the elaborate, which seem characteristic of Scottish psychologies, or of what criticism makes of them.

A poet like W. S. Graham, for example, addressed his often difficult subject of communication in a language that is rarely very far from an accented and demotic spokenness. 'Baldy Bane' might even suggest that a balladic momentum is an aspect of literary Scottishness that many poets have been unable or unwilling to get away from entirely. As Graham wrote in 'The Dark Dialogues',

> . . . always language
> Is where the people are.

Hart Crane, Joyce, Marianne Moore, Dylan Thomas and Beckett might have been among Graham's sources. So, too, were Scottish ballads, and there was room left for a native, perhaps even specifically Greenockian bias to the language of a poet otherwise instinctively preoccupied with modernity and far from prone to placing his nationality in a poem's foreground.

Graham has been less influential than a poet of his importance would at first lead you to believe. His style is eccentric, or individual, close to being a special case, like MacDiarmid's poetry in English, or Muir's. It begins to become clearer that it is characteristic of the best Scottish poets that their work contains an instinctively inimitable quality, or an audible signature.

Other, more disagreeable reasons, help to explain why Graham has been neglected in Scotland. Those antithetical 'characteristics' could tend to exclude poetry which illustrates them less obviously than an insecure taste might prefer. 'Scottishness' is a quality open to crass exaggeration as well as more subtle forms of garbled excess. Graham's appetite for language and poetry – surely the best 'characteristic' of the Scottish poetic gift – is visible on just about every page of his *Collected Poems*. Scottish people and places are quite clearly implicated in his struggle with 'seeing new' (as he called it), or with 'the jungle of mistakes of communication'. However, he lived furth of Scotland for most of his adult life, and loved Cornwall. His relative neglect is due to more than the quirk of having been not-quite-obviously-Scottish-enough; he had the cheek to live somewhere else. Andrew Young, Edwin Muir, and several others, have been treated to petty discriminations of a similar kind.

Graham published young, in 1942, but fifteen years were to elapse between *The Nightfishing* (1955) – the same year as MacDiarmid's *In Memoriam James Joyce* – and *Malcolm Mooney's Land* (1970). *Riding Lights* (1955), which announced Norman MacCaig's first mature style, appeared when he was in his mid-forties. Edwin Morgan was around the same age when he re-invented his talent by writing the poems that appeared in *The Second Life* (1968). Bearing in mind Sorley MacLean's delayed reputation, and Robert Garioch's, and Derick Thomson's – outside a handful of readers – the career pattern that seems to be revealed suggests that Scottish poetry underwent a difficult mid-century phase which subsequent success has tended to obscure. No doubt publishing was part of the trouble. Scottish imprints no longer represented the proud industry of former years – Nelson, Blackie, Collins, Blackwoods, Chambers, Oliver & Boyd. Whatever else they were doing, the support of native talent was not a priority. MacDiarmid was issuing his books from Castle Wynd Printers, for the most part work written years earlier: the impression is that he was exhausted by his efforts of the 1930s, and experiences of the 1940s. Garioch's poetry, and Goodsir Smith's, was not easy to come by. Nor, for that matter, was MacDiarmid's. It was a period of *cognoscenti*, adepts and coteries. In retrospect it seems remarkable that poetic society should have been so enclosed when much of its work was robust. For the best part of twenty years Scottish literary culture showed all the symptoms of provincial decline, even when, as far as writing itself was concerned, it was far from moribund. It indicates the undeserved slump into which the poetry of a small country can fall when its housekeeping is in bad order.

Prior to 1968 Edwin Morgan's work was well-known in literary circles, but chiefly on the strength of magazine appearances and small press publications. In all likelihood he was less known as a poet than as a reviewer and translator (especially of *Beowulf*). Critics have found it hard to pin him down. Wisely, they have stopped trying, and admitted that his various kinds of poetry not only resist theme-spotting but represent the fluid, transformational wagers which are of its essence. Much of his importance – and, like MacCaig, he has been generally influential – stems from his obvious up-to-dateness. After that momentary torpor of the 1950s Morgan's internationalism and experimental verve (concrete poetry, sound poetry etc.) were needed as much as MacCaig's perfected intellectual lyrics and Garioch's hearty Scots. Morgan, however, uses formal versification when it suits him (as in his many sonnets) as well as free verse. He has been a vigorous translator* and essayist. Openness to change, humour and liveliness have made his work attractive to younger readers, especially in Glasgow. His urban *joie de vivre* provides a balance to MacCaig's predilection for more rural and natural settings and celebrations.

Scottish literature has not always been the city's friend. Gaelic culture expressed a distinctive civilization, but it did not create a city, nor could it have done so without contradicting its essential spirit. Until well into the twentieth century, Scottish cities were depicted as stone wildernesses into which rural Lowlanders, displaced Highlanders and immigrant Irish families drifted in search of a livelihood, becoming industrial fodder. Slums, squalor and urban hardships tended and still tend to be depicted in Scottish poetry and fiction, if only because their obviousness invites them. Few countries are as afflicted as Scotland with stark contrasts of urban scale and rural extensiveness within a relatively small but extremely various territory. It is part of the drama of modern Scottish literature. MacDiarmid, for instance, loathed Glasgow as a recalcitrant hotbed of the social conditions that produced just about everything except the energy required for its revolutionary redemption. In what might be his shortest poem, the unpleasant 'Placenta Previa; or, the Case of Glasgow', he wrote:

> It'll be no easy matter to keep the dirt in its place
> And get the Future out alive in *this* case!

For all his cerebral, intellectual reach and pretensions, MacDiarmid was as prime an example of Scottish small-town and village man as you could have found in his day. It took Garioch's eighteenth-century, Fergussonian Edinburgh sensibility to

*See especially his Scots versions of Mayakovksy, *Wi the Haill Voice*, Carcanet Press, 1972. His translations are collected in *Rites of Passage*, Carcanet Press, 1976. I have excluded translations from the anthology as the subject is taken care of elsewhere. A useful measure of the demotic vigour of Scots, however, can be acquired by comparing Morgan's Mayakovsky, or Garioch's Belli, with English versions.

re-introduce to Scottish poetry a critical urbanity rooted in a real city and the present tense. Many of MacCaig's poems, however, are set in Edinburgh, while Goodsir Smith's are stamped with Edinburgh citizenship.

Although one of the best-known cities of the world, to Scots Edinburgh can feel like a lapsed capital, a city of history riddled with picturesque and turbulent resonances, the architectural digest of historical tomes in three volumes. Despite its ancient beauty, 'hie-heapit' as Lewis Spence evoked it in a memorable phrase, or its ordered, Georgian neo-classical loveliness, much of Edinburgh is low-down, dark and shadowy; it can feel like the dungeons of Scottish time. Alastair Reid has noticed – accurately, it seems to me – that the Castle Rock looks suspiciously like the chip on Scotland's shoulder. An easy city to poeticize in general, it is a hard one about which to be poetically specific. Glasgow is, too, but for different reasons. Its past is one of Atlantic trade, and the industrial revolution (which was to a large extent a creation of Scottish technology). Only since Edwin Morgan's poetry of the 1960s has Glasgow been imagined in a significantly modern way. Once known as Juteopolis, or the City of Dreadful Knights, Dundee delivers its own harsh industrial, imperial and working-class heartbreak. Relaxed, aesthetic approaches to poetry are far from impossible in Scottish writing, but the effort required in order to clear the necessary imaginative space is considerable when you bear in mind what might have to be left out of the poetic reckoning. As the city of the North East, 'The Silver City', Aberdeen's long-lived business with the North Sea, the Baltic, and a large agricultural hinterland, have brought about yet another distinctive city. All four are water-cities (with Leith the port for Edinburgh). All four, too, prospered on international contacts. Scotland might seem remote, but its artistic and intellectual character is founded on the opposite of the insularity that its history might seem to invite. Internal linguistic complexity might even have predisposed scholars to lexicography and linguistics in general, and its writers to translation.

At the other extreme, George Mackay Brown's work – Brown has seldom left his native Orkney Islands – could be the outstanding example in recent poetry in the British Isles of an extended chronicle of remote place and a traditional way of life. As with Edwin Muir, for whose poetry and personality Brown maintains a strong affection, the nationality is Orcadian and Norse more than Scottish. A Catholic religious faith is part of his poetry's confidence, which is unusual in a country where a poetic religious impulse tends to be stifled in infancy. Otherwise much of Brown's energy is drawn from a refusal of deracination. Modern life is portrayed as the bestower of unwanted changes on traditional communities whose contentments were sustained by harmonious if also hazardous transactions with the land and the sea. He is an unashamed storyteller, a poet who has taken the risk of assuming his people's lore, legends, character and destiny. As a result, the time-scale of his poetry runs from the dawn of time to the present era of pollution. Brown's poetry is a brave gesture of time and place, a heave of the allegedly remote up against the distempers of modernity. Within Scottish or any other poetry there could hardly be a greater contrast between Brown's inspiration and Edwin Morgan's. Brown's beliefs are all on the side of traditional values, the natural round of the seasons, the organic community; Morgan's convictions relate to the city, science, technology, and the future. Both have imagined Armageddon. In Brown's case it takes the form of a Black Pentecost, which returns the traditional world to its first principles (much as in Muir's poem, 'The Horses'). Morgan envisages a post-Apocalypse Glasgow as Clydegrad, perhaps a riskily optimistic echo of MacDiarmid's communist hopes.

A rural and island inspiration is continued by Iain Crichton Smith whose poetry and fiction have appeared in both Gaelic and English. 'Law' and 'grace', to use Smith's terms, indicate the tensions which he exploited in his earlier work but which survive, too, in his more recent writing. By 'law' he means the authoritarian Christianity of the United Free Church as well as secular systems designed to inhibit individual freedom. 'Grace' signifies the world of art, love, human choice, beauty, philosophy, poetry, and the glamorous self-confidence of those who seize opportunity unhindered by inherited restrictions. His contemporary instances are often set against the heroes and heroines of Rome and Greece or the classics of English literature and found wanting. In a section of his sequence 'At the Sea', for example, denizens of a public park are re-modelled as Helen and Achilles, while 'a fat loud Ajax' waddling up to bowl'. Larkin's presence can be detected gloomily in the shadows behind some of Smith's writing in that vein, in his powers of observation and the emphasis put on them if not in Smith's lavish use of the 'myth-kitty'. In the same sequence the US naval base at the Holy Loch is said to be defending

> the clattering tills, the taxis, thin pale girls
> who wear at evening their Woolworth pearls
> and from the dewed railings gaze at the world's end.

He can also be humorously satirical (see 'The White Air of March'), while in 'Chinese Poem' a native Gaelic dilemma is wittily transposed into the manner of another culture.

Smith has been hospitable to many influences, especially from recent poetry. George Mackay Brown is less eclectic – his sources include the sagas, ballads, Catholic liturgy, Hopkins (in Brown's earlier work) and Edwin Muir, whose poetry is often close to balladic narrative modified by allegory or the mythology and symbolism which bespeak poetry as an eternal craft. Contemporaneity can be an awkward issue in a country where history and national identity are partly unresolved. Writers can be drawn back into time in an effort to overwhelm what Smith calls the 'impenetrable dullness' of an ingrained philistinism, a repressive religiosity, a love of the couthy, the homely, and an infatuation with the second-rate. Significantly, though, Smith mounts his challenge in a passage about the dreaded McGonagall. Poetic contempt is directed, not at the worst poet in the world, but at the hypocritical mentality that reserves a place for 'poetic gems'. In laughing at McGonagall, the Scottish habit is to mock the idea of poetry itself, not just an obvious example of its pathetic delusions.

For many Scots, Burns is not only the National Poet; he is The Only Poet, a conviction which is often expressed with much whisky-o-lated jauntiness but not a lot of reading. Burns is still read by men and women with little or no pretension to cultivated literary taste, read closely, and memorized, as he should be. Edwin Muir was probably right when he remarked that Burns is an 'object-lesson in what poetic popularity really means – the prime object-lesson in the poetry of the world, perhaps the unique instance'. Serious consequences for Scottish poetry, some good, others dismal, have followed in the train of Burns's enduring prestige in the popular mind. MacDiarmid, for example, was probably right in the justification which underlay his slogan – 'Not Burns – Dunbar!' It was the calculated misunderstanding of Burns which irritated MacDiarmid, and which, in its turn, was used to denigrate other kinds of poetry. Literatures sometimes stand in need of punishing reassessment, and what MacDiarmid attempted was the redirection of Scottish taste to Dunbar's more cultivated and comprehensive artistry. Unfortunately, he also intended by it the need to reconstruct that pre-1707 Scottish psyche, which, as I've suggested already, smacks of an intellectually conceived regression on a heroic scale and may anyway be impossible. Perhaps all it amounts to is a dismissal of Englishness. He also underrated Burns's artistry, an aspect of the national poet which has been appreciated only in relatively recent times.

Much of Burns's democratic and egalitarian spirit is continued by Scottish writing in both verse and prose. After all, Burns came from the common people, not from a privileged section of society, as, too, did MacDiarmid, and as have many Scottish writers since. Most Scottish poetry, when compared with its English counterpart, stands in a closer relationship to its potential audience. A natural, uncourted ease of popularity is self-evident, to those who have experienced it, in MacCaig, MacLean (and, possibly, poetry by native speakers of Gaelic in general), Morgan, Smith, and some younger writers like Tom Leonard and Liz Lochhead. Garioch enjoyed it, as did Goodsir Smith and Douglas Young. But by *A Drunk Man Looks at the Thistle* MacDiarmid was set on a course plotted to avoid vulgar repute.

It is too soon to be sure of what Scottish poetry (or any other) might be like in even a decade's time; but there are good grounds for believing that it will continue to merge demotic with more aesthetic approaches. Robin Fulton, Kenneth White and Stewart Conn occupy what Europeans call 'the middle generation'. Of the three I've mentioned Conn is closest to the examples of his predecessors, while Fulton and White have founded most of their work on eclectic resources. Fulton lives in Scandinavia; in addition to his own poetry he is the translator of Tomas Tranströmer and other Swedish writers. Kenneth White lives and works in France, and is widely travelled, an experience which has helped him to form his idea of 'geo-poetics', or what Norman Douglas called 'intellectual nomadism'. His work was re-introduced to British readers as recently as 1989, although it had been appearing consistently in France in bilingual editions. There was nothing new about the postponement of White's reputation in Scotland. What was surprising was, and perhaps still is, his importance in France, in contrast to his (relative) neglect at home. His work shows a more modernist style as well as a more spiritual and philosophical bias than most Scottish poetry of his time. Equally interesting is that he counts MacDiarmid's poetry in English among his other influences.

Another version of vernacular Scots, urban Glaswegian speech, has been released by Tom Leonard. His concern with langwij ('the langwij a thi guhtr') contests political and other forms of condescension with a humour that emphasizes rather than disguises his indignation. He could have been assisted in this liberating act of local discovery by the climate of experiment and self-confidence established by Edwin Morgan. Other sources of energy, however, include William Carlos Williams, the guidance provided by socio-linguistics and the support of a growing number of writers in Glasgow, of both verse and prose. Political as Leonard's poetry is, it opens up the wider issues of indigenous speech. 'Fathers and Sons' exposes class shame and general pressures on personal and poetic identity more damaging than the use of phonetic urban dialect which he is questioned about at a poetry reading:

> I remember being ashamed of my father
> when he whispered the words out loud
> reading the newspaper.

In a country where the majority of writers are born to non-literary families, the subsequent distance which education can put between them and their origins is often painfully vivid. Accent is an audible yardstick for gauging social origins throughout the British Isles; but in Scotland it can seem as if the social controllers have turned up the volume. Leonard's poetry has contributed towards an improved equanimity in a society which used to be more than vulnerable to condescension and discouragement.

As with James Kelman's novels and stories it could come to be regarded as a major innovation in recent Scottish writing. If so, it was one which could hardly have been predicted, in the light of what preceded it – MacDiarmid's imperiously intellectual perspectives on just-about-everything; the use of a Scots diction rooted in the past and remote from modern city life; the rural associations of MacCaig, Smith, Brown and the Gaelic poets.

However, there is a connection between Leonard's Glaswegian idiom and Scots language in general. When Lord Cockburn described the speech of the ruthless judge Lord Braxfield (d. 1799) as one of a 'cherished coarseness', he pointed to an aspect of the Scots vernacular of which readers and writers have since proved themselves shy. As well as a sonorous dignity, it has a bias towards a raspingly reductive indignation and low humour. Perhaps that is true of most languages; but it seems peculiar to Scotland that it should be enjoyed, the evidence being the extent to which it seeps across class barriers while remaining identified with one class. In his Glaswegian poems, Leonard writes through that single class, the Glasgow working class, relishing the degree to which he exposes himself to charges of impropriety as he proceeds, and showing these accusations as vulnerable, class-informed assumptions.

Leonard's style is a difficult one for younger writers to emulate without at the same time announcing where it was found. Once again it is the distinctiveness of the best Scottish poets that asserts itself; it is as if an intuitive, anti-canonical urge runs through a major part of Scottish poetry in this century, which, if true, suggests the extent to which an anxious seriousness lies just beneath the surface of a good deal of the poetry that has appeared, or even an obligation to contribute to a culture worthy of a writer's best redemptive effort. The value of Leonard's work lies in how it castigates social shame and the encumbrances of inferiorist points of view directed at poetry in either English, Scots or Gaelic. It adds to the voice's confidence. Time-dishonoured customs locate the Glasgow voice and its idiom in low comedy or brutalized social circumstances; it is a voice which convention steeps in shame, squalor, crime, frustration and violence. Leonard's poetry takes these predictable attitudes and stands them on their heads. As in W. S. Graham's very different poetry, the energy flows from an intuitive emphasis on everything suggested by 'always language / Is where the people are;' or, as Leonard says, perhaps tongue-in-cheekily, 'all living language is sacred' – an easy piety to utter, but a more difficult one to demonstrate in poetry. Leonard's work tries to show that a demotic urban dialect is as fitted for poetry as more predictable forms of language.

Equally colloquial in its reliance on accent and an actual speaking voice (or voices), Liz Lochhead's poetry appears to have drawn its justifications from the poetry-reading performance as much as from anything in print that has gone into its making. In her work, freer, if punchily rhythmical passages of writing tend to evolve into snappily metrical and rhyming clusters. Her verve is that of a story-teller. Live listeners seem taken for granted, as if the poet was quite unafraid of her audience, whether her purpose is to entertain or deliver more critical perspectives on her feminine subjects. Even if they describe accurately what has been written in the past, the so-called characteristics of a country's poetry may end up inhibiting new work, and it could be wise to be wary of them.* Directness, immediacy of address, the sense of an audience, combine, however, into what does seem to be a permanent feature of much if not all Scottish poetry, a distinctive part of *praefervidum ingenium Scotorum*.

Earlier in the century women poets were prominent – Rachel Annand Taylor, Violet Jacob, Marion Angus and H. B. Cruickshank being the best known. Until the 1960s, however, literary women might have been discouraged by a conspi-cuously male-centred poetic country. Liz Lochhead, Valerie Gillies, Kathleen Jamie and a number of others have corrected that imbalance, a development which could be as important as the banishing of stigma from the Scottish voice.

'Did I ever hear him mention Scotland?' Geoffrey Grigson wrote of Norman Cameron in his *Recollections*:†

It was himself he insisted on, not a Scotch self; a human self. I knew vaguely he had been at school at Fettes, which was no more than a name to me. Otherwise he seemed as much a Southern Englishman, as much a user of the English language as any of us. Partition or a cultural sub-nationalism would have seemed to him pointless, even ridiculous. His English, the English he spoke, the English he wrote, had no trace of Scotch accent or Scotch peculiarity.

Relatively few Scottish writers would care to deserve the kind of compliment that Grigson paid his friend. What Grigson reveals is a wrinkled eighteenth-century distrust of too much dissimilarity; it emanates from a state of mind foreshadowed in Boswell's *Life of Johnson*, where, as Boswell makes clear, nervousness at differences in accent and vocabulary constituted a powerful fear among Scots for whom Scotland was too small for their ambitions. Advancement in England and the Empire was understood to demand a transformation of self and language. 'Scotticisms' were dreaded as tell-tale signs of social and intellectual inferiority. Merely to mention that most Scottish poets did not attend Fettes or any other public school can sound like labouring the point. Grigson's attitude would seem

---

* Such multiple 'characteristics' can be encountered in Kurt Wittig's *The Scottish Tradition in Literature*, Oliver & Boyd, 1958.
† Chatto & Windus, 1985.

to suggest that Scottish writing ought not to be taken seriously unless its language is as much that of a Southern Englishman as his own and that of others of his milieu. 'Scotch self' and 'Scotch peculiarity' give him away as having been misled by social class and nationality – his own. At the other extreme, it can hardly be denied that in this war of the accents the Scots are well capable of returning the insult with the same mindless prejudice. Over-strenuous insistences on a 'Scotch self' can result in the staging of highly unpleasant caricatures. Nationality, and its chum, patriotism, encourage unedifying hyperbole. In a country like Scotland, where nationalism is an active political force, and not just in the Scottish National Party, the temptation is that Scottish subjects should be foregrounded explicitly and at the expense of poetry's inclusiveness.

Younger writers have succeeded in circumventing the cruder embarrassments (to poetry) of what at times can appear to be a depressing political scene. In the relatively recent past, Scottish poetry tended to look like too much of a special case. It suffered from its own introverted publicity. Poets like Stewart Conn and Robin Fulton can seem unusual in the Scottish context in that they have been content to write what they write. Liz Lochhead and poets younger than her have shown a similar lack of embarrassment with their own subjects. Andrew Greig, Gerald Mangan and Frank Kuppner reflect a local personality, but there is rarely any sense of their having gone out of their way to get it into a poem. If anything explains the unclenched nationalism, or refusal of any kind of nationalism on a poem's surface, it is the eclectic reading and wider range of influences to which younger writers have exposed themselves. Greig, for example, admits John Berryman among his formative sources. Robert Crawford's work is usually very Scottish in subject matter, but its panache derives chiefly from the treatment of Scottish incidents and personalities with a newer confidence. A wide frame of literary experience is self-evident in MacCaig, Smith and Morgan, but it has taken some time for it to percolate through to the general advantage of younger generations of writers. It seems narrower and more aboriginal in the work of Scots-writing poets like Garioch and Goodsir Smith, despite their translating. While Raymond Vettese's poetry in Scots sometimes ruminates about the language he uses and whether the struggle is worth the sweat, there are signs of a newer kind of formal engagement in his work, as there is in W. N. Herbert's.

Whatever else it might be, a poetry that includes MacDiarmid, Muir, MacLean, MacCaig, Soutar, Garioch, Goodsir Smith, Morgan, Graham, Brown, Thomson and Iain Crichton Smith, is not weak or lacking in variety. In this century Scottish poetry has come a long way indeed from those 'analphabetic versifiers of post-Burnsian Scotland' whose ghosts were hunted down by MacDiarmid. 'Myopic toe-the-line all-in patrioteering' has been shut away in the Caledonian cupboard, too, where, however, it hangs in the shape of a skeleton.

Poetry in Scots has survived its worst history; since MacDiarmid, it has been less prone to sound like the affectation of the national stammer. That poetry in Gaelic should not only have survived, but enjoyed a renascence, is little short of miraculous. At one time a Scottish poet writing in English could be bullied into believing that his or her language was not a native tongue. Similarly, the translating-back-in-time feeling of the Scots language, with its sometimes extruded diction, could generate unsettling questions about the authenticity of what seemed an archaizing mode. Hectoring issues such as these now appear to have been settled, and the liberty of three languages established. To continue to use Eliot's outline, contemporary poetry in Scotland amounts to a *sixth* phase in its history. It is one which enjoys enough self-confidence to be able to reject historical summaries such as Eliot's; and it can accommodate individual acceptances or rejections of the positions taken by its major figures. It is markedly open to the stimulus of poetry from beyond the British Isles. It might even have developed an easier relationship with English poetry, while, at the same time, maintaining that the differences between Scottish and English literature are obvious, in whatever language. It speaks for itself that Eliot's fourth phase of Scottish literature should have been erased (it was always doubtful, in any case), and replaced with another, with yet another growing from it. It has been a hectic century for Scottish poetry, one filled with thrilling turbulence, and in which the stakes have been high – the survival of a national identity.

Douglas Dunn, Ferry-port-on-Craig, April 1992

Alasdair Maclean withdrew his poems, on political grounds, from this paperback edition. Several new poets have been added.

D. D.

Twentieth-Century Scottish Poetry

Snow

I

'Who affirms that crystals are alive?'
  I affirm it, let who will deny: –
Crystals are engendered, wax and thrive,
  Wane and wither; I have seen them die.

Trust me, masters, crystals have their day,
  Eager to attain the perfect norm,
Lit with purpose, potent to display
  Facet, angle, colour, beauty, form.

II

Water-crystals need for flower and root
  Sixty clear degrees, no less, no more;
Snow, so fickle, still in this acute
  Angle thinks, and learns no other lore:

Such its life, and such its pleasure is,
  Such its art and traffic, such its gain,
Evermore in new conjunctions this
  Admirable angle to maintain.

Crystalcraft in every flower and flake
  Snow exhibits, of the welkin free:
Crystalline are crystals for the sake,
  All and singular, of crystalry.

Yet does every crystal of the snow
  Individualize, a seedling sown
Broadcast, but instinct with power to grow
  Beautiful in beauty of its own.

Every flake with all its prongs and dints
  Burns ecstatic as a new-lit star:
Men are not more diverse, finger-prints
  More dissimilar than snow-flakes are.

Worlds of men and snow endure, increase,
  Woven of power and passion to defy
Time and travail: only races cease,
  Individual men and crystals die.

III

Jewelled shapes of snow whose feathery showers,
  Fallen or falling wither at a breath,
All afraid are they, and loth as flowers
  Beasts and men to tread the way to death.

Once I saw upon an object-glass,
  Martyred underneath a microscope,
One elaborate snow-flake slowly pass,
  Dying hard, beyond the reach of hope.

Still from shape to shape the crystal changed,
  Writhing in its agony; and still,
Less and less elaborate, arranged
  Potently the angle of its will.

Tortured to a simple final form,
  Angles six and six divergent beams,
Lo, in death it touched the perfect norm
  Verifying all its crystal dreams!

IV

Such the noble tragedy of one
  Martyred snow-flake. Who can tell the fate
Heinous and uncouth of showers undone,
  Fallen in cities! – showers that expiate

Errant lives from polar worlds adrift
  Where the great millennial snows abide;
Castaways from mountain-chains that lift
  Snowy summits in perennial pride;

Nomad snows, or snows in evil day
  Born to urban ruin, to be tossed,
Trampled, shovelled, ploughed and swept away
  Down the seething sewers: all the frost

Flowers of heaven melted up with lees,
  Offal, recrement, but every flake
Showing to the last in fixed degrees
  Perfect crystals for the crystal's sake.

                    V

Usefulness of snow is but a chance
  Here in temperate climes with winter sent,
Sheltering earth's prolonged hibernal trance:
  All utility is accident.

Sixty clear degrees the joyful snow,
  Practising economy of means,
Fashions endless beauty in, and so
  Glorifies the universe with scenes

Arctic and antarctic: stainless shrouds,
  Ermine woven in silvery frost, attire
Peaks in every land among the clouds
  Crowned with snows to catch the morning's fire.

VIOLET JACOB (1863–1946)

The Baltic

'Whaur are ye gaen sae fast, my bairn,
　　It's no tae the schule ye'll win?'
'Doon tae the shore at the fit o' the toon
　　Tae bide till the brigs come in.'

'Awa' noo wi' ye and turn ye hame,
　　Ye'll no hae the time tae bide;
It's twa lang months or the brigs come back
　　On the lift o' a risin' tide.'

beam of light

'I'll sit me doon at the water's mou'
　　Till there's niver a blink o' licht,
For my feyther bad' me tae tryst wi' him
　　In the dairkness o' yesternicht.

' "Rise ye an' rin tae the shore", says he,
　　"At the cheep o' the waukin' bird,
And I'll bring ye a tale o' a foreign land
　　The like that ye niver heard." '

stop your nonsense

'Oh, haud yer havers, ye feckless wean,
　　It was but a dream ye saw,
For he's far, far north wi' the Baltic men

violent fall

　　I' the hurl o' the Baltic snaw;

And what did he ca' yon foreign land?'
　　'He tell'tna its name tae me,
But I doot it's no by the Baltic shore,
　　For he said there was nae mair sea.'

MARION ANGUS (1866–1946)

Alas! Poor Queen

She was skilled in music and the dance
And the old arts of love
At the court of the poisoned rose
And the perfumed glove,
And gave her beautiful hand
To the pale Dauphin
A triple crown to win –
And she loved little dogs
    And parrots
  And red-legged partridges
And the golden fishes of the Duc de Guise
And a pigeon with a blue ruff
She had from Monsieur d'Elbœuf.

Master John Knox was no friend to her;
She spoke him soft and kind,
Her honeyed words were Satan's lure
The unwary soul to bind
'Good sir, doth a lissome shape
And a comely face
Offend your God His Grace
Whose Wisdom maketh these
Golden fishes of the Duc de Guise?'

She rode through Liddesdale with a song;
'Ye streams sae wondrous strang,
Oh, mak' me a wrack as I come back
But spare me as I gang,'
While a hill-bird cried and cried
Like a spirit lost
By the grey storm-wind tost.

Consider the way she had to go.
Think of the hungry snare,
The net she herself had woven,

Aware or unaware,
Of the dancing feet grown still,
The blinded eyes –
Queens should be cold and wise,
And she loved little things,
     Parrots
   And red-legged partridges
And the golden fishes of the Duc de Guise
And the pigeon with the blue ruff
She had from Monsieur d'Elbœuf.

LEWIS SPENCE (1874–1955)

The Prows O' Reekie

fine

O wad this braw hie-heapit toun
Sail aff like an enchanted ship,
Drift owre the warld's seas up and doun,
And kiss wi' Venice lip to lip,
Or anchor into Naples' Bay
A misty island far astray
Or set her rock to Athens' wa',
Pillar to pillar, stane to stane,
The cruikit spell o' her backbane,
Yon shadow-mile o' spire and vane,

would surpass them all
lose

Wad ding them a', wad ding them a'!
Cadiz wad tine the admiralty

emerald

O' yonder emerod fair sea,
Gibraltar frown for frown exchange

elbow

Wi' Nigel's crags at elbuck-range,
The rose-red banks o' Lisbon make
Mair room in Tagus for her sake.

A hoose is but a puppet-box
To keep life's images frae knocks,

scrape
stepped gables

But mannikins scrieve oot their sauls
Upon its craw-steps and its walls;
Whaur hae they writ them mair sublime
Than on yon gable-ends o' time?

The Carse

It is a thousand sunsets since I lay
In many-birded Gowrie,* and did know
Its shadow for my soul, that passionate Tay
Out of my heart did flow.

* *Carse of Gowrie* low-lying river-land

The immortal hour the hate of time defies.
Men of my loins a million years away
Shall have the gloom of Gowrie in their eyes,
And in their blood the Tay.

Great Tay of the Waves

O that yon river micht nae mair
   Rin through the channels o' my sleep;
too sorely   My bluid has felt its tides owre sair,
   Its waves hae drooned my dreams owre deep.

O why should Tay be a' my day
   And Buddon links be a' my nicht,
The warld o' a' my walks be gray
   Wi' yon far sands' unwarldly licht?

sea mists   As haars the windless waters find
   The unguarded instant falls a prey
innocent   To sakeless shadows o' the mind,
   And a' my life rins back to Tay.

Deep in the saul the early scene –
   Ah, let him play wi' suns wha can,
The cradle's pented on the een,
quarter   The native airt resolves the man!

The Stown Bairn
stolen

O dinna ye spy yon castel braw
beyond/crests   Ayont the gress-green riggs o'sea,
inside it There's a tower intil't and a bower intil't
   And a louping lyon has power intil't
Rampin' amang the win's that thraw
rowdily   Yon banner bousteouslie.
mother O whaten a castel is yon, ma minnie,

compels   That harles the hert's bluid oot o' me
                         And beckons me owre a warld o' watters
fate   To seek its weird or dee?

                   Yon castel braw, ma bonny bit hinny,
magic   It is the Scottis Glamourie;
                   There's a spell intil't and a well intil't
                  And the sang o' a siller bell intil't,
barren and gorse-choked   But the braes abune it are dowf and whinny,
                  And the bracken buries the lea.
sea mist   It's noo a ship wi' the haar for sail,
then a stronghold   And syne a strength, as ye may see,
besides   Forbye it's a hill wi' a hollow ha',
                  Whaur the fludes sough eerilie.

                   O minnie, see yon mune-white steed
swims   That sowms sae soople owre the sea;
                 Wi' a horn on his heid, he mak's sic speid
exclusively   As alanerlie the clan o' the deid,
fond   And I ken he's fain o' me.
                  O whaur are ye, ma gentle bairn
                  This moment was upon ma knee?
                   I cuddled ye i' the cruik o' ma airm,
                  And noo ye're awa frae me!

RACHEL ANNAND TAYLOR (1876–1960)

The Princess of Scotland

'Who are you that so strangely woke,
  And raised a fine hand?'
Poverty wears a scarlet cloke
      In my land.

'Duchies of dreamland, emerald, rose
  Lie at your command?'
Poverty like a princess goes
      In my land.

'Wherefore the mask of silken lace
  Tied with a golden band?'
Poverty walks with wanton grace
      In my land.

'Why do you softly, richly speak
  Rhythm so sweetly-scanned?'
Poverty hath the Gaelic and Greek
      In my land.

'There's a far-off scent about you seems
  Born in Samarkand.'
Poverty hath luxurious dreams
      In my land.

'You have wounds that like passion-flowers you hide:
  I cannot understand.'
Poverty hath one name with Pride
      In my land.

'Oh! Will you draw your last sad breath
  'Mid bitter bent and sand?'
Poverty begs from none but Death
      In my land.

SIR ALEXANDER GRAY (1882–1967)

Scotland

Here in the uplands
The soil is ungrateful;
The fields, red with sorrel,
Are stony and bare.
A few trees, wind-twisted –
Or are they but bushes? –
Stand stubbornly guarding
A home here and there.

Scooped out like a saucer,
The land lies before me,
The waters, once scattered,
Flow orderly now
Through fields where the ghosts
Of the marsh and the moorland
Still ride the old marches,
Despising the plough.

The marsh and the moorland
Are not to be banished;
The bracken and heather,
The glory of broom,
Usurp all the balks
And the field's broken fringes,
And claim from the sower
Their portion of room.

This is my country,
The land that begat me.
These windy spaces
Are surely my own.
And those who here toil
In the sweat of their faces
Are flesh of my flesh
And bone of my bone.

Hard is the day's task —
Scotland, stern Mother! —
Wherewith at all times
Thy sons have been faced —
Labour by day,
And scant rest in the gloaming
With want an attendant
Not lightly outpaced.

Yet do thy children
Honour and love thee,
Harsh is thy schooling
Yet great is the gain.
True hearts and strong limbs,
The beauty of faces
Kissed by the wind
And caressed by the rain.

ANDREW YOUNG (1885–1971)

On the Pilgrims' Road

That I had hit the Road
    I partly knew
From a great Roman snail
    And sombre yew;
But that my steps went from
    And not towards
The shrine of good St Thomas,
    I thought of afterwards.

So I adored today
    No, not his ghost,
But the saints in Westwell window,
    And her the most
Who knelt there with no head
    But was so very
Adorable a saint
    In dress of crushed strawberry.

The Stockdoves

They rose up in a twinkling cloud
And wheeled about and bowed
To settle on the trees
Perching like small clay images.

Then with a noise of sudden rain
They clattered off again
And over Ballard Down
They circled like a flying town.

Though one could sooner blast a rock
Than scatter that dense flock
That through the winter weather
Some iron rule has held together,

Yet in another month from now
Love like a spark will blow
Those birds the country over
To drop in trees, lover by lover.

A Heap of Faggots

Faggots of ash, elm, oak
That dark loose snowflakes touch and soak,
An unlit fire they lie
With cold inhospitality.

Nothing will light them now,
Sticks that with only lichen glow
And crumble to touchwood
Soft and unfit for fire's food.

And with wren, finch and tit
And all the silent birds that sit
In this snow-travelled wood
I warm myself at my own blood.

A Prehistoric Camp

It was the time of year
   Pale lambs leap with thick leggings on
Over small hills that are not there,
   That I climbed Eggardon.

The hedgerows still were bare,
   None ever knew so late a year;
Birds built their nests in the open air,
   Love conquering their fear.

But there on the hill-crest,
   Where only larks or stars look down,
Earthworks exposed a vaster nest,
   Its race of men long flown.

Passing the Graveyard

I see you did not try to save
The bouquet of white flowers I gave;
So fast they wither on your grave.

Why does it hurt the heart to think
Of that most bitter abrupt brink
Where the low-shouldered coffins sink?

These living bodies that we wear
So change by every seventh year
That in a new dress we appear;

Limbs, spongy brain and slogging heart,
No part remains the selfsame part;
Like streams they stay and still depart.

You slipped slow bodies in the past;
Then why should we be so aghast
You flung off the whole flesh at last?

Let him who loves you think instead
That like a woman who has wed
You undressed first and went to bed.

Sudden Thaw

When day dawned with unusual light,
Hedges in snow stood half their height
And in the white-paved village street
Children were walking without feet.

But now by their own breath kept warm
Muck-heaps are naked at the farm
And even through the shrinking snow
Dead bents and thistles start to grow.

The Shepherd's Hut

The smear of blue peat smoke
That staggered on the wind and broke,
The only sign of life,
Where was the shepherd's wife,
Who left those flapping clothes to dry,
Taking no thought for her family?
For, as they bellied out
And limbs took shape and waved about,
I thought, She little knows
That ghosts are trying on her children's clothes.

HELEN B. CRUICKSHANK (1886–1975)

The Ponnage Pool

'. . . *Sing*
Some simple silly sang
O' willows or o' mimulus
A river's banks alang.'
  Hugh MacDiarmid

remember

[place name]

I mind o' the Ponnage Pule,
The reid brae risin',
Morphie Lade,
An' the saumon that louped the dam,
A tree i' Martin's Den
Wi' names carved on it;
But I ken na wha I am.

one

Ane o' the names was mine,
An' still I own it.
Naething it kens
O' a' that mak's up me.
Less I ken o' mysel'
Than the saumon wherefore
It rins up Esk frae the sea.

I am the deep o' the pule,
The fish, the fisher,
The river in spate,
The broon o' the far peat-moss,
The shingle bricht wi' the flooer
O' the yellow mim'lus,
The martin fleein' across.

I mind o' the Ponnage Pule
On a shinin' mornin',
The saumon fishers
Nettin' the bonny brutes –
I' the slithery dark o' the boddom
O' Charon's Coble

one   Ae day I'll faddom my doobts.

EDWIN MUIR (1887–1959)

Childhood

Long time he lay upon the sunny hill,
　To his father's house below securely bound.
Far off the silent, changing sound was still,
　With the black islands lying thick around.

He saw each separate height, each vaguer hue,
　Where the massed islands rolled in mist away,
And though all ran together in his view
　He knew that unseen straits between them lay.

Often he wondered what new shores were there.
　In thought he saw the still light on the sand,
The shallow water clear in tranquil air,
　And walked through it in joy from strand to
　　　　　　　　　　　　　　　　　　strand.

Over the sound a ship so slow would pass
　That in the black hill's gloom it seemed to lie.
The evening sound was smooth like sunken glass,
　And time seemed finished ere the ship passed by.

Grey tiny rocks slept round him where he lay,
　Moveless as they, more still as evening came,
The grasses threw straight shadows far away,
　And from the house his mother called his name.

The Town Betrayed

Our homes are eaten out by time,
　Our lawns strewn with our listless sons,
Our harlot daughters lean and watch
　The ships crammed down with shells and guns.

Like painted prows far out they lean:
  A world behind, a world before.
The leaves are covering up our hills,
  Neptune has locked the shore.

Our yellow harvests lie forlorn
  And there we wander like the blind,
Returning from the golden field
  With famine in our mind.

Far inland now the glittering swords
  In order rise, in order fall,
In order on the dubious field
  The dubious trumpets call.

Yet here there is no word, no sign
  But quiet murder in the street.
Our leaf-light lives are spared or taken
  By men obsessed and neat.

We stand beside our windows, see
  In order dark disorder come,
And prentice killers duped by death
  Bring and not know our doom.

Our cattle wander at their will.
  To-day a horse pranced proudly by.
The dogs run wild. Vultures and kites
  Wait in the towers for us to die.

At evening on the parapet
  We sit and watch the sun go down,
Reading the landscape of the dead,
  The sea, the hills, the town.

There our ancestral ghosts are gathered.
  Fierce Agamemnon's form I see,
Watching as if his tents were time
  And Troy eternity.

We must take order, bar our gates,
  Fight off these phantoms. Inland now
Achilles, Siegfried, Lancelot
  Have sworn to bring us low.

Scotland 1941

We were a tribe, a family, a people.
Wallace and Bruce guard now a painted field,
And all may read the folio of our fable,
Peruse the sword, the sceptre and the shield.
A simple sky roofed in that rustic day,
The busy corn-fields and the haunted holms,
The green road winding up the ferny brae.
But Knox and Melville clapped their preaching palms
And bundled all the harvesters away,
Hoodicrow Peden in the blighted corn
Hacked with his rusty beak the starving haulms.
Out of that desolation we were born.

Courage beyond the point and obdurate pride
Made us a nation, robbed us of a nation.
Defiance absolute and myriad-eyed
That could not pluck the palm plucked our
                                         damnation.
We with such courage and the bitter wit
To fell the ancient oak of loyalty,
And strip the peopled hill and the altar bare,
And crush the poet with an iron text,
How could we read our souls and learn to be?
Here a dull drove of faces harsh and vexed,
We watch our cities burning in their pit,
To salve our souls grinding dull lucre out,
We, fanatics of the frustrate and the half,
Who once set Purgatory Hill in doubt.
Now smoke and dearth and money everywhere,
Mean heirlooms of each fainter generation,
And mummied housegods in their musty niches,
Burns and Scott, sham bards of a sham nation,

And spiritual defeat wrapped warm in riches,
No pride but pride of pelf. Long since the young
Fought in great bloody battles to carve out
This towering pulpit of the Golden Calf,
Montrose, Mackail, Argyle, perverse and brave,
Twisted the stream, unhooped the ancestral hill.
Never had Dee or Don or Yarrow or Till
Huddled such thriftless honour in a grave.

Such wasted bravery idle as a song,
Such hard-won ill might prove Time's verdict wrong,
And melt to pity the annalist's iron tongue.

The Ring

Long since we were a family, a people,
The legends say; an old kind-hearted king
Was our foster father, and our life a fable.

Nature in wrath broke through the grassy ring
Where all our gathered treasures lay in sleep —
Many a rich and many a childish thing.

She filled with hoofs and horns the quiet keep.
Her herds beat down the turf and nosed the shrine
In bestial wonder, bull and adder and ape,

Lion and fox, all dressed by fancy fine
In human flesh and armed with arrows and spears;
But on the brow of each a secret sign

That haughtily put aside the sorrowful years
Or struck them down in stationary rage;
Yet they had tears that were not like our tears,

And new, all new, for Nature knows no age.
Fatherless, sonless, homeless haunters, they
Had never known the vow and the pilgrimage,

Poured from one fount into the faithless day.
We are their sons, but long ago we heard
Our fathers or our fathers' fathers say

Out of their dream the long-forgotten word
That rounded again the ring where sleeping lay
Our treasures, still unrusted and unmarred.

The Castle

All through that summer at ease we lay,
And daily from the turret wall
We watched the mowers in the hay
And the enemy half a mile away.
They seemed no threat to us at all.

For what, we thought, had we to fear
With our arms and provender, load on load,
Our towering battlements, tier on tier,
And friendly allies drawing near
On every leafy summer road.

Our gates were strong, our walls were thick,
So smooth and high, no man could win
A foothold there, no clever trick
Could take us, have us dead or quick.
Only a bird could have got in.

What could they offer us for bait?
Our captain was brave and we were true . . .
There was a little private gate,
A little wicked wicket gate.
The wizened warder let them through.

Oh then our maze of tunnelled stone
Grew thin and treacherous as air.
The cause was lost without a groan,
The famous citadel overthrown,
And all its secret galleries bare.

How can this shameful tale be told?
I will maintain until my death
We could do nothing, being sold;
Our only enemy was gold,
And we had no arms to fight it with.

The Labyrinth

Since I emerged that day from the labyrinth,
Dazed with the tall and echoing passages,
The swift recoils, so many I almost feared
I'd meet myself returning at some smooth corner,
Myself or my ghost, for all there was unreal
After the straw ceased rustling and the bull
Lay dead upon the straw and I remained,
Blood-splashed, if dead or alive I could not tell
In the twilight nothingness (I might have been
A spirit seeking his body through the roads
Of intricate Hades) – ever since I came out
To the world, the still fields swift with flowers, the
                                                              trees
All bright with blossom, the little green hills, the sea,
The sky and all in movement under it,
Shepherds and flocks and birds and the young and
                                                              old,
(I stared in wonder at the young and the old,
For in the maze time had not been with me;
I had strayed, it seemed, past sun and season and
                                                              change,
Past rest and motion, for I could not tell
At last if I moved or stayed; the maze itself
Revolved around me on its hidden axis
And swept me smoothly to its enemy,
The lovely world) – since I came out that day,
There have been times when I have heard my
                                                              footsteps
Still echoing in the maze, and all the roads
That run through the noisy world, deceiving streets
That meet and part and meet, and rooms that open

Into each other – and never a final room –
Stairways and corridors and antechambers
That vacantly wait for some great audience,
The smooth sea-tracks that open and close again,
Tracks undiscoverable, indecipherable,
Paths on the earth and tunnels underground,
And bird-tracks in the air – all seemed a part
Of the great labyrinth. And then I'd stumble
In sudden blindness, hasten, almost run,
As if the maze itself were after me
And soon must catch me up. But taking thought,
I'd tell myself, 'You need not hurry. This
Is the firm good earth. All roads lie free before you.'
But my bad spirit would sneer, 'No, do not hurry.
No need to hurry. Haste and delay are equal
In this one world, for there's no exit, none,
No place to come to, and you'll end where you are,
Deep in the centre of the endless maze.'

I could not live if this were not illusion.
It is a world, perhaps; but there's another.
For once in a dream or trance I saw the gods
Each sitting on the top of his mountain-isle,
While down below the little ships sailed by,
Toy multitudes swarmed in the habours, shepherds
drove
Their tiny flocks to the pastures, marriage feasts
Went on below, small birthdays and holidays,
Ploughing and harvesting and life and death,
And all permissible, all acceptable,
Clear and secure as in a limpid dream.
But they, the gods, as large and bright as clouds,
Conversed across the sounds in tranquil voices
High in the sky above the untroubled sea,
And their eternal dialogue was peace
Where all these things were woven, and this our life
Was as a chord deep in that dialogue,
As easy utterance of harmonious words,
Spontaneous syllables bodying forth a world.

That was the real world; I have touched it once,
And now shall know it always. But the lie,
The maze, the wild-wood waste of falsehood, roads
That run and run and never reach an end,
Embowered in error – I'd be prisoned there
But that my soul has birdwings to fly free.

Oh these deceits are strong almost as life.
Last night I dreamt I was in the labyrinth,
And woke far on. I did not know the place.

The Combat

It was not meant for human eyes,
That combat on the shabby patch
Of clods and trampled turf that lies
Somewhere beneath the sodden skies
For eye of toad or adder to catch.

And having seen it I accuse
The crested animal in his pride,
Arrayed in all the royal hues
Which hide the claws he well can use
To tear the heart out of the side.

Body of leopard, eagle's head
And whetted beak, and lion's mane,
And frost-grey hedge of feathers spread
Behind – he seemed of all things bred.
I shall not see his like again.

As for his enemy, there came in
A soft round beast as brown as clay;
All rent and patched his wretched skin;
A battered bag he might have been,
Some old used thing to throw away.

Yet he awaited face to face
The furious beast and the swift attack.

Soon over and done. That was no place
Or time for chivalry or for grace.
The fury had him on his back.

And two small paws like hands flew out
To right and left as the trees stood by.
One would have said beyond a doubt
This was the very end of the bout,
But that the creature would not die.

For ere the death-stroke he was gone,
Writhed, whirled, huddled into his den,
Safe somehow there. The fight was done,
And he had lost who had all but won.
But oh his deadly fury then.

A while the place lay blank, forlorn,
Drowsing as in relief from pain.
The cricket chirped, the grating thorn
Stirred, and a little sound was born.
The champions took their posts again.

And all began. The stealthy paw
Slashed out and in. Cold nothing save
These rags and tatters from the claw?
Nothing. And yet I never saw
A beast so helpless and so brave.

And now, while the trees stand watching, still
The unequal battle rages there.
The killing beast that cannot kill
Swells and swells in his fury till
You'd almost think it was despair.

One Foot in Eden

One foot in Eden still, I stand
And look across the other land.
The world's great day is growing late,

Yet strange these fields that we have planted
So long with crops of love and hate.
Time's handiworks by time are haunted,
And nothing now can separate
The corn and tares compactly grown.
The armorial weed in stillness bound
About the stalk; these are our own.
Evil and good stand thick around
In the fields of charity and sin
Where we shall lead our harvest in.

Yet still from Eden springs the root
As clean as on the starting day.
Time takes the foliage and the fruit
And burns the archetypal leaf
To shapes of terror and of grief
Scattered along the winter way.
But famished field and blackened tree
Bear flowers in Eden never known.
Blossoms of grief and charity
Bloom in these darkened fields alone.
What had Eden ever to say
Of hope and faith and pity and love
Until was buried all its day
And memory found its treasure trove?
Strange blessings never in Paradise
Fall from these beclouded skies.

To Franz Kafka

If we, the proximate damned, presumptive blest,
Were called one day to some high consultation
With the authentic ones, the worst and best
Picked from all time, how mean would be our

station.
Oh we could never bear the standing shame,
Equivocal ignominy of non-election;
We who will hardly answer to our name,
And on the road direct ignore direction.

But you, dear Franz, sad champion of the drab
And half, would watch the tell-tale shames drift in
(As if they were troves of treasure) not aloof,
But with a famishing passion quick to grab
Meaning, and read on all the leaves of sin
Eternity's secret script, the saving proof.

The Difficult Land

This is a difficult land. Here things miscarry
Whether we care, or do not care enough.
The grain may pine, the harlot weed grow haughty,
Sun, rain, and frost alike conspire against us:
You'd think there was malice in the very air.
And the spring floods and summer droughts: our
                                                        fields
Mile after mile of soft and useless dust.
On dull delusive days presaging rain
We yoke the oxen, go out harrowing,
Walk in the middle of an ochre cloud,
Dust rising before us and falling again behind us,
Slowly and gently settling where it lay.
These days the earth itself looks sad and senseless.
And when next day the sun mounts hot and lusty
We shake our fists and kick the ground in anger.
We have strange dreams: as that, in the early
                                                        morning
We stand and watch the silver drift of stars
Turn suddenly to a flock of black-birds flying.
And once in a lifetime men from over the border,
In early summer, the season of fresh campaigns,
Come trampling down the corn, and kill our cattle.
These things we know and by good luck or guidance
Either frustrate or, if we must, endure.
We are a people; race and speech support us,
Ancestral rite and custom, roof and tree,
Our songs that tell of our triumphs and disasters
(Fleeting alike), continuance of fold and hearth,
Our names and callings, work and rest and sleep,

And something that, defeated, still endures –
These things sustain us. Yet there are times
When name, identity, and our very hands,
Senselessly labouring, grow most hateful to us,
And we would gladly rid us of these burdens,
Enter our darkness through the doors of wheat
And the light veil of grass (leaving behind
Name, body, country, speech, vocation, faith)
And gather into the secrecy of the earth
Furrowed by broken ploughs lost deep in time.

We have such hours, but are drawn back again
By faces of goodness, faithful masks of sorrow,
Honesty, kindness, courage, fidelity,
The love that lasts a life's time. And the fields,
Homestead and stall and barn, springtime and

autumn.
(For we can love even the wandering seasons
In their inhuman circuit.) And the dead
Who lodge in us so strangely, unremembered,
Yet in their place. For how can we reject
The long last look on the ever-dying face
Turned backward from the other side of time?
And how offend the dead and shame the living
By these despairs? And how refrain from love?
This is a difficult country, and our home.

The Horses

Barely a twelvemonth after
The seven days war that put the world to sleep,
Late in the evening the strange horses came.
By then we had made our covenant with silence,
But in the first few days it was so still
We listened to our breathing and were afraid.
On the second day
The radios failed; we turned the knobs; no answer.
On the third day a warship passed us, heading north,
Dead bodies piled on the deck. On the sixth day

A plane plunged over us into the sea. Thereafter
Nothing. The radios dumb;
And still they stand in corners of our kitchens,
And stand, perhaps, turned on, in a million rooms
All over the world. But now if they should speak,
If on a sudden they should speak again,
If on the stroke of noon a voice should speak,
We would not listen, we would not let it bring
That old bad world that swallowed its children quick
At one great gulp. We would not have it again.
Sometimes we think of the nations lying asleep,
Curled blindly in impenetrable sorrow,
And then the thought confounds us with its
                                        strangeness.

The tractors lie about our fields; at evening
They look like dank sea-monsters couched and
                                        waiting.
We leave them where they are and let them rust:
'They'll moulder away and be like other loam'.
We make our oxen drag our rusty ploughs,
Long laid aside. We have gone back
Far past our fathers' land.
                            And then, that evening
Late in the summer the strange horses came.
We heard a distant tapping on the road,
A deepening drumming; it stopped, went on again
And at the corner changed to hollow thunder.
We saw the heads
Like a wild wave charging and were afraid.
We had sold our horses in our fathers' time
To buy new tractors. Now they were strange to us
As fabulous steeds set on an ancient shield
Or illustrations in a book of knights.
We did not dare go near them. Yet they waited,
Stubborn and shy, as if they had been sent
By an old command to find our whereabouts
And that long-lost archaic companionship.
In the first moment we had never a thought
That they were creatures to be owned and used.

Among them were some half-a-dozen colts
Dropped in some wilderness of the broken world,
Yet new as if they had come from their own Eden.
Since then they have pulled our ploughs and borne
                          our loads
But that free servitude still can pierce our hearts.
Our life is changed; their coming our beginning.

HUGH MACDIARMID (Christopher Murray Grieve) (1892–1978)

The Bonnie Broukit Bairn

For Peggy

fine in crimson

Mars is braw in crammasy,
Venus in a green silk goun,
The auld mune shak's her gowden feathers,

a bit of nonsense

Their starry talk's a wheen o' blethers,
Nane for thee a thochtie sparin',

neglected child

Earth, thou bonnie broukit bairn!

but weep
the whole of worthless
humanity

– *But greet, an' in your tears ye'll droun*
The haill clanjamfrie!

The Watergaw

one wet dusk in the ewe-
*tremble**

Ae weet forenicht i' the yow-trummle

rare

I saw yon antrin thing,

a broken rainbow

A watergaw wi' its chitterin' licht

beyond the downpour

Ayont the on-ding;
An' I thocht o' the last wild look ye gied
Afore ye deed!

no quarrel in the lark's house

There was nae reek i' the laverock's hoose
That nicht – an' nane i' mine;
But I hae thocht o' that foolish licht

since then

Ever sin' syne;
An' I think that mebbe at last I ken
What your look meant then.

The Eemis Stane

unsteady

at the very heart/harvest

I' the how-dumb-deid o' the cauld hairst nicht
The warl' like an eemis stane

in the sky

Wags i' the lift;

yow-trummle a cold spell in summer after sheep-shearing

snow blown in the air

An' my eerie memories fa'
Like a yowdendrift.

Like a yowdendrift so's I couldna read
The words cut oot i' the stane
moss   Had the fug o' fame
lichen   An' history's hazelraw
buried   No' yirdit thaim.

disgust

Scunner

hides   Your body derns
In its graces again
dreary earth As dreich grun' does
In the gowden grain,
And oot o' the daith
O' pride you rise
Wi' beauty yet
For a hauf-disguise.

sparkling   The skinklan' stars
Are but distant dirt.
very close   Tho' fer owre near
sometimes   You are still – whiles – girt
Wi' the bonnie licht
you should have lost You bood ha'e tint
– And I lo'e Love
Wi' a scunner in't.

Empty Vessel

beyond the hillock I met ayont the cairney
unkempt   A lass wi' tousie hair
Singin' till a bairnie
That was nae langer there.

winds   Wunds wi' warlds to swing
Dinna sing sae sweet,

The licht that bends owre a' thing
Is less ta'en up wi't.

from A Drunk Man Looks at the Thistle

lines 101–44

if she's not here   *Jean! Jean!* Gin *she's* no' here it's no' *oor* bed,
Or else I'm dreamin' deep and canna wauken,
very   But it's a fell queer dream if this is no'
A real hillside – and thae things thistles and bracken!

holding   It's hard wark haud'n by a thocht worth ha'en'
every man   And harder speakin't, and no' for ilka man;
Maist Thocht's like whisky – a thoosan' under proof,
And a sair price is pitten on't even than.

As Kirks wi' Christianity ha'e dune,
Burns Clubs wi' Burns – wi' a'thing it's the same,
anything   The core o' ocht is only for the few,
busy   Scorned by the mony, thrang wi'ts empty name.

And a' the names in History mean nocht
To maist folk but 'ideas o' their ain,'
The vera opposite o' onything
The Deid 'ud awn gin they cam' back again.

A greater Christ, a greater Burns, may come.
The maist they'll dae is to gi'e bigger pegs
To folly and conceit to hank their rubbish on.
truly!   They'll cheenge folks' talk but no' their natures, fegs!

I maun feed frae the common trough ana'
Whaur a' the lees o' hope are jumbled up;
While centuries like pigs are slorpin' owre't
Sall my wee 'oor by cryin': 'Let pass this cup'?

pig's snout   In wi' your gruntle then, puir wheengin' saul,
cattle-piss/the rest   Lap up the ugsome aidle wi' the lave,

What gin it's your ain vomit that you swill
yawning   And frae Life's gantin' and unfaddomed grave?

very much   I doot I'm geylies mixed, like Life itsel',
                 But I was never ane that thocht to pit
*pint-pot**   An ocean in a mutchkin. As the haill's
                 Mair than the pairt sae I than reason yet.

                 I dinna haud the warld's end in my heid
                 As maist folk think they dae; nor filter truth
                 In fishy gills through which its tides may poor
                 For ony *animalcula* forsooth.

laugh   I lauch to see my crazy little brain
                 – And ither folks' – tak'n' itsel' seriously,
blaze   And in a sudden lowe o' fun my saul
dazed   Blinks dozent as the owl I ken't to be.

                 I'll ha'e nae hauf-way hoose, but aye be whaur
                 Extremes meet – it's the only way I ken
                 To dodge the curst conceit o' bein' richt
                 That damns the vast majority o' men.

                 lines 477–512

                 [MAN AND THE INFINITE]

throbs   Nerves in stounds o' delight,
                 Muscles in pride o' power,
arrayed   Bluid as wi' roses dight
prominent   Life's toppin' pinnacles owre,
                 The thistle yet'll unite
                 Man and the Infinite!

nimble and swift with vigour   Swippert and swith wi' virr
hollows   In the howes o' man's hert
great   Forever its muckle roots stir
astir   Like a Leviathan astert,
                 Till'ts coils like a thistle's leafs

* *mutchkin* quarter of a Scottish pint (i.e. three-quarters of an imperial pint)

lightning   Sweep space wi' levin sheafs.

lowest   Frae laichest deeps o' the ocean
                               It rises in flight upon flight,
                               And yont its uttermaist motion
                               Can still set roses alight,
                               As else unreachable height
                               Fa's under its triumphin' sight.

                               Here is the root that feeds
*stalk**   The shank wi' the blindin' wings
*dwindling overhead to sparks** Dwinin' abundheid to gleids
*nimbuses**   Like stars in their keethin' rings,
                               And blooms in sunrise and sunset
gate   Inowre Eternity's yett.

                               Lay haud o' my hert and feel
stars   Fountains ootloupin' the starns
                               Or see the Universe reel
ardent brains   Set gaen' by my eident harns,
shoulder   Or test the strength o' my spauld
weight   The wecht o' a' thing to hauld!

                               – The howes o' Man's hert are bare,
                               The Dragon's left them for good,
                               There's nocht but naethingness there,
                               The hole whaur the Thistle stood,
                               That rootless and radiant flies
                               A Phoenix in Paradise! . . .

                               lines 612–35

                               [O WHA'S THE BRIDE?]

                               O wha's the bride that cairries the bunch
glimmering   O' thistles blinterin' white?
suspects   Her cuckold bridegroom little dreids
                               What he sall ken this nicht.

---

* *shank* also, a salmon after spawning (see keethin'); *gleids* or, something glimpsed through having been forced to
squint (?); *keethin'* turbulence in water made by fish

husband

For closer than gudeman can come
And closer to'r than hersel',
Wha didna need her maidenheid
Has wrocht his purpose fell.

O wha's been here afore me, lass,
And hoo did he get in?
  — *A man that deed or I was born*
  This evil thing has din.

And left, as it were on a corpse,
Your maidenheid to me?
  — *Nae lass, gudeman, sin' Time began*
has had   *'S hed ony mair to gi'e.*

But I can gi'e ye kindness, lad,
And a pair o' willin' hands,
And you sall ha'e my briests like stars,
My limb like willow wands,

And on my lips ye'll heed nae mair,
And in my hair forget,
The seed o' a' the men that in
My virgin womb ha'e met . . .

lines 636–43

[REPETITION COMPLEX]

Millions o' wimmen bring forth in pain
Millions o' bairns that are no' worth ha'en.

Wull ever a wumman be big again
Wi's muckle's a Christ? Yech, there's nae sayin'.

Gin that's the best that you ha'e comin',
faith   Fegs but I'm sorry for you, wumman!

Yet a'e thing's certain. – Your faith is great.

shy Whatever happens, you'll no' be blate! . . .

lines 644–51

[THE PROBLEM CHILD]

childbed Mary lay in jizzen
As it were claith o' gowd.

rags But it's in orra duds
every other birth* is wrapped Ilka ither bairntime's row'd.

Christ had never toothick,
Christ was never seeck,

troublesome But Man's a fiky bairn
colic, diarrhoea and toothache Wi' bellythraw, ripples, and worm-i'-the-cheek! . . .

lines 1219–30

[THE THISTLE'S CHARACTERISTICS]

The language that but sparely flooers
And maistly gangs to weed;
The thocht o' Christ and Calvary

going backwards and forwards Aye liddenin' in my heid;
And a' the dour provincial thocht
That merks the Scottish breed
– These are the thistle's characters,

argue To argie there's nae need.
Hoo weel my verse embodies
The thistle you can read!
– But will a Scotsman never
Frae this vile growth be freed? . . .

lines 1334–60

A black leaf owre a white leaf twirls,
flutters A grey leaf flauchters in atween,
Sae ply my thochts aboot the stem

---

*bairntime 'a woman's breeding time' (MacDiarmid); labour or lying-in

coagulated   O' loppert slime frae which they spring.
                                The thistle like a snawstorm drives,
                                Or like a flicht o' swallows lifts,
                                Or like a swarm o' midges hings,
                                A plague o' moths, a starry sky,
                                But's naething but a thistle yet,
                                And still the puzzle stands unsolved.
                                Beauty and ugliness alike,
                                And life and daith and God and man,
                                Are aspects o't but nane can tell
                                The secret that I'd fain find oot
                                O' this bricht hive, this sorry weed,
                                The tree that fills the universe,
like a dried herring shrinks Or like a reistit herrin' crines.

if   Gin I was sober I micht think
                                It was like something drunk men see!

                                The necromancy in my bluid
                                Through a' the gamut cheenges me
                                O' dwarf and giant, foul and fair,
                                But winna let me be mysel'
                                – My mither's womb that reins me still
test for occult authenticity Until I tae can prick the witch
                                And 'Wumman' cry wi' Christ at last,
                                'Then what hast thou to do wi' me?'

                                lines 1451–1548

                                [*part of* A STICK-NEST IN YGDRASIL*]

in every direction   Thou art the facts in ilka airt
force a way through   That breenge into infinity.
                                Criss-crossed wi' coontless ither facts
                                Nae man can follow, and o' which
                                He is himsel' a helpless pairt.
                                Held in their tangle as he were
                                A stick-nest in Ygdrasil!

---

* *stick-nest* probably MacDiarmid's poetic compound imaging a nest like a magpie's, in *Ygdrasil*, the world ash tree of ancient Norse myth

The less man sees the mair he is
Content wi't, but the mair he sees
The mair he kens hoo little o'
A' that there is he'll ever see,
And hoo it mak's confusion aye
The waur confoondit till at last
His brain inside his heid is like
bobbin   Ariadne wi' an empty pirn,
spinning   Or like a birlin' reel frae which
A whale has rived the line awa'.

abandoned   What better's a forhooied nest
loose straw Than shasloch scattered owre the grun'?

O hard it is for man to ken
He's no creation's goal nor yet
A benefitter by't at last –
A means to ends he'll never ken,
And as to michtier elements
The slauchtered brutes he eats to him
Or forms o' life owre sma' to see
Wi' which his heedless body swarms,
And a' man's thocht nae mair to them
spider's web Than ony moosewob to a man,
glittering   His Heaven to them the blinterin' o'
shithoose   A snail-trail on their closet wa'!

For what's an atom o' a twig
That tak's a billion to an inch
abundance   To a' the routh o' shoots that mak'
The bygrowth o' the Earth aboot
The michty trunk o' Space that spreids
small branches Ramel o' licht that ha'e nae end,
– The trunk wi' centuries for rings,
Comets for fruit, November shooers
For leafs that in its Autumns fa'
such   – And Man at maist o' sic a twig
Ane o' the coontless atoms is!

sinews	My sinnens and my veins are but
much	As muckle o' a single shoot
unweave	Wha's fibre I can ne'er unwaft
	O' my wife's flesh and mither's flesh
	And a' the flesh o' humankind,
ravelled threads	And revelled thrums o' beasts and plants
	As gangs to mak' twixt birth and daith
	A'e sliver for a microscope;
	And a' the life o' Earth to be
	Can never lift frae underneath
	The shank o' which oor destiny's pairt
as high as/facing	As heich's to stand forenenst the trunk
straw*	Stupendous as a windlestrae!
	I'm under nae delusions, fegs!
whopping sucker	The whuppin' sooker at wha's tip
	Oor little point o' view appears,
honeycomb	A midget coom o' continents
blobs	Wi' blebs o' oceans set, sends up
	The braith o' daith as weel as life,
and we must sprout	And we maun braird anither tip
	Oot owre us ere we wither tae,
wooden*	And join the sentrice skeleton
build	As coral insects big their reefs.
	What is the tree? As fer as Man's
	Concerned it disna maitter
	Gin but a giant thistle 'tis
	That spreids eternal mischief there,
	As I'm inclined to think.
	Ruthless its sends its solid growth
	Through mair than he can e'er conceive,
asunder	And braks his warlds abreid and rives
	His Heavens to tatters on its horns.
	The nature or the purpose o't
bother to ask	He needna fash to spier, for he

* *windlestrae* withered grass, anything weak or slender, worthless; *sentrice* timbers used to support an arch in the process of building

Is destined to be sune owre grown
And hidden wi' the parent wud
cover   The spreidin' boughs in darkness hap,
And a' its future life'll be
Ootwith'm as he's ootwith his banes.

Juist as man's skeleton has left
behind   Its ancient ape-like shape ahint,
Sae states o' mind in turn gi'e way
To different states, and quickly seem
Impossible to later men.
And Man's mind in its final shape
Or lang'll seem a monkey's spook,
very   And, strewth, to me the vera thocht
extreme   O Thocht already's fell like that!
Yet still the cracklin' thorns persist
In fitba' match and peepy show;
To antic hay a dog-fecht's mair
Than Jacob *v.* the Angel;
And through a cylinder o' wombs,
puddle   A star reflected in a dub,
brains   I see as 'twere my ain wild harns
intestines The ripple o' Eve's moniplies.

lines 2216–35

[FAREWELL TO DOSTOEVSKI]

over us   *The wan leafs shak' atour us like the snaw.*
heavy snowfall/lost *Here is the cavaburd in which Earth's tint.*
There's naebody but Oblivion and us,
vagrants   *Puir gangrel buddies, wanderin' hameless in't.*

remains   *The stars are larochs o' auld cottages,*
blinding snow   *And a' Time's glen is fu' o' blinnin stew.*
window glimmers *Nae freen'ly lozen skimmers: and the wund*
*Rises and separates even me and you.**

* Dostoevski

I ken nae Russian and you ken nae Scots.
We canna tell oor voices frae the wund.
The snaw is seekin' everywhere: oor herts
hearths   *At last like roofless ingles it has f'und,*

And gethers there in drift on endless drift,
Oor broken herts that it can never fill;
And still – its leafs like snaw, its growth like wund –
The thistle rises and forever will! . . .

The thistle rises and forever will,
Getherin' the generations under't.
This is the monument o' a' they were,
And a' they hoped and wondered.

lines 2482–2529

[*part of* THE GREAT WHEEL]

whit   Nae verse is worth a ha'et until
It can join issue wi' the Will
That raised the Wheel and spins it still,

But a' the music that mankind
'S made yet is to the Earth confined,
Poo'erless to reach the general mind,

next   Poo'erless to reach the neist star e'en,
That as a pairt o'ts sel' is seen,
And only men can tell between.

Yet I exult oor sang has yet
To grow wings that'll cairry it
beyond Ayont its native speck o' grit,

And I exult to find me
The thocht that this can ever be,
A hope still for humanity.

if the sum   For gin the sun and mune at last
       Are as a neebor's lintel passed,
lose   The wheel'll tine its stature fast,

spin   And birl in time inside oor heids
sparks   Till we can thraw oot conscious gleids
       That draw an answer to oor needs,

       Or if nae answer still we find
       Brichten till a' thing is defined
       In the huge licht-beams o' oor kind,

       And if we still can find nae trace
behind   Ahint the Wheel o' ony Face,
       There'll be a glory in the place,

perhaps   And we may aiblins swing content
       Upon the wheel in which we're pent
       In adequate enlightenment.

       Nae ither thocht can mitigate
       The horror o' the endless Fate
       A'thing's whirled in predestinate.

       O whiles I'd fain be blin' to it,
       As men wha through the ages sit,
off the one spot And never move frae aff the bit,

       Wha hear a Burns or Shakespeare sing,
their own little jingles Yet still their ain bit jingles string,
       As they were worth the fashioning.

       Whatever Scotland is to me,
       Be it aye pairt o' a' men see
       O' Earth and o' Eternity

       Wha winna hide their heids in't till
       It seems the haill o' Space to fill,
       As 'twere an unsurmounted hill.

He canna Scotland see wha yet
Canna see the Infinite,
And Scotland in true scale to it.

lines 2614–46

[*part of* THE GREAT WHEEL]

endure
nondescript
hush

'Mercy o' Gode, I canna thole
Wi' sic an orra mob to roll.'
— *'Wheesht! It's for the guid o' your soul.'*

'But what's the meanin', what's the sense?'
— *'Men shift but by experience.*
'Twixt Scots there is nae difference.

They canna learn, sae canna move,
But stick for aye to their auld groove
— The only race in History who've

Bidden in the same category
Frae stert to present o' their story,
And deem their ignorance their glory.

capsize

The mair they differ, mair the same.
The wheel can whummle a' but them,
— They ca' their obstinacy "Hame",

And "Puir Auld Scotland" bleat wi' pride,
And wi' their minds made up to bide
A thorn in a' the wide world's side.

who have had

There ha'e been Scots wha ha'e ha'en thochts.
They're strewn through maist o' the various lots
— Sic traitors are nae langer Scots!'

'But in this huge ineducable
Heterogeneous hotch and rabble,
Why am *I* condemned to squabble?'

'A Scottish poet maun assume
The burden o' his people's doom,
And dee to brak' their livin' tomb.

Mony ha'e tried, but a' ha'e failed.
Their sacrifice has nocht availed.
Upon the thistle they're impaled.

You maun choose but gin ye'd see
Anither category ye
must lose   Maun tine your nationality.'

First Hymn to Lenin

To Prince D. S. Mirsky

Few even o' the criminals, cravens, and fools
Wha's voices vilify a man they ken
They've cause to fear and are unfit to judge
As they're to stem his influence again
But in the hollows where their herts should be
    Foresee your victory.

Churchills, Locker-Lampsons, Beaverbrooks'll be
In history's perspective less to you
(And them!) than the Centurions to Christ
Of whom, as you, at least this muckle's true
— 'Tho' pairtly wrang he cam' to richt amang's
    Faur greater wrangs.'

Christ's cited no' by chance or juist because
You mark the greatest turnin'-point since him
But that your main redress has lain where he's
Least use — fulfillin' his sayin' lang kept dim
That whasae followed him things o' like natur'
    'Ud dae — and greater!

Certes nae ither, if no' you's dune this.
It maitters little. What you've dune's the thing,
No' hoo't compares, corrects, or complements

The work of Christ that's taen owre lang to bring
Sic a successor to keep the reference back
    Natural to mak'.

Great things ha'e aye ta'en great men in the past
In some proportion to the work they did,
But you alane to what you've dune are nocht
Even as the poo'ers to greater ends are hid
In what's ca'd God, or in the common man,
    Withoot your plan.

Descendant o' the unkent Bards wha made
Sangs peerless through a' post-anonymous days
I glimpse again in you that mightier poo'er
troubles   Than fashes wi' the laurels and the bays
But kens that it is shared by ilka man
    Since time began.

Great things, great men – but at faur greater's cost!
If first things first had had their rightfu' sway
Life and Thocht's misused poo'er might ha' been ane
For a' men's benefit – as still they may
Noo that through you this mair than elemental force
    Has f'und a clearer course.

Christ said: 'Save ye become as bairns again.'
common run   Bairnly eneuch the feck o' us ha' been!
Your work needs men; and its worst foes are juist
The traitors wha through a' history ha' gi'en
compelled   The dope that's gar'd the mass o' folk pay heed
    And bide bairns indeed.

As necessary, and insignificant, as death
Wi' a' its agonies in the cosmos still
The Cheka's horrors are in their degree;
And'll end suner! What maitters 't wha we kill
To lessen that foulest murder that deprives
    Maist men o' real lives?

For now in the flower and iron of the truth
To you we turn; and turn in vain nae mair,
Ilka fool has folly eneuch for sadness
But at last we are wise and wi' laughter tear
The veil of being, and are face to face
    Wi' the human race.

Here lies your secret, O Lenin, – yours and oors,
No' in the majority will that accepts the result
But in the real will that bides its time and kens

inmost

The benmaist resolve is the poo'er in which we exult
Since naebody's willingly deprived o' the good;

crowd

    And, least o' a', the crood!

Water Music

To William and Flora Johnstone

hush

Wheesht, wheesht, Joyce, and let me hear
    Nae Anna Livvy's lilt.
But Wauchope, Esk, and Ewes again,

with its own rhythms to it

    Each wi' its ain rhythms till't.

I

*flowing smoothly here and
tumultuous there
volatile or orderly*

Archin' here and arrachin there,
    Allevolie or allemand,

*sometimes compliant, sometimes
troublesome*

Whiles appliable, whiles areird,
    The polysemous poem's planned.

downcast, between, between

Lively, louch, atweesh, atween,

*reduced to a thread or in full
flood*

    Auchimuty or aspate,

through the heather stems

Threidin' through the averins

ample in the outcome

    Or bightsom in the aftergait.

wanton or perverse

Or barmybrained or barritchfu',

like a spider

    Or rinnin' like an attercap,

like a coin*

Or shinin' like an Atchison,

with a cry or with a surge

    Wi' a blare or wi' a blawp.

* *Atchison* old copper coin washed with silver

all that opens and shuts

They ken a' that opens and steeks,
    Frae Fiddleton Bar to Callister Ha',
And roon aboot for twenty miles,

make rings, bubble and make waves

    They bead and bell and swaw.

straight or circuitous or crooked

Brent on or boutgate or beshacht

hesitant or headlong

    Bellwaverin' or borne-heid,

they pose and pout,* or cry and cringe

They mimp and primp, or bick and birr,
    Dilly-dally or show speed.

impulsive or slovenly, ruffted, smooth*
outrageous or austere

Brade-up or sclafferin', rouchled, sleek,
    Abstraklous or austerne,

in whirlpools below the banks*

In belths below the brae-hags

and carousals* in the fern

    And bebbles in the fern.

Bracken, blaeberries, and heather

know their babble and chatter

    Ken their amplefeysts and toves,

here goes one with spangles*

Here gangs ane wi' aiglets jinglin',

another struggles through a gorge

    Through a gowl anither goves.

Lint in the bell whiles hardly vies

with one the wind disturbs

    Wi' ane the wind amows,

down eroded steeps decorated with gold another pours

While blithely doon abradit linns
    Wi' gowd begane anither jows.

hacking, hawking, choking and croaking
flattery in one another's throats

Cougher, blocher, boich and croichle,
    Fraise in ane anither's witters,

with vortexes, currents, side-channels
light brown or bluish

Wi' backthraws, births, by-rinnin's,
    Beggar's-broon or blae – the critters!

or brown, holly green, dark green, mottled*

Or burnet, holine, watchet, chauve,
    Or wi' a' the colours dyed

of the sky above

O' the lift abune and plants and trees
    That grow on either side.

---

*mimp speak or act affectedly; *primp* behave prudishly or affectedly; *bick* sob or cry, *birr* move energetically or be in turmoil, *bick and birr* (trad.) to imitate the cry of a grouse; *sleek* smoothly, with cunning (as a noun it can mean ooze on a river bed); *brae-hags* wooded overhanging banks of a stream; *bebbles* sips, drinks, tipples; *aiglets* points (i.e. metal tips or ornaments on the ends of laces or cords); *chauve* having white and black hair more or less equally (used of cattle)

pitted	Or coinyelled wi' the midges,
	Or swallows a'aboot,
	The shadow o' an eagle,
the splash of a trout	The aiker o' a troot.
distorting	Toukin' ootrageous face
winding stair	The turn-gree o' your mood,
climbed	I've climmed until I'm lost
	Like the sun ahint a clood.
a pop-gun from the elder	*But a tow-gun frae the boon-tree,*
	A whistle frae the elm,
	A spout-gun frae the hemlock,
	And, back in this auld realm,
colt's-foot	*Dry leafs o' dishielogie*
'crab's claw'*	*To smoke in a 'partan's tae'!*
	And you've me in your creel again,
dull or bright	Brim or shallow, bauch or bricht,
	Singin' in the mornin',
murmuring	Corrieneuchin' a' the nicht.

II

on the turf	Lappin' on the shirrel,
bursting down the glen	Or breengin' doon the cleuch,
chequerboard*	Slide-thrift for stars and shadows,
come to grief over the crag*	Or sun-'couped owre the heuch'.
	Wi' the slughorn o' a folk,
lookouts*	Sightsmen for a thoosand years,
in spate or serene*	In fluther or at shire
	O' the Border burns' careers,
let them bubble, let them purl	Let them popple, let them pirl,
	Plish-plash and plunk and plop and ploot,
in risky quagmire* or fish sanctuary	In quakin' quaw or fish-currie
	I ken a' they're aboot.

*'*partan's tae*' a short, stubby pipe (or 'cutty-clay'); *slide-thrift* the game of 'first off the board' at draughts; *heuch* crag, cliff, hollow, or deep glen; *sight(s)men* fishermen posted as lookouts for salmon; *at shire* clear, not muddy; *quaw* also a hole from which peats have been cut

caper

dance

And 'twixt the pavvy o' the Wauchope,
    And the paspey o' the Ewes,
And the pavane o' Esk itsel',
    It's no' for me to choose.

lively

like striped satin or cream*

a toy mill*

make all the country toil

Be they querty, be they quiet,
    Flow like railya or lamoo,
Only turn a rashmill or
    Gar a' the country tew,

snowing*
or pours pipestems and chimney cowls
so Waich Water flashes and swarms*

romps, and ruptures and rages

As it's froggin' in the hills,
    Or poors pipestapples and auld wives,
Sae Waich Water glents and scrows,
    Reels and ratches and rives.

Some day they say the Bigly Burn

will jump out from its scrub and overwhelm the lovely birch wood

all to wrack and ruin

    'll loup oot frae its scrabs and thistles,
And ding the bonnie birken shaw
    A' to pigs and whistles.

And there's yon beck – I winna name't –
    That hauds the fish that aince was hookit

a century ago

and abandoned all his gear

A century syne – the fisher saw't,
    And flew, and a' his graith forsookit.

And as for Unthank Water,

reeds and rushes*

it's still up to thieving*

the golden-eye duck's eggs

    That seeps through miles o' reeds and seggs,
It's aye at pilliewinkie syne
    Wi' the gowdnie's eggs.

than you yourself could piss

Nae mair than you could stroan yoursel'
    The biggest o' them you may say,

yet famous and I still see them sprouting*

Yet lood and still I see them stoan
    To oceans and the heaven's sway.

---

* *lamoo* anything easily swallowed; *rashmill* toy mill made of rushes; *froggin'* snowing or sleeting at intervals; *scrows* or, possibly, tears apart; *seggs* various plants with sword-shaped leaves – yellow iris, etc. *pilliewinkie* children's cruel pastime of raiding birds' nests for eggs and younglings; *stoan* send out shoots, tendrils, suckers – here 'tributaries'

Fleetin' owre the meadows,
    Or cleitchin' in the glaur,
The haill world answers to them,
    And they rein the faurest star.

falling [?] in the mud

the furthest star

Humboldt, Howard, Maury,
    Hildebrandsson, Hann, and Symons,
A digest o' a' their work's
    In these dour draps or diamonds.

in these stubborn drops

And weel I ken the air's wild rush
    As it comes owre the seas,
Clims up and whistles 'twixt the hills,
    Wi' a' the weather gi'es

O' snaw and rain and thunder,
    Is a single circle spun
By the sun's bricht heat and guided by
    Earth's spin and the shapes o' the grun'.

of the ground

Lappin' on the shirrel,
    Or breengin' doon the cleuch,
I can listen to the waters
    Lang – and no' lang – eneuch.

*Wheesht, wheesht, Joyce, and let me hear
    No' Anna Livvy's lilt,
But Wauchope, Esk, and Ewes again,
    Each wi' its ain rhythms till't.*

Ho, My Little Sparrow

Ho, my little sparrow! For well I know
The profound and subtle soft lights in your eyes
Mean no more than two grains of wheat
In a basin full of water. And so
    I call you my little sparrow,
    For so a sparrow's wings go.

Ho, my little sparrow! Sparrows are common
Yet who can describe their thousand and one changes
Of colour as they quiver in the sun
Like thoughts of old rainbows? But what omen
    Is this? – All the live arc at home in
      Your look again, woman!

On a Raised Beach

To James H. Whyte

All is lithogenesis – or lochia,
Carpolite fruit of the forbidden tree,
Stones blacker than any in the Caaba,
Cream-coloured caen-stone, chatoyant pieces,
Celadon and corbeau, bistre and beige,
Glaucous, hoar, enfouldered, cyathiform,
Making mere faculae of the sun and moon
I study you glout and gloss, but have
No cadrans to adjust you with, and turn again
From optik to haptik and like a blind man run
My fingers over you, arris by arris, burr by burr,
Slickensides, truité, rugas, foveoles,
Bringing my aesthesis in vain to bear,
An angle-titch to all your corrugations and coigns,
Hatched foraminous cavo-relievo of the world,
Deictic, fiducial stones. Chiliad by chiliad
What bricole piled you here, stupendous cairn?
What artist poses the Earth écorché thus,
Pillar of creation engouled in me?
What eburnation augments you with men's bones,
Every energumen an Endymion yet?
All the other stones are in this haecceity it seems,
But where is the Christophanic rock that moved?
What Cabirian song from this catasta comes?

Deep conviction or preference can seldom
Find direct terms in which to express itself.
Today on this shingle shelf
I understand this pensive reluctance so well,

This not discommendable obstinacy,
These contrivances of an inexpressive critical feeling,
These stones with their resolve that Creation shall
                                                    not be
Injured by iconoclasts and quacks. Nothing has
                                                    stirred
Since I lay down this morning an eternity ago
But one bird. The widest open door is the least liable
                                                    to intrusion,
Ubiquitous as the sunlight, unfrequented as the sun.
The inward gates of a bird are always open.
It does not know how to shut them.
That is the secret of its song,
But whether any man's are ajar is doubtful.
I look at these stones and know little about them.
But I know their gates are open too,
Always open, far longer open, than any bird's can be,
That every one of them has had its gates wide open
                                                    far longer
Than all birds put together, let alone humanity,
Though through them no man can see,
No man nor anything more recently born than
                                                    themselves
And that is everything else on the Earth.
I too lying here have dismissed all else.
Bread from stones is my sole and desperate dearth,
From stones, which are to the Earth as to the sunlight
Is the naked sun which is for no man's sight.
I would scorn to cry to any easier audience
Or, having cried, to lack patience to await the
                                                    response.
I am no more indifferent or ill-disposed to life than
                                                    death is;
I would fain accept it all completely as the soil does;
Already I feel all that can perish perishing in me
As so much has perished and all will yet perish in
                                                    these stones.
I must begin with these stones as the world began.

Shall I come to a bird quicker than the world's course
                                                    ran?
        To a bird, and to myself, a man?
        And what if I do, and further?
I shall only have gone a little way to go back again
And be like a fleeting deceit of development,
Iconoclasts, quacks. So these stones have dismissed
All but all of evolution, unmoved by it,
(Is there anything to come they will not likewise
                                            dismiss?)
As the essential life of mankind in the mass
Is the same as their earliest ancestors yet.

Actual physical conflict or psychological warfare
        Incidental to love or food
Brings out animal life's bolder and more brilliant
                                                patterns
        Concealed as a rule in habitude.
        There is a sudden revelation of colour,
        The protrusion of a crest,
        The expansion of an ornament,
— But no general principle can be guessed
From these flashing fragments we are seeing,
These foam-bells on the hidden currents of being.
The bodies of animals are visible substances
And must therefore have colour and shape, in the
                                            first place
Depending on chemical composition, physical
                        structure, mode of growth,
Psychological rhythms and other factors in the case,
But their purposive function is another question.
Brilliant-hued animals hide away in the ocean deeps;
The mole has a rich sexual colouring in due season
Under the ground; nearly every beast keeps
Brighter colours inside it than outside.
What the seen shows is never anything to what it's
                                        designed to hide,
The red blood which makes the beauty of a maiden's
                                                cheek
Is as red under a gorilla's pigmented and hairy face.

Varied forms and functions though life may seem to
                             have shown
They all come back to the likeness of stone,
So to the intervening stages we can best find a clue
In what we all came from and return to.
There are no twirly bits in this ground bass.

We must be humble. We are so easily baffled by
                             appearances
And do not realise that these stones are one with the
                             stars.
It makes no difference to them whether they are high
                             or low,
Mountain peak or ocean floor, palace, or pigsty.
There are plenty of ruined buildings in the world but
                           no ruined stones.
No visitor comes from the stars
But is the same as they are.
— Nay, it is easy to find a spontaneity here,
An adjustment to life, an ability
To ride it easily, akin to 'the buoyant
Prelapsarian naturalness of a country girl
Laughing in the sun, not passion-rent,
But sensing in the bound of her breasts vigours to
                             come
Powered to make her one with the stream of earthlife
                             round her,'
But not yet as my Muse is, with this ampler scope,
This more divine rhythm, wholly at one
With the earth, riding the Heavens with it, as the
                             stones do
And all soon must.
But it is wrong to indulge in these illustrations
Instead of just accepting the stones.
It is a paltry business to try to drag down
The arduous furor of the stones to the futile
                             imaginings of men,
To all that fears to grow roots into the common
                             earth,
As it soon must, lest it be chilled to the core,

As it will be – and none the worse for that.
Impatience is a poor qualification for immortality.
Hot blood is of no use in dealing with eternity.
It is seldom that promises or even realisations
Can sustain a clear and searching gaze.
But an emotion chilled is an emotion controlled;
This is the road leading to certainty,
Reasoned planning for the time when reason can no
                                  longer avail.
It is essential to know the chill of all the objections
That come creeping into the mind, the battle between
                                  opposing ideas
Which gives the victory to the strongest and most
                                  universal
Over all others, and to wage it to the end
With increasing freedom, precision, and detachment
A detachment that shocks our instincts and ridicules
                                  our desires.
All else in the world cancels out, equal, capable
Of being replaced by other things (even as all the
                                  ideas
That madden men now must lose their potency in a
                                  few years
And be replaced by others – even as all the religions,
All the material sacrifices and moral restraints,
That in twenty thousand years have brought us no
                                  nearer to God
Are irrelevant to the ordered adjustments
Out of reach of perceptive understanding
Forever taking place on the Earth and in the
                            unthinkable regions around it;
This cat's cradle of life; this reality volatile yet
                                  determined;
This intense vibration in the stones
That makes them seem immobile to us)
But the world cannot dispense with the stones.

They alone are not redundant. Nothing can replace
them
Except a new creation of God.

I must get into this stone world now.
Ratchel, striae, relationships of tesserae,
    Innumerable shades of grey,
    Innumerable shapes,
And beneath them all a stupendous unity,
Infinite movement visibly defending itself
Against all the assaults of weather and water,
Simultaneously mobilised at full strength
At every point of the universal front,
    Always at the pitch of its powers,
    The foundation and end of all life.
I try them with the old Norn words – hraun
Duss, rønis, queedaruns, kollyarum:
They hvarf from me in all directions
Over the hurdifell – klett, millya, hellya, hellyina
bretta,
Hellyina wheeda, hellyina grø, bakka, ayre, –
    And lay my world in kolgref.

This is no heap of broken images.
Let men find the faith that builds mountains
Before they seek the faith that moves them. Men
cannot hope
To survive the fall of the mountains
Which they will no more see than they saw their rise
Unless they are more concentrated and determined,
Truer to themselves and with more to be true to,
Than these stones, and as inerrable as they are.
Their sole concern is that what can be shaken
Shall be shaken and disappear
And only the unshakable be left.
What hardihood in any man has part or parcel in the
latter?
It is necessary to make a stand and maintain it
forever.

These stones go through Man, straight to God, if
                                        there is one.
What have they not gone through already?
Empires, civilisations, aeons. Only in them
If in anything, can His creation confront Him.
They came so far out of the water and halted forever.
That larking dallier, the sun, has only been able to
                                        play
With superficial by-products since;
The moon moves the waters backwards and
                                        forwards,
But the stones cannot be lured an inch farther
Either on this side of eternity or the other.
Who thinks God is easier to know than they are?
Trying to reach men any more, any otherwise, than
                                        they are?
These stones will reach us long before we reach them.
Cold, undistracted, eternal and sublime.
They will stem all the torrents of vicissitude forever
With a more than Roman peace.
Death is a physical horror to me no more.
I am prepared with everything else to share
Sunshine and darkness and wind and rain
And life and death bare as these rocks though it be
In whatever order nature may decree,
But, not indifferent to the struggle yet
Nor to the ataraxia I might get
By fatalism, a deeper issue see
Than these, or suicide, here confronting me.
It is reality that is at stake.
Being and non-being with equal weapons here
Confront each other for it, non-being unseen
But always on the point, it seems, of showing clear,
Though its reserved contagion may breed
This fancy too in my still susceptible head
And then by its own hidden movement lead
Me as by aesthetic vision to the supposed
Point where by death's logic everything is
                                        recomposed,
Object and image one, from their severance freed,

As I sometimes, still wrongly, feel 'twixt this storm
beach and me.
What happens to us
Is irrelevant to the world's geology
But what happens to the world's geology
Is not irrelevant to us.
We must reconcile ourselves to the stones,
Not the stones to us.
Here a man must shed the encumbrances that muffle
Contact with elemental things, the subtleties
That seem inseparable from a humane life, and go
apart
Into a simple and sterner, more beautiful and more
oppressive world,
Austerely intoxicating; the first draught is
overpowering;
Few survive it. It fills me with a sense of perfect form,
The end seen from the beginning, as in a song.
It is no song that conveys the feeling
That there is no reason why it should ever stop,
But the kindred form I am conscious of here
Is the beginning and end of the world,
The unsearchable masterpiece, the music of the
spheres,
Alpha and Omega, the Omnific Word.
These stones have the silence of supreme creative
power,
The direct and undisturbed way of working
Which alone leads to greatness.
What experience has any man crystallised,
What weight of conviction accumulated,
What depth of life suddenly seen entire
In some nigh supernatural moment
And made a symbol and lived up to
With such resolution, such Spartan impassivity?
It is a frenzied and chaotic age,
Like a growth of weeds on the site of a demolished
building.
How shall we set ourselves against it,

Imperturbable, inscrutable, in the world and yet not
                                        in it,
    Silent under the torments it inflicts upon us,
        With a constant centre,
With a single inspiration, foundations firm and
                                        invariable;
        By what immense exercise of will,
Inconceivable discipline, courage, and endurance,
        Self-purification and anti-humanity,
            Be ourselves without interruption,
                Adamantine and inexorable?
It will be ever increasingly necessary to find
In the interests of all mankind
Men capable of rejecting all that all other men
        Think, as a stone remains
Essential to the world, inseparable from it,
        And rejects all other life yet.
Great work cannot be combined with surrender to
                                        the crowd.
        – Nay, the truth we seek is as free
From all yet thought as a stone from humanity.
Here where there is neither haze nor hesitation
Something at least of the necessary power has entered
                                        into me.
I have still to see any manifestation of the human
                                        spirit
That is worthy of a moment's longer exemption than
                                        it gets
From petrifaction again – to get out if it can.
All is lithogenesis – or lochia;
And I can desire nothing better,
An immense familiarity with other men's imaginings
Convinces me that they cannot either
(If they could, it would instantly be granted
– The present order must continue till then)
Though, of course, I still keep an open mind,
A mind as open as the grave.
You may say that the truth cannot be crushed out,
That the weight of the whole world may be tumbled
                                        on it,

And yet, in puny, distorted, phantasmal shapes albeit,
It will braird again; it will force its way up
Through unexpectable fissures? look over this beach.
What ruderal and rupestrine growth is here?
What crop confirming any credulities?
Conjure a fescue to teach me with from this
And I will listen to you, but until then
Listen to me – Truth is not crushed;
It crushes, gorgonises all else into itself.
The trouble is to know it when you see it?
You will have no trouble with it when you do.
Do not argue with me. Argue with these stones.
Truth has no trouble in knowing itself.
This is it. The hard fact. The inoppugnable reality,
Here is something for you to digest.
Eat this and we'll see what appetite you have left
For a world hereafter.
I pledge you in the first and last crusta,
The rocks rattling in the bead-proof seas.

O we of little faith,
As romanticists viewed the philistinism of their days
As final and were prone to set over against it
Infinite longing rather than manly will –
Nay, as all thinkers and writers find
The indifference of the masses of mankind, –
So are most men with any stone yet,
Even those who juggle with lapidary's, mason's,
                                        geologist's words
      And all their knowledge of stones in vain,
Tho' these stones have far more differences in colour,
                                        shape and size
      Than most men to my eyes –
Even those who develop precise conceptions to
                                        immense distances
      Out of these bleak surfaces.
All human culture is a Goliath to fall
To the least of these pebbles withal.
A certain weight will be added yet
To the arguments of even the most foolish

And all who speak glibly may rest assured
That to better their oratory they will have the whole
                        earth
For a Demosthenean pebble to roll in their mouths.

I am enamoured of the desert at last,
The abode of supreme serenity is necessarily a desert.
My disposition is towards spiritual issues
Made inhumanly clear; I will have nothing interposed
Between my sensitiveness and the barren but
                        beautiful reality;
The deadly clarity of this 'seeing of a hungry man'
Only traces of a fever passing over my vision
Will vary, troubling it indeed, but troubling it only
In such a way that it becomes for a moment
Superhumanly, menacingly clear – the reflection
Of a brightness through a burning crystal.
A culture demands leisure and leisure presupposes
A self-determined rhythm of life; the capacity for
                        solitude
Is its test; by that the desert knows us.
It is not a question of escaping from life
But the reverse – a question of acquiring the power
To exercise the loneliness, the independence, of
                        stones,
And that only comes from knowing that our function
                        remains
However isolated we seem fundamental to life as
                        theirs.
     We have lost the grounds of our being,
     We have not built on rock.
Thinking of all the higher zones
Confronting the spirit of man I know they are bare
Of all so-called culture as any stone here;
Not so much of all literature survives
As any wisp of scriota that thrives
On a rock – (interesting though it may seem to be
As de Bary's and Schwendener's discovery
Of the dual nature of lichens, the partnership,
Symbiosis, of a particular fungus and particular alga).

These bare stones bring me straight back to reality.
　　I grasp one of them and I have in my grip
The beginning and the end of the world,
My own self, and as before I never saw
The empty hand of my brother man,
The humanity no culture has reached, the mob.
Intelligentsia, our impossible and imperative job!

'Ah!' you say, 'if only one of these stones would
　　　　　　　　　　　　　　　　　　move
— Were it only an inch — of its own accord.
　　This is the resurrection we await,
— The stone rolled away from the tomb of the Lord.
　　I know there is no weight in infinite space,
　　　　No impermeability in infinite time,
But it is as difficult to understand and have patience
　　　　　　　　　　　　　　　　　　here
　　　　As to know that the sublime
Is theirs no less than ours, no less confined
To men than men's to a few men, the stars of their
　　　　　　　　　　　　　　　　　　kind.'
　　　　(The masses too have begged bread from stones,
　　　　　From human stones, including themselves,
　　　　And only got it, not from their fellow-men,
　　　　　But from stones such as these here — if then.)
Detached intellectuals, not one stone will move,
Not the least of them, not a fraction of an inch. It is
　　　　　　　　　　　　　　　　　　not
　　　　The reality of life that is hard to know.
It is nearest of all and easiest to grasp,
But you must participate in it to proclaim it.
— I lift a stone; it is the meaning of life I clasp
Which is death, for that is the meaning of death;
How else does any man yet participate
　　　　In the life of a stone,
How else can any man yet become
Sufficiently at one with creation, sufficiently alone,
Till as the stone that covers him he lies dumb
And the stone at the mouth of his grave is not
　　　　　　　　　　　　　　　　　　overthrown?

– Each of these stones on this raised beach,
   Every stone in the world,
Covers infinite death, beyond the reach
Of the dead it hides; and cannot be hurled
Aside yet to let any of them come forth, as love
    Once made a stone move
  (Though I do not depend on that
    My case to prove).
So let us beware of death; the stones will have
Their revenge; we have lost all approach to them,
But soon we shall become as those we have betrayed,
And they will seal us fast in our graves
As our indifference and ignorance seals them;
    But let us not be afraid to die.
No heavier and colder and quieter then,
No more motionless, do stones lie
    In death than in life to all men.
It is not more difficult in death than here
– Though slow as the stones the powers develop
To rise from the grave – to get a life worth having;
And in death – unlike life – we lose nothing that is
                        truly ours.

Diallage of the world's debate, end of the long
                        auxesis,
Although no ébrillade of Pegasus can here avail,
I prefer your enchorial characters – the futhorc of the
                        future –
To the hieroglyphics of all the other forms of Nature.
Song, your apprentice encrinite, seems to sweep
The Heavens with a last entrochal movement;
And, with the same word that began it, closes
Earth's vast epanadiplosis.

Harry Semen

I ken these islands each inhabited
Forever by a single man
Livin' in his separate world as only

In dreams yet maist folk can.

dogfish Mine's like the moonwhite belly o' a hoo
Seen in the water as a fisher draws in his line.
I canna land it nor can it ever brak awa'.
It never moves, yet seems a' movement in the brine;
A movin' picture o' the spasm frae which I was born,
It writhes again, and back to it I'm willy-nilly torn.
A' men are similarly fixt; and the difference 'twixt
      The sae-ca'd sane and insane
Is that the latter whiles ha'e glimpses o't
      And the former nane.

Particle frae particle'll brak asunder,

each one/next Ilk ane o' them mair livid than the neist.
A separate life? – incredible war o' equal lichts,
Nane o' them wi' ocht in common in the least.
Nae threid o' a' the fabric o' my thocht
Is left alangside anither; a pack

mangling O' leprous scuts o' weasels riddlin' a plaid
loose ends   Sic thrums could never mak'.

went Hoo mony shades o' white gaed curvin' owre
bluish To yon blae centre o' her belly's flower?
Scottish bluebell Milk-white, and dove-grey, wi' harebell veins.
one Ae scar in fair hair like the sun in sunlicht lay,
And pelvic experience in a thin shadow line;
such soft Thocht canna mairry thocht as sic saft shadows dae.

Grey ghastly commentaries on my puir life,
A' the sperm that's gane for naething rises up to
                                                    damn
In sick-white onanism the single seed
Frae which in sheer irrelevance I cam.
What were the odds against me? Let me coont.
What worth am I to a' that micht ha'e been?
To a' the wasted slime I'm capable o'
Appeals this lurid emission, whirlin' lint-white and
                                                    green.
Am I alane richt, solidified to life,
Disjoined frae a' this searin' like a white-het knife,

And vauntin' my alien accretions here,
Boastin' sanctions, purpose, sense the endless tide
I cam frae lacks — the tide I still sae often feed?
O bitter glitter; wet sheet and flowin' sea — and what
                                  beside?

festering
in all directions

Sae the bealin' continents lie upon the seas,
    Sprawlin' in shapeless shapes a' airts,
Like ony splash that ony man can mak'
    Frae his nose or throat or ither pairts,
Fantastic as ink through blottin' paper rins.

wild cherry

But this is white, white like a flooerin' gean,
Passin' frae white to purer shades o' white,
Ivory, crystal, diamond, till nae difference is seen
Between its fairest blossoms and the stars
Or the clear sun they melt into,
And the wind mixes them amang each ither
Forever, hue upon still mair dazzlin' hue.

Sae Joseph may ha'e pondered; sae a snawstorm
Comes whirlin' in grey sheets frae the shadowy sky
And only in a sma' circle are the separate flakes seen.
White, whiter, they cross and recross as capricious
                        they fly,
Mak' patterns on the grund and weave into wreaths,
Load the bare boughs, and find lodgments in corners
                         frae
The scourin' wind that sends a snawstorm up frae the
                        earth
To meet that frae the sky, till which is which nae
                        man can say.
They melt in the waters. They fill the valleys. They
                        scale the peaks.
There's a tinkle o' icicles. The topmaist summit
                        shines oot.
Sae Joseph may ha'e pondered on the coiled fire in
                        his seed,
The transformation in Mary, and seen Jesus tak' root.

WILLIAM SOUTAR (1898–1943)

The Tryst

softly

O luely, luely cam she in
And luely she lay doun:

cool

I kent her by her caller lips
And her breists sae sma' and roun'.

A' thru the nicht we spak nae word

parted bone from bone

Nor sinder'd bane frae bane:
A' thru the nicht I heard her hert
Gang soundin' wi' my ain.

wakeful

It was about the waukrife hour
Whan cocks begin to craw

slipped away

That she smool'd saftly thru the mirk
Afore the day wud daw.

Sae luely, luely, cam she in
Sae luely was she gaen
And wi' her a' my simmer days
Like they had never been.

The Guns

Now, on the moors where the guns bring down
The predestinated birds,
Shrill, wavering cries pass
Like the words of an international peace;
And I would that these cries were heard in every
town,
Astounding the roar of the wheel
And the lying mouth of the news:
And I would that these cries might more and more
increase
Until the machine stood still;
And men, despairing in the deathly queues,

Heard their own heart-beats
Shouting aloud, in the silence of the streets:
'Are we not also hand-fed in a wilderness:
What are we waiting for?'

The Hungry Mauchs

a sickly, mother maggot   There was a moupit, mither mauch
Wha hadna onie meat;
always quick to laugh   And a' her bairns, aye gleg to lauch,
to weep   Were gether'd round to greet.

who was that   'O mither, mither, wha was yon
That breisted on through bluid:
who broke crowns and wrecked towns   Wha crackit crouns, and wrackit touns,
And was our faithers' pride?

'O mither, mither, wha was yon
bold   That was sae frack and fell?'
'My loves, it was Napoleon
in ruins   But he's sma' brok himsel'.'

bow low   'Noo lat us a' lowt on our knees,'
The spunkiest shaver said:
'And prig upon the Lord to gie's
Napoleon frae the dead.'

The mither mauch began to lauch:
fuss or complain   'Ye needna fash nor wurn:
pressed down and covered over   He's clappit doun, and happit roun',
iron chest   And in a kist o' airn.'

'O whaur, O whaur's my faither gaen?'
smallest   The peeriest bairn outspak.
'Wheesht, wheesht, ye wee bit loonickin,
wonder   He'll fetch a ferlie back.'

'Will he bring hame Napoleon's head
make my stomach better To cockle up my kite?'
hothead 'He'll bring ye hame the wuff o' bluid
That's reid and rinnin yet.'

Song

bridge Whaur yon broken brig hings owre;
Whaur yon water maks nae soun';
in dust Babylon blaws by in stour:
go down Gang doun wi' a sang, gang doun.

for any Deep, owre deep, for onie drouth:
gloomy Wan eneuch an ye wud droun:
salty or pleasant Saut, or seelfu', for the mouth;
Gang doun wi' a sang, gang doun.

Babylon blaws by in stour
Whaur yon water maks nae soun':
Darkness is your only door;
Gang doun wi' a sang, gang doun.

The Makar

the poet

Nae man wha loves the lawland tongue
wrestles But warsles wi' the thocht –
There are mair sangs that bide unsung
Nor a' that hae been wrocht.

below the wastefulness Ablow the wastrey o' the years,
shackle The thorter o' himsel',
Deep buried in his bluid he hears
loyal A music that is leal.

And wi' this lealness gangs his ain;
And there's nae ither gait
all his comrades were foreign Though a' his feres were fremmit men
Wha cry: *Owre late, owre late.*

WILLIAM MONTGOMERIE (b. 1904)

The Edge of the War (1939–)

On the esplanade
the deck-chair hirer
watches his summer
shovelled into sandbags
till at high tide
the beach is flooded to the Promenade

Our submarines like five alligators
pass
always at dusk
to the North Sea
where a German plane has sown surface mines

One mine circles the harbour slowly
missing the pier
again and again and again
until defused by a simple twist of the wrist

The whelk-seller leaves his bag and barrow
to pull a mine up the beach
and dies
'Stretchers! Stretchers here!'
they shout from the Castle

A policeman arrests one mine on the shore
and drags it halfway to the police-station
his tombstone a cottage gable-end
pocked with holes packed with red putty

Casks of brandy butter and ham
float on to the beach
from a mined ship

A grocer's van parks at dusk
by the Castle railings

Sergeant MacPherson pins on his notice-board
'Flotsam butter from the beach
must be left immediately
at the police-station'

For days the streets are sweet
with the smell of shortbread

Blue-mould butter
is dumped on the counter
or thrown at night
over the wall of the station
where greased door-handles will not turn

A German plane
following the wrong railway
dumps his bombs on an up-country farm

A plane from the North-Sea sunrise
machine-gunning our little fishing fleet
brushes a wing against a mast
and ditches

'Hilfe! Hilfe!'

'Take your time lads!'
shouts a skipper
to a drifter turning toward the sinking plane

'One of our planes
has sunk a German U-boat
off Montrose'

A war-rumour

The submarine
one of ours
dented
is in dry-dock
in Dundee

Bennet from Stratford-on-Avon
one of the crew
cycles to our house
with no lights
sings to us
of Boughton's Lordly Ones
from *The Immortal Hour*
talks of his wife in Stratford
and of the night they watched Birmingham burning

After late supper
he returns to the night
having left his ration of pipe-tobacco
on the piano

If his submarine sinks
he knows how to escape
and is found afloat
on the Pacific Ocean
drowned

On Tents Muir
across the Tay estuary
parachutes are falling
from war planes

We talk of the Second Front

One parachute does not open

Broughty Ferry

NORMAN CAMERON (1905–53)

She and I

She and I, we thought and fought
And each of us won by the other's defeat;
She and I, we danced and pranced
And lost by neglect the use of our feet;
She and I caught ills and chills
And were cured or dead before we could cough;
She and I, we walked and talked
Half an hour after our heads were cut off.

Forgive Me, Sire

Forgive me, Sire, for cheating your intent,
That I, who should command a regiment,
Do amble amiably here, O God,
One of the neat ones in your awkward squad.

A Visit to the Dead

I bought (I was too wealthy for my age)
A passage to the dead ones' habitat,
And learnt, under their tutelage,
To twitter like a bat

In imitation of their dialect.
Crudely I aped their subtle practices;
By instinct knew how to respect
Their strict observances.

The regions of the dead are small and pent,
Their movements faint, sparing of energy.
Yet, like an exiled Government,
With so much jealousy

As were the issue a campaign or Crown,
They hold debates, wage Cabinet intrigues,
Move token forces up and down,
Turn inches into leagues.

Long I was caught up in their twilit strife.
Almost they got me, almost had me weaned
From all my memory of life.
But laughter supervened:

Laughter, like sunlight in the cucumber,
The innermost resource, that does not fail.
I, Marco Polo, traveller,
Am back, with what a tale!

Green, Green is El Aghir

Sprawled on the crates and sacks in the rear of the
                                                    truck,
I was gummy-mouthed from the sun and the dust of
                                               the track.
And the two Arab soldiers I'd taken on as hitch-
                                                  hikers
At a torrid petrol-dump, had been there on their
                                                 hunkers
Since early morning. I said, in a kind of French
'On m'a dit, qu'il y a une belle source d'eau fraîche.
Plus loin, à El Aghir' . . .

                    It was eighty more kilometres
Until round a corner we heard a splashing of waters,
And there, in a green, dark street, was a fountain
                                         with two faces
Discharging both ways, from full-throated faucets
Into basins, thence into troughs and thence into
                                                brooks.
Our negro corporal driver slammed his brakes,
And we yelped and leapt from the truck and went at
                                             the double

To fill our bidons and bottles and drink and dabble.
Then, swollen with water, we went to an inn for
                                                    wine.
The Arabs came, too, though their faith might have
                                          stood between.
'After all,' they said, 'it's a boisson,' without
                                            contrition.

Green, green is El Aghir. It has a railway-station,
And the wealth of its soil has borne many another
                                                fruit,
A mairie, a school and an elegant Salle de Fêtes.
Such blessings, as I remarked, in effect, to the waiter,
Are added unto them that have plenty of water.

ROBERT GARIOCH (Robert Garioch Sutherland) (1909–81)

*Edinburgh to the frolic**   Embro to the Ploy

                            In simmer, whan aa sorts foregether
                            in Embro to the ploy,
people/chinwag   fowk seek out friens to hae a blether,
enemies   or faes they'd fain annoy;
smothered/smoke   smorit wi British Railways' reek
                            frae Glesca or Glen Roy
                            or Wick, they come to hae a week
                            of cultivatit joy,
                                            or three,
                            in Embro to the ploy.

plenty   Americans wi routh of dollars,
                            wha drink our whisky neat,
                            wi Sasunachs and Oxford Scholars
eager   are eydent for the treat
                            of music sedulously high-tie
                            at thirty-bob a seat;
                            Wop opera performed in Eytie
                            to them's richt up their street,
                                            they say,
                            in Embro to the ploy.

expatriate   Furthgangan Embro folk come hame
                            for three weeks in the year,
                            and find Auld Reekie no the same,
in a frenzy   fu sturrit in a steir.
buildings   The stane-faced biggins whaur they froze
took in poorhouse learning and suppit puirshous leir
yesterday's staple culture,
reheated   of cultural cauld-kale and brose
antics disconcerting   see cantraips unco queer
                                            thae days
                            in Embro to the ploy.

*i.e. the Edinburgh Festival

The tartan tred wad gar ye lauch;　*trade/laugh*
nae problem is owre teuch.　*too difficult*
Your surname needna end in -*och*;
they'll cleik ye up the cleuch.　*hook you up to the high places*
A puckle dollar bills will aye　*few*
prieve Hiram Teufelsdrockh　*prove*
a septary of Clan McKay,
it's maybe richt eneuch,
　　　　　verfluch!
in Embro to the ploy.

The auld High Schule, whaur monie a skelp　*blow*
of triple-tonguit tawse
has gien a hyst-up and a help
towards Doctorates of Laws,
nou hears, for Ramsay's cantie rhyme,　*cheerful*
loud pawmies of applause　*palm-strokes*
frae folk that pey a pund a time
to sit on wudden raws
　　　　　gey hard　*very*
in Embro to the ploy.

The haly kirk's Assembly-haa
nou fairly coups the creel　*makes a mess of it*
wi Lindsay's Three Estaitis, braw　*fine*
devices of the Deil.
About our heids the satire stots　*bounces*
like hailstanes till we reel;
the bawrs are in auld-farrant Scots,　*jokes/old-fashioned*
it's maybe jist as weill,
　　　　　imphm,
in Embro to the ploy.

The Epworth Haa wi wunner did
behold a piper's bicker;　*quarrel*
wi *hadarid* and *hindarid*
the air gat thick and thicker.
Cumha na Cloinne pleyed on strings
torments a piper quicker
to get his dander up, by jings,

than thirty u.p. liquor,
hooch aye!
in Embro to the ploy.

The Northern British Embro Whigs
that stayed in Charlotte Square,
lost   they fairly wad hae tined their wigs
to see the Stuarts there,
bleeding/everyone else   the bleidan Earl of Moray and aa
well-painted/very   weill-pentit and gey bare;
beautifully adorned   Our Queen and Princess, buskit braw,
enjoyed the hale affair
(see Press)
in Embro to the ploy.

Whan day's anomalies are cled
in decent shades of nicht,
the Castle is transmogrified
by braw electric licht.
shelters   The toure that bields the Bruce's croun
presents an unco sicht
kin   mair sib to Wardour Street nor Scone,
wae's me for Scotland's micht,
says I
in Embro to the ploy.

prank   A happening, incident, or splore
affrontit them that saw
a thing they'd never seen afore –
in the McEwan Haa:
a lassie in a wheelie-chair
wi naething on at aa,
jist like my luck! I wasna there,
at all   it's no the thing ava,
tut-tut,
in Embro to the ploy.

The Café Royal and Abbotsford
sundry   are filled wi orra folk
written   whaes stock-in trade's the scrievit word,

or twicet-scrievit joke.
Brains, weak or strang, in heavy beer,
or ordinary, soak.
said one/ale   Quo yin: This yill is aafie dear,
coins in purse   I hae nae clinks in poke,
                 nor fauldan-money,
in Embro to the ploy.

The auld Assembly-rooms, whaur Scott
comrades   foregethert wi his fiers,
eye-catching   nou see a gey kenspeckle lot
ablow the chandeliers.
to Edinburgh thirsts (or drunks) Til Embro drouths the Festival Club
a richt godsend appears;
it's something new to find a pub
that gaes on sairvan beers
               eftir hours
in Embro to the ploy.

ejected/drunken   Jist pitten-out, the drucken mobs
taverns   frae howffs in Potterraw,
fleean, to hob-nob wi the Nobs,
ran to this Music Haa,
Register Rachel, Cougait Kate,
nose-less   Nae-neb Nellie and aa
staggered   stauchert about amang the Great,
what fun! I never saw
               the like,
in Embro to the ploy.

They toddle hame doun lit-up streets
filled wi synthetic joy;
oh well/such   aweill, the year brings few sic treats
much   and muckle to annoy.
many spirited   There's monie hartsom braw high-jinks
mixed up in this alloy
in simmer, whan aa sorts foregether
in Embro to the ploy.

To Robert Fergusson

Fergusson, tho twa-hunder year
awa, your image is mair clear
than many things   nor monie things that nou appear
in braid daylicht.
makes   What gars perspective turn sae queer?
What ails my sicht?

Pairtlie, nae dout, because your een
so very   gey clearlie saw the Embro scene
young woman   in times when Embro was a quean
sae weill worth seein
few   that life wi her still had a wheen
sampling   guid things worth preein.

homely
whose life was stirring, hot and   A hameil, Scottish place eneuch,
rough   whas life was steiran, het and reuch
plough   whilst yet the fairmer wi his pleuch
turned owre the sod
whar classie Queen Street and Drumsheugh
trim   nou stand sae snod.

But what a pairtner for your life!
cheerful   Gey like a weill-bred, cantie wife
chilly   wha wears an apron, no cauldrife
false   wi fause gentilitie,
wi mind keen-edgit as a knife,
used wi civilitie.

each   In ae gret tenement or land,*
big building   a muckle rubble biggin, planned
save/found   to hain grund-rent, folk wad be fand
jumbled together   aa mixter-maxter —
lordies and lawyers, no owre grand
baker   to ken a baxter

* *land* building, let out in tenements

or Ramsay wi his curlin-tangs,
guid makar baith of wigs and sangs,
or, Fergusson, yoursel; sae lang's
shy   ye werena blate,
shocks   they were your friens, whatever bangs
served up   were sair'd by fate.

a lawyer's hack by trade   Altho to tred a lawyer's hack
paid by the tuppence or the   peyed by the bodle or the plack
penny
writing   for scrievin till your wrist wad crack,
early   baith ear and late,
                  yet of guid friens ye had nae lack
at every level   in ilk estait.

the Cape [Club]'s   The 'Cape's' self-knichted cavaliers
suchlike   'Sir Scrape-Greystiel' and siclike fiers,
chose/above   they waled ye weill abune their peers
                        for cannie capers
                  whan ye'd got throu, wi nae arrears,
stint   your stent of papers.

sprightly   Hou gleglie they'd kick owre the traces
                  in the Daft Days* or at Leith Races,
                  wi trips to Fife or siccan places
cram   to stech their leisor
alcoholic pranks/pimply faces   wi drouthie ploys, while plookie faces
scorched   birslit wi pleisor.

                  And what a knack ye had of scrievin
in fresh verse/abundance of living   in caller verse yon rowth of levin,
stone world, fighting   your wee stane warld, fechtin, thievin,
working   drinkin and swinkin,
lots of fun and little grieving   wi muckle fun and puckle grievin
plenty   and fowth of thinkin.

                  In praise of Wilkie* ye declared
                  his verses wad be aye revered

* *Daft Days* period of festivity at Christmas and New Year; *Wilkie* William Wilkie (1721–72) professor, poet and
farmer

oxen   while slaw-gaun owsen turned the swaird;
                                    nou ither factors
                          hae shown the doctor gey ill-sair'd —
                                    we dae't wi tractors.

                          But this I'll say: while there's a still
ale   in Scotland, or a pint of yill,
weak   houever washie, fit to swill
                                    atween the tide
                          at Leith Port and the Blackford Hill,
                                    your fame sall byde.

hooked   Whan Daith raxed out his airm and cleikit
gate was shut   Ramsay, folk thocht the yett was steekit,
poet's right to citizenship yet sune your makar's burgess-ticket
                                    gied ye the freedom
joined   of Scottish verse, in whilk were eikit
heart and spirit   baith hert and smeddum.

                          For ye had at your fingernebbs
living   real levan words to weave your webs
frowns   of sound and sense, of smiles and slebs,
young men   whilst Embro callants
turn up their noses   ne'er thocht to runkle up their nebs
                                    at guid braid Lallans.

with perfect certainty And yet, owre surelie did ye ken
                          guid Scots wad mak bad Englishmen
they looked too deeply into England whan owre faur South they keekit ben
                                    and sune were smitten,
                          tho barelie three-score years and ten
                                    had seen Great Britain.

squint-eyed   South-keekan Scots gaed skellie-ee'd
silly head   and tuke it in their tawpie-heid
                          to hae their bairns anglified
force   and gar their stiff tongues
language   transmogrifie their Lallan leid
                                    frae vowels to diphthongs.

Of Heriot's or Watson's* ghaist
which — or yours, I wonder whilk is maist
dumbfounert, dozent and bumbazed
    wi indignation
to see our modern Embro taste
    in education.

guess/bones — We may jalouse George Watson's banes
complain the most with grisly moans — will gowl the maist wi grieslie maens
poverty's children — nou that his schule for puirtith's weans,
    foundit sae weill,
chairges sic fees and taks sic pains
    to be genteel.

No that I'd hae a body think
the worse for being clean — our toun's the waur of bein perjink
in some weys; Embro's famous stink
    is banish'd nou;
forced you to dodge — gane are the shouts, that garred ye jink,
    of 'Gardyloo!'*

our filth's poisoned — Our fulyie's pusionit the Firth
and caused, I dout, an unco dearth
oysters of great size — of thae Pandores of muckle girth
    ye thocht sae fair;
what wad ye think our gain was worth?
    I'm no that shair.

Auld Reekie's bigger, nou, what's mair,
and folk wha hae the greater share
of warldlie gear may tak the air
    in Morningside,
climb — and needna sclim the turnpike stair
    whar ye wad byde.

comfortable — But truth it is, our couthie city
curdled — has cruddit in twa pairts a bittie

*founders of Edinburgh schools; warning call that slops were about to be thrown from a window into the street: French 'gardez (vous de) l'eau'

and speaks twa tongues, ane coorse and grittie,
                    heard in the Cougait,
the tither copied, mair's the pitie,
                    frae Wast of Newgate.

which   Whilk is the crudd and whilk the whey
hard pushed   I wad be kinna sweirt to say,
                 but this I ken, that of the twae
                    the corrupt twang
                 of Cougait is the nearer tae
language   the leid ye sang.

these   Thir days, whan cities seem unreal
conscience   to makars, inwit gars us feel
                 fause as the hauf-inch marble peel
                    in Princes Street
                 whaur new shop-fronts wad shame the Deil
                    wi their deceit.

on the other hand   A conter, we've some rotten riggin
rat-infested tenements in
Cowgate   of ratton-eaten Cougait biggin
long ago the skilled rhythms   that heard langsyne the skeelie jiggin
                              of your new verse.
I chose this direction   Hard-pressed, I wale yon airt to dig in
                              and micht dae worse.

ghost-haunted   Our life's a bogle-hauntit dream
too full of terrors owre thrang wi wirrikows to seem
lightning   quite real; our fun a fireflaucht-gleam
sliced   whang'd throu a nicht
unforeseen evils/furious of gurliewhirkies huge and breme,
clotted with fright   loppert wi fricht.

                 Ye gaed about in guid braid claith
with never a thought/harm wi fient a thocht of want or skaith,
loath   in howffs at hy-jinks never laith
                    to blaw your chanter,
[an Edinburgh madhouse] syne in cursed Darien's bedlam, Daith
wrought your misfortune   wrocht your mishanter.

what made you   What gart ye break throu reason's ice?
sane   Compared wi ye, we're no sae wyce.
used to   Maybe we're yaised wi madness; vice
             and lust for pouer
       bring furth some hellish new device
every other   ilk ither hour.

       Was it the dreidit mental state
earthly   in whilk things yerdlie, smaa and great,
       become irrelevant, and Fate
             dauntin the Kirk,
from the far side of   glowres at a man frae ben Hell's gate
gloom   throu endless mirk?

       Syne even poetrie becomes
remnants   a naething, an affair of thrums
booms   of words, words, a noise that jumms
lying verbosity   wi leean skreed,
lost   the purport tint, man's sperit numbs –
             as weill be deid.

       The flicker-pictur on the screen
       bursts as by boomb-blast, and is gane;
last night   What was sae firm and good yestreen
             seems foul indeed.
then a man bums his books   Syne a man brenns his buiks bedeen,
forthwith   afore he's deid.

trouble yourself   Ye didna hae to fash your thoombs
       wi hydrogen or atom boombs,
swims   nor monie a nesty thocht that soums
             aye in our heid
scares   and flegs us in our flimsie rooms,
             and yet, ye're deid.

oh well/a very long time ago   Aweill, ye're deid, gey lang sinsyne –
       the Scottish elegiac line
       I'll spare ye, tho, as ye ken fine,
             ye scrievit monie

lively/lose

crouse stanzas whan ye'd cam to tine
            some decent cronie.

My ain toun's makar, monie an airt
formed us in common, faur apairt

extremely alike

in time, but fell alike in hert;
            I whiles forget

mud

that ye ligg there ablow the clart
            of Canogait.

great daring

Like me, nae dout, wi muckle darin,

tasted

ye pree'd grim joys at Muschat's cairn*

gruesome

and grugous thochts of Effie's bairn,*
            or, as a laddie,

slid/scratches

ye skliddert doun, for scarts no caring,
            the Guttit Haddie.*

The auld High Schule (gane Royal syne)
your Alma Mater was and mine,
and whar ye construed, line by line,
            the Gallic Weirs
we ken the airt, doun by the Wynd
            of the Black Friars.*

The wind that blaws frae Nor to South,

shrieking

skirlan frae ilka close's* mouth,

chilled both of us

has nithert baith o's in our youth

upended

            and coupt us, whiles,

slaked thirst

as we gaed hame wi slockent drouth
            doun by Sanct Giles'.

But aye we'd rise wi little hairm
and cleik ilk ither by the airm,
singan in unison to chairm

Muschat's cairn a memorial in Holyrood Park to Nichol Muschat who murdered his wife in 1702 after failing to obtain a divorce; *Effie's bairn* Effie Dean's son, known as The Whistler (see Sir Walter Scott's *The Heart of Midlothian*); *Guttit Haddie* exposed rock on Arthur's Seat said to have been caused by a waterspout in 1744; *Wynd of the Black Friars* was on the south side of the Cowgate; *close* common entry to a tenement

harm   awa the skaith,
then seek some antic, happy-go-   syne seek some cantraip, harum-skarum
lucky
loath   and naething laith.

                                        Ye stickit minister,* young Rab,
keep your defiant talk   ye wadnae hain your giff-gaff gab
a schoolmaster or bore   frae me, a dominie or crab
forever disputing it   aye stickan it,
begrudge/thief   nor gruch your brain, nor cry me scab
                                            for pickin it.

                                        To Warld's End Close frae Ramsay Lane*
batter/spine   we'd ding Auld Reekie's black rigg-bane.
Nethergate   Whan Ne'er-gate's ten-hour bell had gane
                                                that wadnae daunt us;
accompany you all the way home I'd gie scotch-convoy back again
                                                to Dawnie Douglas.

                                        Ye'd quote frae Ramsay, I frae Grieve;
I'd fill your belly   wi Happy Days your wame I'd steeve
                                and aye the mair ye'd hae me prieve
                                                your aqua vitae,
deafen   syne we wad rair out sangs to deave
the city breathing loudly in sleep   the swuffan citie.

up went every window with lots
of shrieking   Up gaed ilk sash wi feck of skriekan,
peeping   frae the wee windaes heids were keekan;
complaining   the Embro folk gied owre their gleekin
                                                for very joy;
bright fire-glow/basking   in ae bricht lowe we aa were beekan –
                                                wow! what a ploy!

                                        But ach! the nippie-tongue of morn
puts all such enchantment   pits aa sic glaumerie to scorn;
foolish   I stand here, glaikit and forlorn
                                                in Canogait,

stickit minister minister of the Church of Scotland who never gets a pastoral charge; *stickit* unfinished; i.e. to the
end of the High Street from Edinburgh Castle

determined, yet afraid to beg by force

ettlesome, yet feart to sorn
     on your estait.

my way is steep, not sensible at all

Robert, fareweill; I maun awa.
My gait is stey, no wyce ava,
by Jacob's Ladder,* Burns's smaa
     Greek pepperpat,*
Sanct Andrew's Hous* an' aa an' aa –
     nae mair of that!

panting/language
calm
living/lie dead

woeful wreck

Pechan, I turn, whilst aye your leid
of lowan Scots sounds in my heid
wi levan braith, tho ye ligg deid;
     I glowre faur doun
and see the waesome wrak outspreid
     of your auld toun.

then struggling up the slope once more

Syne trauchlan up the brae yince mair,
frae Canogait, I leave ye there,
whar wee white roses scent the air
     about your grave,

and to
go with the rest of them

and til some suburb new and bare
     gang wi the lave.

The Wire

moor

This day I saw ane endless muir
wi sad horizon, like the sea
around some uncouth landless globe

where/flicker

whaur waters flauchter endlessly.

bilberry

Heather bell and blaeberry
grow on this muir; reid burns rin

sky
mist

in clear daylicht; the luift is free
frae haar, and yet there is nae sun.

Jacob's Ladder steep path, including steps, on Calton Hill; *Burns's smaa Greek pepperpat* on Calton Hill,
monument to Robert Burns raised in 1830, and a copy of the monument of Lysicrates in Athens; *Sanct Andrew's
Hous* St Andrew's House, HQ of the Scottish Office, a sort of cut-price Kremlin

everywhere   Gossamers glint in aa the airts,
flower-heads   criss-cross about the lang flure-heids
grass and thistles of girss and thristles here, and there
                 amang the purpie willow-weeds.

                 Bog-myrtle scent is in the air
honey   heavy wi hinnie-sap and peat
mixed   whiles mellit like uneasy thochts
excrement or sweat wi something human, shairn or sweit.

powder smoke   Nou guns gaun aff, and pouther-reik
dogs   and yappin packs of foetid dugs,
red/blisters   and blobs of cramosie, like blebs
                 of bluid squeezed frae vanilla bugs

knock violently   pash suddenlike intill the licht
that beats   that dings on this unshadowed muir
from every direction, and then are gone frae ilka airt, and syne are gane
whirlwinds/dust   like tourbillions of twisted stour.

                 The criss-cross gossamers, the while,
tight   twang owre the heather, ticht and real;
slender   I ken, houever jimp they seem,
                 that they are spun frae strands of steel.

                 And they are barbed wi twisted spikes
                 wi scant a handsbreidth space atween,
iron   and reinforced wi airn rods
                 and hung about wi bits of tin

                 that hing in pairs alang the Wire,
each one   ilkane three-cornered like a fang:
                 clashin thegither at a touch
unnaturally into the lark's song they break aukwart the lairick's sang.

high   Heich in their sentry-posts, the guairds
who dare not   wha daurna sleep, on pain of daith,
                 watch throu the graticules of guns,
                 cruel and persecuted, baith.

crowded	This endless muir is thrang wi folk
limp in all directions at once	that hirple aye aa airts at aince
	wi neither purport nor content
restless	nor rest, in fidgan impotence.
	They gae in danger of the Wire
but stagger	but staucher on anither mile
	frae line to line of spider steel
to leap	to loup anither deidlie stile.
	A man trips up; the Wire gaes ding,
	tins clash, the guaird lifts up his heid;
very slowly	fu slaw he traverses his gun
	and blatters at him till he's deid.
tearing	The dugs loup on him, reivan flesh,
bones/wood	crunchin the bane as they were wud;
swiftly	swith they come and swith are gane,
	syne nocht is left but pools of bluid.
blood dripping	Bluid dreipan doun amang the roots
is sucked	is soukit up the vampire stem
cruel flowers	and suin the gaudy felloun flures
cheat and mock	begowk the man that nourished them.
	Some pairts the Wires close in and leave
go	smaa space whaur men may freely gang,
	and ilka step is taen in dreid;
	there flures and men maist thickly thrang.
entangled	A man gets taiglit on a barb,
the length of his stomach	endlang his wame the cauld fear creeps;
	he daurna muve, the hert beats hard,
	but beats awa. The sentry sleeps.
energy	Aye! his virr comes back in spate,
sly	as some auld trout this man is slee;
	he hauds himsel still as a stane,
	back comes his ain self-maistery.

Cannily he sets to wark,
warp by warp his sleeve is free,
it hings nou by a single threid:
loud clash the tins and bullets flee.

forward   Forrit and back and in and out
woeful   they darn in waesome figure-dance;
staying/endure   bydin still they canna thole
and each man works and ilk man warks his ain mischance.

They see the Wire, and weill they ken
which   whilk wey it warks. In middle-air
the glintan guns are clear in sicht,
who   tho nae man kens wha set them there.

Impersonal in uniform,
the guairds are neither friens nor faes;
none tries   nane ettles to propitiate
upsets   nor fashes them wi bribes or praise.

Efficient and predictable,
immediately   they cairry out their orders stricht;
here naething happens unforeseen;
it is jist sae, no wrang nor richt.

On this dour mechanistic muir
wi nae land's end, and endless day,
whaur nae thing thraws a shadow, here
sorrowful   the truth is clear, and it is wae.

The crouds that thrang the danger-spots
weill ken what wey their warld's wrocht,
struggle on   but aye the mair they pauchle on
to win release frae nigglin thocht.

Some pairts the pattern of the Wire
leaves clear for fifty yairds and mair
dried up/dust   whaur soil has crined to desert stuir
with stunted shrubs wi scroggie bussels puir and bare.

more sensible than the rest
given to taking fright

spinning
must endure

saunter aimlessly their patch
ponies
mettle

some in odd, ill-favoured directions

to soak the wearisome unmoistened dust

endure
and suffer what happens

in all that alien
slow-going/eyes
as if
reflected marvels

revealed

unusually small

faded away

Here some folk wycer nor the lave
or maybe suiner gien to skar
tether theirsels wi chains to stakes,
sae they may gang, but no owre far.

Birlan in wretchedness aroun
their safe lives' centre, they maun dree
temptation sair to break their chains
for aye they ettle to gang free.

Some stark and strang stravaig their yird
like shelties that hae never taen
the bit; mere smeddum drives them on,
their lives are short, but are their ain.

A wheen in orra ill-faur'd airts
on barren streitches of the muir
gae whaur nae bluid is ever shed
to drouk the dreich unslockent stour.

Within a pentagon of wire
they gang alane, or twae by twae,
thole the condition of their life
and dree the weird as best they may.

Alane in thon hale fremmit globe
thae slaw-gaun folk hae in their een
some sapience, as gin their looks
refleckit ferlies they hae seen

in their ain thochts, the nucleus
of man himsel is keethit there.
Expressed in terms of happiness
are premises of pure despair.

Thae guidlie folk are nae great men;
the best of men are unco smaa
whan in the autumn of despair
irrelevance has dwined awa.

then the leaf   Their syllogisms widdershins
                      wither the petal; syne the leaf
shrink   and stem crine in as life gaes doun
                      intill a corm of prime belief.

mighty thought   Wi utmaist pouer of forcy thocht
                      they crine their life within its core,
                      and what they ken wi certainty
known beside   is kent inby the bracken-spore.

                      And aye alane or twae by twae
vexation   they gang unhurt amang the noy
that cruel/eyes   of thon fell planet, and their een
blaze   lowe wi the licht of inwart joy.

                      Outwartly they seem at rest,
save for   binna the glint of hidden fires.
                      Their warld shaks, but they bide still
vibrating   as nodal points on dirlan wires.

                      In ither airts, whaur folk are thrang,
                      the Wire vibrates, clash gae the tins,
                      flures blume frae bluidie marl, dugs
                      yowl throu the blatter of the guns.

spin   I saw thon planet slawlie birl;
                      I saw it as ane endless muir
                      in daylicht, and I saw a few
dust   guid men bide still amang the stour.

Property

A man should have no thought for property,
he said, and drank down his pint.
Mirage is found in the Desert and elswhere.
Later, in Libya (sand & scrub,
the sun two weeks to midsummer)
he carried all his property over the sand:
socks, knife and spoon, a dixie,

toilet kit, the Works of Shakespeare,
blanket, groundsheet, greatcoat,
and a water-bottle holding no more water.
He walked with other scorched men
in the dryness of this littoral waste land,
a raised beach without even sea water
with a much damned escarpment
unchanged throughout a day's truck-bumping
or a lifetime of walking without water,
confirming our worst fears of eternity.
Two men only went on whistling,
skidding on a beat-frequency.
Tenderness to music's dissonances,
and much experience of distress in art
was distressed, this time, in life.
A hot dry wind rose, moving the sand,
the sand-shifting Khamsin, rustling over
the land, whistling through hardy sandy
scrub, where sand-snails' brittle
shells on the sand, things in themselves,
roll for ever. Suffusing the sand in the
air, the sun burned in darkness.
No man now whistled, only the sandy wind.
The greatcoat first, then blanket discarded
and the other property lay absurd on the Desert,
but he kept his water-bottle.
In February, in a cold wet climate,
he has permanent damp in his bones
for lack of that groundsheet.
He has a different notion of the values of things.

Glisk of the Great

glimpse

I saw him comin out the N.B. Grill,
greasy   creashy and winey, wi his famous voice
joke   crackin some comic bawr to please three choice
magistrates, laughing   notorious bailies, lauchan fit to kill.

then the four merry cronies climbed into

a great big

Syne thae fowre crousie cronies clam intill
a muckle big municipal Rolls-Royce,
and disappeared, aye lauchan, wi a noise
that droont the traffic, towards the Calton Hill.

As they rade by, it seemed the sun was shinin

cheerful

brichter nor usual roun thae cantie three

that well-known magnifico

that wi thon weill-kent Heid-yin had been dinin.

Nou that's the kinna thing I like to see;
tho ye and I look on and canna jyne in,
it gies our toun some tone, ye'll aa agree.

Heard in the Cougate

'Whu's aa thae fflagpoles ffur in Princes Street?
Chwoich! Ptt! Hechyuch! Ab-boannie cairry-on.
Seez-owre the wa'er. Whu' the deevil's thon
inaidie, heh?' 'The Queen's t'meet

The King o Norway wi his royal suite.'
'His royal wh'?' 'The hale jing-bang. It's aw in
the papur. Whaur's ma speck-sh? Aye they're gaun
t'day-cor-ate the toun. It's a fair treat,

something ye dinnae see jist ivry day,
foun'uns in the Gairdens, muckle spates
dancing t'music, an thir's t'be nae

chairge t'gi'in, it aw gaes on the Rates.'
'Ah ddae-ken whu' the pplace is comin tae
wi aw thae, hechyuch! fforeign po'entates.'

At Robert Fergusson's Grave

October 1962

Canongait kirkyaird in the failing year

rose bushes

is auld and grey, the wee roseirs are bare,

gleam

five gulls leam white agin the dirty air:
why are they here? There's naething for them here.

Why are we here oursels? We gaither near
the grave. Fergusons mainly, quite a fair
turn-out, respectfu, ill at ease, we stare
at daith – there's an address – I canna hear.

oh well/mist
went back to the pool
mud

Aweill, we staund bareheidit in the haar,
murnin a man that gaed back til the pool
twa-hunner year afore our time. The glaur

that covers his bones
sorrow
tugs/disparage this if you dare
earth (on a grave)

that haps his banes glowres back. Strang, present
                                       dool
ruggs at my hairt. Lichtlie this gin ye daur:
here Robert Burns knelt and kissed the mool.

Elegy

They are lang deid, folk that I used to ken,

all mouldering and awry

their firm-set lips aa mowdert and agley,
sherp-tempert een rusty amang the cley:

sensible, pleasant

they are baith deid, thae wycelike, bienlie men,

heidmaisters, that had been in pouer for ten

entangling

or twenty year afore fate's taiglie wey

well-educated, shy and fated
just-hatched schoolmaster

brocht me, a young, weill-harnit, blate and fey
new-cleckit dominie, intill their den.

one told me

Ane tellt me it was time I learnt to write –
round-haund, he meant – and saw about my hair:

I remember him well/paunch

I mind of him, beld-heidit, wi a kyte.

Ane sneerit quarterly – I cuidna square
my savings bank – and sniftert in his spite.

if they aren't dead

Weill, gin they arena deid, it's time they were.

In Princes Street Gairdens

barrow

Doun by the baundstaund, by the ice-cream barrie,
there is a sait that says, Wilma is Fab.

give me your talk

Sit doun aside me here and gieze your gab,

a pigeon

jist you and me, a dou, and a wee cock-sparrie.

prosperous
lay slates and paint and cobble

Up in the street, shop-folk sairve and harrie;
weill-daean tredsmen sclate and pent and snab

take notice

and jyne and plaister. We never let dab

dodge

sae lang as we can jink the strait-and-narrie.

A sculptured growp, classical and symbolic,
staunds by the path, maist beautiful to see:
National Savings, out for a bit frolic,

to

peys echt per cent til Thrift and Industry,
but dour Inflatioun, a diabolic
dou, has owrecam, and duin Thrift in the ee.

Merulius Lacrymans*

make you snort

My name is dreidfu. Did it garr ye snirk?
I cam in wi your braith, syne. Whan I'm seen

mad-red

I'm growin, wud-reid, nae Bolshevik, green

suit/gloom

jist wadnae sair me; I bide in the mirk,

dark

nae chlorophyll in me. But in some dirk

corner/you're not keen

neuk of your property ye arena keen

to look into/glows between

to keek intill, my floure-heid lowes atween

fine plaster and cracked joist

braw plaister and crackt jeest, in hous or kirk.

Onie bit weakness whaur the rain may flow
or slocken, even, and it's aa the same,

moisten

suck/under

I'll souk the guid dry timmer frae ablow

*dry rot

your feet, and lay my water-warks. My name?
In France they used to cry me Collabo;
I'm Greitan Muriel whan I'm at hame.

NORMAN MACCAIG (b. 1910)

Summer Farm

Straws like tame lightnings lie about the grass
And hang zigzag on hedges. Green as glass
The water in the horse-trough shines.
Nine ducks go wobbling by in two straight lines.

A hen stares at nothing with one eye,
Then picks it up. Out of an empty sky
A swallow falls and, flickering through
The barn, dives up again into the dizzy blue.

I lie, not thinking, in the cool, soft grass,
Afraid of where a thought might take me – as
This grasshopper with plated face
Unfolds his legs and finds himself in space.

Self under self, a pile of selves I stand
Threaded on time, and with metaphysic hand
Lift the farm like a lid and see
Farm within farm, and in the centre, me.

Drifter

The long net, tasselled with corpses, came
Burning through the water, flowing up.
Dogfish following it to the surface
Turned away slowly to the deep.

The *Daffodil* squatted, slid ahead
Through the red kyle with thirty crans
Of throttled silver in her belly.
Her anchor snored amid its chains.

And memory gathered tarry splinters,
Put shadowy sparkles in her bag,

Slid up her sleeve the hills of Harris
And stole Orion and the Dog.

I sat with that kind thief inside me;
I sat with years I did not know
Heaped on my knees. With these two treasures
I sailed home through the Gaelic sea.

Crofter's Kitchen, Evening

A man's boots with a woman in them
Clatter across the floor. A hand
Long careless of the lives it kills
Comes down and thwacks on newspapers
A long black fish with bloody gills.

The kettle's at her singsong – minor
Prophetess in her sooty cave.
A kitten climbs the bundled net
On the bench, and, curled up like a cowpat,
Purrs on the *Stornoway Gazette*.

The six hooks of a Mackerel Dandy
Climb their thin rope – an exclamation
By the curled question of a gaff.
Three rubber eels cling like a crayfish
On top of an old photograph.

Peats fur themselves in gray. The door
Bursts open, chairs creak, hands reach out
For spectacles, a lamp flairs high . . .
The collie underneath the table
Slumps with a world-rejecting sigh.

Half-built Boat in a Hayfield

A cradle, at a distance, of a kind:
Or, making midget its neat pastoral scene,
A carcass rotted and its bones picked clean.

Rye-grass was silk and sea, whose rippling was
Too suave to rock it. Solid in the sun,
Its stiff ribs ached for voyages not begun.

The gathering word was not completed yet.
The litter of its own genesis lay around,
Sunk in the bearded sea, or on the ground.

As though evolving brilliances could show
In their first utterances what would end as one
Continuous proclamation of a sun.

Only when these clawed timbers could enclose
Their own completing darkness would they be
Phoenixed from It and phoenixed into She.

And fit then, as such noticing reveals,
To split her first wave open and explore
The many ways that all lead to one shore.

Explicit Snow

First snow is never all the snows there were
Come back again, but novel in the sun
As though a newness had but just begun.

It does not fall as rain does from nowhere
Or from that cloud spinnakered on the blue,
But from a place we feel we could go to.

As a great actor steps, not from the wings,
But from the play's extension – all he does
Is move to the seen from the mysterious –

And his performance is the first of all –
The snow falls from its implications and
Stages pure newness on the uncurtained land.

And the hill we've looked out of existence comes
Vivid in its own language; and this tree
Stands self-explained, its own soliloquy.

Celtic Cross

The implicated generations made
This symbol of their lives, a stone made light
By what is carved on it.
                        The plaiting masks,
But not with involutions of a shade,
What a stone says and what a stone cross asks.

Something that is not mirrored by nor trapped
In webs of water or bag-nets of cloud;
The tangled mesh of weed
                        lets it go by.
Only men's minds could ever have unmapped
Into abstraction such a territory.

No green bay going yellow over sand
Is written on by winds to tell a tale
Of death-dishevelled gull
                        or heron, stiff
As a cruel clerk with gaunt writs in his hand
– Or even of light, that makes its depths a cliff.

Singing responses order otherwise.
The tangled generations ravelled out
In links of song whose sweet
                        strong choruses

Are these stone involutions to the eyes
Given to the ear in abstract vocables.

The stone remains, and the cross, to let us know
Their unjust, hard demands, as symbols do.
But on them twine and grow
                              beneath the dove
Serpents of wisdom whose cool statements show
Such understanding that it seems like love.

Feeding Ducks

One duck stood on my toes.
The others made watery rushes after bread
Thrown by my momentary hand; instead,
She stood duck-still and got far more than those.

An invisible drone boomed by
With a beetle in it; the neighbour's yearning bull
Bugled across five fields. And an evening full
Of other evenings quietly began to die.

And my everlasting hand
Dropped on my hypocrite duck her grace of bread.
And I thought, 'The first to be fattened, the first to be
                                                    dead',
Till my gestures enlarged, wide over the darkening
                                                    land.

Things in Each Other

To fake green strokes in water, light fidgets,
A niggling fidget, and the green is there,
Born of a blue and marrying into blue
With clouds blushed pink on it from the upper air.

And water breathing upwards from itself
Sketches an island with blurred pencillings,

A phase of space, a melting out of space:
Mind does this, too, with the pure shapes of things.

Or the mind fidgets and a thought, grown green,
Born of nowhere and marrying nowhere,
Fakes a creation, that is one and goes
Into the world and makes its difference there.

A thing to be regarded: whose pure shape
Blurs in the quality of the noticing mind
And is blushed pink and makes the hard jump from
Created to creator, like human kind.

The Shore Road

The sea pursued
Its beastlike amours, rolling in its sweat
And beautiful under the moon; and a leaf was
A lively architecture in the light.

The space between
Was full, to splitting point, of presences
So oilily adjustable a walking man
Pushed through and trailed behind no turbulence.

The walking man
With octaves in his guts was a quartertone
In octaves of octaves that climbed up and down
Beyond his hearing, to back parts of the moon.

As though things were
Perpetual chronologies of themselves,
He sounded his small history, to make complete
The interval of leaf and rutting waves.

Or so he thought,
And heard his hard shoes scrunching in the grit,
Smelt salt and iodine in the wind and knew
The door was near, the supper, the small lamplight.

Byre

The thatched roof rings like heaven where mice
Squeak small hosannahs all night long,
Scratching its golden pavements, skirting
The gutter's crystal river-song.

Wild kittens in the world below
Glare with one flaming eye through cracks,
Spurt in the straw, are tawny brooches
Splayed on the chests of drunken sacks.

The dimness becomes darkness as
Vast presences come mincing in,
Swagbellied Aphrodites, swinging
A silver slaver from each chin.

And all is milky, secret, female.
Angels are hushed and plain straws shine.
And kittens miaow in circles, stalking
With tail and hindleg one straight line.

Loch Sionascaig

Hard to remember how the water went
Shaking the light,
Until it shook like peas in a riddling plate.

Or how the islands snored into the wind,
Or seemed to, round
Stiff, plunging headlands that they never cleared.

Or how a trout hung high its drizzling bow
For a count of three –
Heraldic figure on a shield of spray.

Yet clear the footprint in the puddled sand
That slowly filled
And rounded out and smoothed and disappeared.

July Evening

A bird's voice chinks and tinkles
Alone in the gaunt reedbed –
    Tiny silversmith
Working late in the evening.

I sit and listen. The rooftop
With a quill of smoke stuck in it
    Wavers against the sky
In the dreamy heat of summer.

Flowers' closing time: bee lurches
Across the hayfield, singing
    And feeling its drunken way
Round the air's invisible corners.

And grass is grace. And charlock
Is gold of its own bounty.
    The broken chair by the wall
Is one with immortal landscapes.

Something has been completed
That everything is part of,
    Something that will go on
Being completed forever.

Porpoises

In twos and threes and fives
they made a circus-ring of the Minch,
wheeling over, and leaving behind them in the air
two puffs, three puffs, five puffs –
audible plumes.

One looked to see on their backs
or in the carved car they might well be pulling
some plump mythical boy
or sea-green sea-nymph
or Arion himself, twangling from his lyre
audible spray.

But not
these days.

All the same, I myself
(in a mythical sort of way)
have been drawn over metaphorical waters
by these curving backs, till,
filled with an elation
I don't want to have explained to me,
I lifted a pagan face and shouted
audible nonsense.

Looking Down on Glen Canisp

The summer air is thick, is wads
that muffle the hill burn's voice
and stifle colours
to their cloudier selves – and
bright enough: the little loch
is the one clear pane
in a stained-glass window.

The scent of thyme and bog myrtle
is so thick
one listens for it, as though it might be
a drowsy honey-hum
in the heavy air.

Even the ravens
have sunk into the sandstone cliffs
of Suilven, that are dazed blue
and fuzz into the air around them –

as my mind does, till I hear
a thin far clatter and
look down to where two stags
canter across the ford, splashing up before them
antlers of water.

Blue Tit on a String of Peanuts

A cubic inch of some stars
weighs a hundred tons – Blue tit,
who could measure the power
of your tiny spark of energy? Your hair-thin legs
(one north-east, one due west) support
a scrap of volcano, four inches
of hurricane: and, seeing me, you make the sound
of a grain of sawdust being sawn
by the minutest of saws.

Old Edinburgh

Down the Canongate
down the Cowgate
go vermilion dreams
snake's tongues of bannerets
trumpets with words from their mouths
saying *Praise me, praise me.*

Up the Cowgate
up the Canongate
lice on the march
tar on the amputated stump
Hell speaking with the tongue of Heaven
a woman tied to the tail of a cart.

And history leans by a dark entry
with words from his mouth
that say *Pity me, pity me
but never forgive.*

Basking Shark

To stub an oar on a rock where none should be,
To have it rise with a slounge out of the sea
Is a thing that happened once (too often) to me.

But not too often – though enough. I count as gain
That once I met, on a sea tin-tacked with rain,
That roomsized monster with a matchbox brain.

He displaced more than water. He shoggled me
Centuries back – this decadent townee
Shook on a wrong branch of his family tree.

Swish up the dirt and, when it settles, a spring
Is all the clearer. I saw me, in one fling,
Emerging from the slime of everything.

So who's the monster? The thought made me grow
                                                    pale
For twenty seconds while, sail after sail,
The tall fin slid away and then the tail.

Intruder in a Set Scene

The way the water goes is blink blink blink.
That heap of trash was once
a swan's throne. The swans now lean their chests
against the waves that spill on Benbecula.
On the towpath a little girl
peers over the handle of the pram she's pushing.
Her mother follows her, reading a letter.

Everything is winter, everything
is a letter from another place, measuring
absence. Everything laments
the swan, drifting and dazzling on a western sealoch.

– But the little girl, five years of self-importance,
walks in her own season, not noticing
the stop-go's of water, the mouldering swan-throne,
the tears turning cold in the eyes of her mother.

No Interims in History

Barbarians! growled Attila
as the pile of skulls mounted higher.
What fun! squealed Robespierre,
shaking the gloved hand of Monsieur Guillotin.
The sword of the Lord! roared Cromwell
while the church and the people in it
became a stack of fire.

It would be good to think
that Attila felt a headache coming on,
that Monsieur Guillotin fingered the crick in his neck,
that Cromwell had a grey taste on his tongue

– while, as now, the dove
flew wildly over the world
finding nowhere to land,
growing weaker and weaker.

SOMHAIRLE MACGILL-EAIN/SORLEY MACLEAN (b. 1911)

Gaoir na h-Eòrpa

A nighean a' chùil bhuidhe, throm-bhuidh òr-bhuidh,
fonn do bheòil-sa 's gaoir na h-Eòrpa,
a nighean gheal chasurlach aighearach bhòidheach
cha bhiodh masladh ar latha-ne searbh 'nad phòig-sa.

An tugadh t' fhonn no t' àilleachd ghlòrmhor
bhuam-sa gràinealachd mharbh nan dòigh seo,
a' bhrùid 's am meàirleach air ceann na h-Eòrpa
's do bhial-sa uaill-dhearg 'san t-seann òran?

An tugadh corp geal is clàr gréine
bhuam-sa cealgaireachd dhubh na bréine,
nimh bhùirdeasach is puinnsean créide
is dìblidheachd ar n-Albann éitigh?

An cuireadh bòidhchead is ceòl suaimhneach
bhuam-sa breòiteachd an aobhair bhuain seo,
am mèinear Spàinnteach a' leum ri cruadal
is' anam mórail dol sìos gun bhruaillean?

Dé bhiodh pòg do bheòil uaibhrich
mar ris gach braon de 'n fhuil luachmhoir
a thuit air raointean reòta fuara
nam beann Spàinnteach bho fhòirne cruadhach?

Dé gach cuach de d' chual òr-bhuidh
ris gach bochdainn, àmhghar 's dórainn
a thig 's a thàinig air sluagh na h-Eòrpa
bho Long nan Daoine gu daors' a' mhór-shluaigh?

The Cry of Europe

Girl of the yellow, heavy-yellow, gold-yellow hair,
the song of your mouth and Europe's shivering cry,
fair, heavy-haired, spirited, beautiful girl,
the disgrace of our day would not be bitter in your
                                                        kiss.

Would your song and splendid beauty take
from me the dead loathsomeness of these ways,
the brute and the brigand at the head of Europe
and your mouth red and proud with the old song?

Would white body and forehead's sun take
from me the foul black treachery,
spite of the bourgeois and poison of their creed
and the feebleness of our dismal Scotland?

Would beauty and serene music put
from me the sore frailty of this lasting cause,
the Spanish miner leaping in the face of horror
and his great spirit going down untroubled?

What would the kiss of your proud mouth be
compared with each drop of the precious blood
that fell on the cold frozen uplands
of Spanish mountains from a column of steel?

What every lock of your gold-yellow head
to all the poverty, anguish and grief
that will come and have come on Europe's people
from the Slave Ship to the slavery of the whole
                                                        people?

Am Bata Dubh

A bhàta dhuibh, a Ghreugaich choimhlionta,
cluas siùil, balg siùil làn is geal,
agus tu fhéin gu foirfeach ealanta,
sàmhach uallach gun ghiamh gun ghais;
do chùrsa réidh gun bhròn gun fhaireachadh;
cha b' iadsan luingis dhubha b' ealanta
a sheòl Odysseus a nall á Itaca
no Mac Mhic Ailein a nall á Uidhist,
cuid air muir fìon-dhorcha
's cuid air sàl uaine-ghlas.

The Black Boat

Black boat, perfect Greek,
sail tack, sail belly full and white,
and you yourself complete in craft,
silent, spirited, flawless;
your course smooth, sorrowless, unfeeling;
they were no more skilled black ships
that Odysseus sailed over from Ithaca,
or Clanranald over from Uist,
those on a wine-dark sea,
these on a grey-green brine.

Ban-Ghàidheal

Am faca Tu i, Iùdhaich mhóir,
ri 'n abrar Aon Mhac Dhé?
Am fac' thu 'coltas air Do thriall
ri strì an fhìon-lios chéin?

An cuallach mhiosan air a druim,
fallus searbh air mala is gruaidh;
's a' mhios chreadha trom air cùl
a cinn chrùibte bhochd thruaigh.

Chan fhaca Tu i, Mhic an t-saoir,
ri 'n abrar Rìgh na Glòir,
a miosg nan cladach carrach siar,
fo fhallus cliabh a lòin.

An t-earrach so agus so chaidh
's gach fichead earrach bho 'n an tùs
tharruing ise 'n fheamainn fhuar
chum biadh a cloinne 's duais an tùir.

'S gach fichead foghar tha air triall
chaill i samhradh buidh nam blàth;
is threabh an dubh-chosnadh an clais
tarsuinn mìnead ghil a clàir.

Agus labhair T' eaglais chaomh
mu staid chaillte a h-anama thruaigh;
agus leag an cosnadh dian
a corp gu sàmhchair dhuibh an uaigh.

Is thriall a tìm mar shnighe dubh
a' drùdhadh tughaidh fàrdaich bochd;
mheal ise an dubh-chosnadh cruaidh;
is glas a cadal suain an nochd.

A Highland Woman

Hast Thou seen her, great Jew,
who art called the One Son of God?
Hast Thou seen on Thy way the like of her
labouring in the distant vineyard?

The load of fruits on her back,
a bitter sweat on brow and cheek,
and the clay basin heavy on the back
of her bent poor wretched head.

Thou hast not seen her, Son of the carpenter,
who art called the King of Glory,
among the rugged western shores
in the sweat of her food's creel.

This Spring and last Spring
and every twenty Springs from the beginning,
she has carried the cold seaweed
for her children's food and the castle's reward.

And every twenty Autumns gone
she has lost the golden summer of her bloom,
and the Black Labour has ploughed the furrow
across the white smoothness of her forehead.

And Thy gentle church has spoken
about the lost state of her miserable soul,
and the unremitting toil has lowered
her body to a black peace in a grave.

And her time has gone like a black sludge
seeping through the thatch of a poor dwelling:
the hard Black Labour was her inheritance;
grey is her sleep to-night.

Calbharaigh

Chan eil mo shùil air Calbharaigh
no air Betlehem an àigh
ach air cùil ghrod an Glaschu
far bheil an lobhadh fàis,
agus air seòmar an Dùn-éideann,
seòmar bochdainn 's cràidh,
far a bheil an naoidhean creuchdach
ri aonagraich gu bhàs.

Calvary

My eye is not on Calvary
nor on Bethlehem the Blessed,
but on a foul-smelling backland in Glasgow,
where life rots as it grows;
and on a room in Edinburgh,
a room of poverty and pain,
where the diseased infant
writhes and wallows till death.

My Een Are Nae on Calvary

Frae the Gaelic o Sorley MacLean

My een are nae on Calvary
or the Bethlehem they praise,
but on the shitten back-lands in Glesga toun
whaur growan life decays,
and a stairheid room in an Embro land,
a chalmer o puirtith and skaith,
whaur monie a shilpet bairnikie
gaes smoorit doun til daith.

trans. Douglas Young

Clann Ghill-Eain

Chan e iadsan a bhàsaich
an àrdan Inbhir-chéitein
dh'aindeoin gaisge is uabhair
ceann uachdrach ar sgeula;
ach esan bha 'n Glaschu,
ursann-chatha nam feumach,
Iain mór MacGill-Eain,
ceann is fèitheam ar sgeula.

The Clan MacLean

Not they who died
in the hauteur of Inverkeithing
in spite of valour and pride
the high head of our story;
but he who was in Glasgow
the battle-post of the poor,
great John MacLean,
the top and hem of our story.

Dol an Iar

Tha mi dol an iar 'san Fhàsaich
is mo thàmailt air mo ghuaillean,
gun d' rinneadh a' chuis-bhùrta dhiom
on a bha mi mar bu dual dhomh.

An gaol 's an t-iomrall bu mhotha
an onair mheallta mo mhilleadh,
le sgleò na laige air mo léirsinn,
claonadh an éiginn a' chinne.

'S fhada bhuam-sa an t-Eilean
is gealach ag éirigh air Catàra,
's fhada bhuam an Aird Ghiuthais
is rudhadh maidne air an Fhàsaich.

Tha Camus Alba fada bhuam
agus daorsa na Roinn-Eòrpa.
fada bhuam 'san Aird an Iarthuath
na sùilean glas-ghorma 's bòidhche.

'S fhada bhuam-sa an t-Eilean
agus gach ìomhaigh ghaoil an Alba,
tha gainmheach choigreach anns an Eachdraidh
a' milleadh innealan na h-eanchainn.

'S fhada bhuam Belsen's Dachau
Rotterdam is Cluaidh is Pràga
is Dimitrov air bialaibh cùirte
a' bualadh eagail le ghlag gàire.

Tha Guernica fhéin glé fhada
bho chuirp neoichiontach nan Nàsach
a tha 'nan laighe ann an greibheal
's an gainmhich lachduinn na Fàsaich.

Chan eil gamhlas 'na mo chridhe
ri saighdearan calma 'n Nàmhaid
ach an càirdeas a tha eadar
fir am prìosan air sgeir-thràghad,

a' fuireach ris a' mhuir a' lìonadh
's a' fuarachadh na creige blàithe,
agus fuaralachd na beatha
ann an gréin theth na Fàsaich.

Ach 's e seo an spàirn nach seachnar,
éiginn ghoirt a' chinne-daonna,
's ged nach fuath liom armailt Roimeil
tha sùil na h-eanchainn gun chlaonadh.

Agus biodh na bha mar bha e,
tha mi de dh'fhir mhór' a' Bhràighe,
de Chloinn Mhic Ghille Chaluim threubhaich,
de Mhathanaich Loch Aills nan geurlann,
agus fir m' ainme – có bu tréine
nuair dh' fhàdadh uabhar an léirchreach?

Going Westwards

*I go westwards in the Desert
with my shame on my shoulders,
that I was made a laughing-stock
since I was as my people were.*

*Love and the greater error,
deceiving honour spoiled me,
with a film of weakness on my vision,
squinting at mankind's extremity.*

*Far from me the Island
when the moon rises on Quattara,
far from me the Pine Headland
when the morning ruddiness is on the Desert.*

Camus Alba is far from me
and so is the bondage of Europe,
far from me in the North-West
the most beautiful grey-blue eyes.

Far from me the Island
and every loved image in Scotland,
there is a foreign sand in History
spoiling the machines of the mind.

Far from me Belsen and Dachau,
Rotterdam, the Clyde and Prague,
and Dimitrov before a court
hitting fear with the thump of his laugh.

Guernica itself is very far
from the innocent corpses of the Nazis
who are lying in the gravel
and in the khaki sand of the Desert.

There is no rancour in my heart
against the hardy soldiers of the Enemy,
but the kinship that there is among
men in prison on a tidal rock

waiting for the sea flowing
and making cold the warm stone;
and the coldness of life
in the hot sun of the Desert.

But this is the struggle not to be avoided,
the sore extreme of human-kind,
and though I do not hate Rommel's army
the brain's eye is not squinting.

And be what was as it was,
I am of the big men of Braes,
of the heroic Raasay MacLeods,
of the sharp-sword Mathesons of Lochalsh;

and the men of my name – who were braver
when their ruinous pride was kindled?

Glac a' Bhàis

Thubhairt Nàsach air choireigin gun tug am Furair air ais do fhir
na Gearmailte 'a' chòir agus an sonas bàs fhaotainn anns an
àraich'

'Na shuidhe marbh an 'Glaic a' Bhàis'
fo Dhruim Ruidhìseit,
gill' òg 's a logan sìos m' a ghruaidh
's a thuar grìsionn.

Smaoinich mi air a' chòir's an àgh
a fhuair e bho Fhurair,
bhith tuiteam ann an raon an àir
gun éirigh tuilleadh;

air a' ghreadhnachas's air a' chliù
nach d' fhuair e 'na aonar,
ged b' esan bu bhrònaiche snuadh
ann an glaic air laomadh

le cuileagan mu chuirp ghlas'
air gainmhich lachduinn
's i salach-bhuidhe 's làn de raip
's de sprùidhlich catha.

An robh an gille air an dream
a mhàb na h-Iùdhaich
's na Comunnaich , no air an dream
bu mhotha, dhiùbh-san

a threòraicheadh bho thoiseach àl
gun deòin gu buaireadh
agus bruaillean cuthaich gach blàir
air sgàth uachdaran?

Ge b'e a dheòin-san no a chàs,
a neoichiontas no mhìorun,
cha do nochd e toileachadh 'na bhàs
fo Dhruim Ruidhìseit.

Death Valley

Some Nazi or other has said that the Fuehrer had restored to German manhood the 'right and joy of dying in battle'

Sitting dead in 'Death Valley'
below the Ruweisat Ridge
a boy with his forelock down about his cheek
and his face slate-grey;

I thought of the right and the joy
that he got from his Fuehrer,
of falling in the field of slaughter
to rise no more;

of the pomp and the fame
that he had, not alone,
though he was the most piteous to see
in a valley gone to seed

with flies about grey corpses
on a dun sand
dirty yellow and full of the rubbish
and fragments of battle.

Was the boy of the band
who abused the Jews
and Communists, or of the greater
band of those

led, from the beginning of generations,
unwillingly to the trial
and mad delirium of every war
for the sake of rulers?

Whatever his desire or mishap,
his innocence or malignity,
he showed no pleasure in his death
below the Ruweisat Ridge.

Curaidhean

Chan fhaca mi Lannes aig Ratasbon
no MacGill-Fhinnein aig Allt Eire
no Gill-Iosa aig Cuil-Lodair,
ach chunnaic mi Sasunnach 'san Eiphit.

Fear beag truagh le gruaidhean pluiceach
is glùinean a' bleith a chéile,
aodann guireanach gun tlachd ann –
còmhdach an spioraid bu tréine.

Cha robh buaidh air " 'san tigh-òsda
'n àm nan dòrn a bhith 'gan dùnadh",
ach leóghann e ri uchd a' chatha,
anns na frasan guineach mùgach.

Thàinig uair-san leis na sligean,
leis na spealgan-iaruinn beàrnach,
anns an toit is anns an lasair,
ann an crith is maoim na h-àraich.

Thàinig fios dha 'san fhrois pheileir
e bhith gu spreigearra 'na dhiùlnach:
is b'e sin e fhad 's a mhair e,
ach cha b' fhada fhuair e dh' ùine.

Chum e ghunnachan ris na tancan,
a' bocail le sgriach shracaidh stàirnich
gus an d' fhuair e fhéin mu 'n stamaig
an deannal ud a chuir ri làr e,
bial sìos an gainmhich 's an greabhal,
gun diog o ghuth caol grànnda.

Cha do chuireadh crois no meadal
ri uchd no ainm no g' a chàirdean:
cha robh a bheag dhe fhòirne maireann,
's nan robh cha bhiodh am facal làidir;
's có dhiubh, ma sheasas ursann-chatha
leagar móran air a shàilleabh
gun dùil ri cliù, nach iarr am meadal
no cop 'sam bith á bial na h-àraich.

Chunnaic mi gaisgeach mór á Sasuinn,
fearachan bochd nach laigheadh sùil air;
cha b' Alasdair á Gleanna Garadh –
is thug e gal beag air mo shùilean.

Heroes

I did not see Lannes at Ratisbon
nor MacLennan at Auldearn
nor Gillies MacBain at Culloden,
but I saw an Englishman in Egypt.

A poor little chap with chubby cheeks
and knees grinding each other,
pimply unattractive face –
garment of the bravest spirit.

He was not a hit 'in the pub
in the time of the fists being closed',
but a lion against the breast of battle,
in the morose wounding showers.

His hour came with the shells,
with the notched iron splinters,
in the smoke and flame,
in the shaking and terror of the battlefield.

Word came to him in the bullet shower
that he should be a hero briskly,

and he was that while he lasted
but it wasn't much time he got.

He kept his guns to the tanks,
bucking with tearing crashing screech,
until he himself got, about the stomach,
that biff that put him to the ground,
mouth down in sand and gravel,
without a chirp from his ugly high-pitched voice.

No cross or medal was put to his
chest or to his name or to his family;
there were not many of his troop alive,
and if there were their word would not be strong.
And at any rate, if a battle post stands
many are knocked down because of him,
not expecting fame, not wanting a medal
or any froth from the mouth of the field of slaughter.

I saw a great warrior of England,
a poor manikin on whom no eye would rest;
no Alasdair of Glen Garry;
and he took a little weeping to my eyes.

Hallaig

'Tha tìm, am fiadh, an coille Hallaig'

Tha bùird is tàirnean air an uinneig
troimh 'm faca mi an Aird an Iar
's tha mo ghaol aig Allt Hallaig
'na craoibh bheithe, 's bha i riamh

eadar an t-Inbhir 's Poll a' Bhainne,
thall 's a bhos mu Bhaile-Chùirn:
tha i 'na beithe, 'na calltuinn,
'na caorunn dhìreach sheang ùir.

Ann an Screapadal mo chinnidh,
far robh Tarmad 's Eachunn Mór,

tha 'n nigheanan 's am mic 'nan coille
ag gabhail suas ri taobh an lóin.

Uaibhreach a nochd na coilich ghiuthais
ag gairm air mullach Cnoc an Rà,
dìreach an druim ris a' ghealaich –
chan iadsan coille mo ghràidh.

Fuirichidh mi ris a' bheithe
gus an tig i mach an Càrn,
gus am bi am bearradh uile
o Bheinn na Lice f' a sgàil.

Mura tig 's ann theàrnas mi a Hallaig
a dh'ionnsaigh sàbaid nam marbh,
far a bheil an sluagh a' tathaich,
gach aon ghinealach a dh' fhalbh.

Tha iad fhathast ann a Hallaig,
Clann Ghill-Eain's Clann MhicLeòid,
na bh' ann ri linn Mhic Ghille-Chaluim:
Chunnacas na mairbh beò.

Na fir 'nan laighe air an lianaig
aig ceann gach taighe a bh' ann,
na h-igheanan 'nan coille bheithe,
direach an druim, crom an ceann.

Eadar an Leac is na Feàrnaibh
tha 'n rathad mór fo chóinnich chiùin,
's na h-igheanan 'nam badan sàmhach
s' dol a Chlachan mar o thùs.

Agus a' tilleadh as a' Ghlachan,
á Suidhisnis 's á tir nam beò;
a chuile té òg uallach
gun bhristeadh cridhe an sgeòil.

O Allt na Feàrnaibh gus an fhaoilinn
tha soilleir an dìomhaireachd nam beann

chan eil ach coimhthional nan nighean
ag cumail na coiseachd gun cheann.

A' tilleadh a Hallaig anns an fheasgar,
anns a' chamhanaich bhalbh bheò'
a' lìonadh nan leathadan casa,
an gàireachdaich 'nam chluais 'na ceò,

's am bòidhche 'na sgleò air mo chridhe
mun tig an ciaradh air na caoil,
's nuair theàrnas grian air cùl Dhùn Cana
thig peileir dian á gunna Ghaoil;

's buailear am fiadh a tha 'na thuaineal
a' snòtach nan làraichean feòir;
thig reothadh air a shùil 'sa' choille:
chan fhaighear lorg air fhuil ri m' bheò.

Hallaig

'Time, the deer, is in the wood of Hallaig'

The window is nailed and boarded
through which I saw the West
and my love is at the Burn of Hallaig,
a birch tree, and she has always been

between Inver and Milk Hollow,
here and there about Baile-chuirn:
she is a birch, a hazel,
a straight, slender young rowan.

In Screapadal of my people
where Norman and Big Hector were,
their daughters and their sons are a wood
going up beside the stream.

Proud tonight the pine cocks
crowing on the top of Cnoc an Ra,

straight their backs in the moonlight –
they are not the wood I love.

I will wait for the birch wood
until it comes up by the cairn,
until the whole ridge from Beinn na Lice
will be under its shade.

If it does not, I will go down to Hallaig,
to the Sabbath of the dead,
where the people are frequenting,
every single generation gone.

They are still in Hallaig,
MacLeans and MacLeods,
all who were there in the time of Mac Gille Chaluim
the dead have been seen alive.

The men lying on the green
at the end of every house that was,
the girls a wood of birches,
straight their backs, bent their heads.

Between the Leac and Fearns
the road is under mild moss
and the girls in silent bands
go to Clachan as in the beginning,

and return from Clachan,
from Suisnish and the land of the living;
each one young and light-stepping,
without the heartbreak of the tale.

From the Burn of Fearns to the raised beach
that is clear in the mystery of the hills,
there is only the congregation of the girls
keeping up the endless walk,

coming back to Hallaig in the evening,
in the dumb living twilight,

filling the steep slopes,
their laughter a mist in my ears,

and their beauty a film on my heart
before the dimness comes on the kyles,
and when the sun goes down behind Dun Cana
a vehement bullet will come from the gun of Love;

and will strike the deer that goes dizzily,
sniffing at the grass-grown ruined homes;
his eye will freeze in the wood,
his blood will not be traced while I live.

SYDNEY TREMAYNE (1912–86)

Legend

When I grew strong to climb
Over the high stone wall,
First needling through the cushat wood,
Led by a cushat's call,
I reached the slope of a black hill
That wore a cloud for shawl.

I saw the sun prick through the cloud,
I heard the water run
Under the roots of the long grass
That hid the chuckling stone.
I cupped some water in my hands
And raised them to the sun.

The world and both my shining hands
Brightened my mouth to sing.
The little chipping birds as well
Went skipping on the wing
And donkey thistles kicked their heels,
Mocking the highland fling.

Never I guessed I was alone
Until the sun went in
And with a whistling wind there stooped
A dark bird from the rain.
The ground rushed by me as I swung
From talons cold as chain.

So long ago, so far from here
The rainbird let me fall
I have been trudging through the world
To find that high stone wall:
Restlessly turning round and round,
A beetle in a bowl.

Here is the wall, you wandering man;
Never this side you'll climb.
Look, there the dandelions grow
Unchanging since the game
When you were three feet low, and blew
Their white heads for the time.

And there's the black bull-shouldered hill
With all its trees cut down,
But through the roots of the long grass
You'll hear the water run.
Go catch the water in your hands,
And lift them to the sun.

A Burial

Of one who was much to me,
Nothing to anyone else,
I shall have least to say,
For silence is not false.
Once when I walked in iron
Through dead formalities,
I wished that I need not summon
The barbarous preaching voice.
So simple an act as death
Needs no pomp to excuse,
Nor any expense of breath
To magnify what is.
The sun shot the red apples,
Flies swung on summer air,
The world swam in green ripples
As a slow sea might stir.
There is no more to do
But to turn and go away,
Turn and finally go
From one who was much to me,
Nothing to anyone else.
Often it must be so
And always words be false.

Child, do you blame what is?
Child, do you blame what was?

Wanting News

Crystals of fog have frozen on the thorns,
Black trees stand coated in a web of white
As though a snow had fallen overnight
But missed the red field where the bracken burns.

A ridge of rime bevels all spiky things,
Barbed wire and holly, brambles, the one pine,
And wind out of the north makes a low whine,
A thin glissando played on icy strings.

Across the stoneless landscape of long hills
Midwinter daylight has no sun to shed:
All last year's nettle stalks are touched instead
Into unsparkling lightness, stiff as quills.

My house is hard to find, green lichen stains
The wooden box for letters. Far from roads
The wintry silence grips the rigid woods
Against mind's fidgetting, discordant strains,

Waiting for words to fall into the box
And ice to drop from hedges, wanting news.
Missing your voice, cold stillness builds unease:
The eye looks round for movement, like a fox.

DOUGLAS YOUNG (1913–73)

For a Wife in Jizzen

in childbed

Lassie, can ye say
    whaur ye ha been,
whaur ye ha come frae,
marvels   whatna ferlies seen?

Eftir the bluid and swyte,
struggling   the warsslin o yestreen,
exhausted ye ligg forfochten, whyte,
than   prouder nor onie Queen.

although Albeid ye hardly see me
    I read it i your een,
sae saft blue and dreamy,
remembering   mindan whaur ye've been.

only Anerly wives ken
the roots of joy and grief   the ruits o joy and tene,
        the march o daith and birth,
        the tryst o love and strife
midnight sunshine i the howedumbdeidsuinsheen,
    fire, air, water, yirth
mixing   mellan to mak new life,
laughing and weeping, passionate lauchan and greetan, feiman and serene.

hide from all men Dern frae aa men
    the ferlies ye ha seen.

Sainless

incurable [and, unblessed]

quiet I hae stuid an hour o the lown midsimmer nicht
twelve o'clock
magic light livelong til twal o the knock i the leelang glamarie-licht
looking all round by the cherry-tree at the midden, luikan aa round.
over by the farm buildings There's never a steer owreby at the ferm-toun,

smoke/in the sky/soft　the reek gangs straucht i the luift, that's lither and
　　　　　　　　　　　　　　　　　　　　　　　　　　　　　　　gray,
occasional patch of gold　wi an auntran gair o gowd i the North by the Tay.
　　　　　　　　　　The whyte muin owre Drumcarro, the Lomond
　　　　　　　　　　　　　　　　　　　　　　　　　　　　　shawan
lone curlew calling　purpie i the West, and a lane whaup caaan.

active　The ither birds are duin, but thon whaup's aye busy,
vibrating　wi the dirlan bubble-note that maks ye dizzy,
　　　　　　the daft cratur's in luve, tho it's late i the year,
unusual fuss　aa round Lucklaw he's fleean wi an unco steer.
a few bullocks　There's a wheen stots owre i the park by the
　　　　　　　　　　　　　　　　　　　　　　　　mansion-hous,
shambling/sleepy and gentle　skemblan about whiles, dozent and douce,
　　　　　　and a rabbit nibbles amang our raspberry canes
and the rest　for aa our wire and our traps and the lave o our
　　　　　　　　　　　　　　　　　　　　　　　　　　pains.

most/gaped　But the feck o the hour I hae gowpit owre the dyke,
over there　taen up wi a sicht thonder that I dinna like,
colt　a day-auld cowt liggan doun i the gress
　　　and the Clydesdale mear standan there motionless.
　　　The hale hour she has made never a steer,
　　　but stuid wi her heid forrit, rigid wi fear,
　　　it's a wonder onie beast can haud sae still.
suspects　The fermer douts the cowt has the joint-ill,
healed/ask if　that canna be sained. Ye'd speir gin his mither kens?
　　　Ay, beasts hae their tragedies as sair as men's.

The Shepherd's Dochter

Written on the occasion described in Fife in 1949

gaping　Lay her and lea her here i the gantan grund,
　　　　the blythest, bonniest lass o the countryside,
shrunk in a timber shift, covered　crined in a timber sark, hapt wi the pride
　　　o hothous flouers, the dearest that could be fund.

　　　Her faither and brithers stand, as suddentlie stunned
weight of sorrow; gentle　wi the wecht o dule; douce neebours side by side

wrench and fidget askance –
looking, reluctant to stay
performing and his passionate
words

    wriest and fidge, sclent-luikan, sweirt tae bide
while the Minister's duin and his threep gane wi the
                             wind.

scatter

[graveyard] earth

dance/solidly

labour

The murners skail, thankfu tae lea thon place
    whar the blythest, bonniest lass liggs i the mouls,
    Lent lilies lowp and cypresses stand stieve.
Time tae gae back tae the darg, machines and tools
    and beasts and seeds, the things men uis tae live,
and lea the puir lass there in her state o Grace.

RUTHVEN TODD (1914–1978)

Trout Flies

for J.K.M.

Ten years of age and intent upon a tea-brown burn
Across a moor in Lanarkshire, brass reel and
                                        greenheart
Rod, my first, I tried them out and came to learn
These magic names, from which I now can never
                                        part.

The insignificant ones were best, so ran the story
Of the old man who slowly taught me how to cast:
Dark Snipe, perhaps, Cow Dung, or favourite
                                Greenwell's Glory,
Would attract the sleek trout that moved so fast

To attack and suck the right and only fly.
Gaudy Partridge & Orange could be used, he said,
By those who fished on lochs, *his* fish would shy
From bright Butcher, Cardinal, or Teal & Red.

Now, on a clear day, a Wickham's Fancy might
Deceive a hungry trout, or even a Red Spinner,
But Coch-y-Bondu, or March Brown, in failing light,
Were more certain to bring home the dinner.

Watching the dull fly settle gently on the water
I would await the tug and make my strike,
While these names became a permanent mortar
Between my memories, names that I like

And tongue familiarly, Black Midge and August Dun,
Blue Upright, Cinnamon Sedge, Coachman and
                                Pheasant Tail,
Red Ant, Red Hackle, Furnace Palmer, and Yellow
                                Sally, in the sun,
Ghost, Green Midge, Half Stone and, sometimes,
                                Never Fail.

Of Moulds and Mushrooms

Agrippina, well aware of Claudius' greed
For Caesar's mushroom, knew also that it looked
Like death-cap or destroying angel, so a god
Made room on earth for Nero, whose joke,
'Food of the gods', allowed for deadly poison.

Some still, with unreasoning fear, disgust,
Kick or switch down the mushrooms by their path.
Leaving the amanita rudely shattered, gills
Like fallen feathers scattered, veil and volva
Broken, and all this symmetry destroyed.

The lack of chlorophyll suggests the parasite
Which guilty man so readily despises.
These are strange fruit of the thin mycellium,
That webs this world beneath the surface,
And which can persist in its invisibility

Breaking down discard of leaves and timber,
Which otherwise would overtop the wood
Extinguishing everything, so that the seed
May sprout to nourishment, and the cycle
Of death, decay and rebirth still go on.

And I, aesthetic and somewhat botanical,
Would note and praise the diversity
Of shapes, variety of colours of the fungi,
Ball, club, shelf, parasol, cup and horn,
And the suave velvet of the different moulds.

I would recall the fungi in their settings:
Fly-agaric, scarlet with wrinkled creamy warts,
In birch woods of Dumbartonshire, but lemon-
Yellow in New England, toxic they said to flies,
But intoxicant for the Kamchatka tribesman.

Near Selkirk once I found a monstrous puff ball,
Far bigger than my younger brother's head,
A gleaming baldpate beckoning me across the field
To find and greet poor Yorick's vegetable skull,
Solitary underneath the well-clipped hazel hedge.

Where anciently the monks had had their abbey,
Beside my Essex farmhouse, clustered blewits
Were palely violet below the dark-fruited sloes,
And the old gnarled oaks within the woods
Were sometimes richly shelved with beefsteaks;

And I, in a strictly rationed world,
Welcomed and ate these, and others that I found,
Spongy cèpe, chanterelle and honeycombed morel,
Grey oyster-mushroom and tall dignified parasol,
Which I again met later on a Chilmark lawn.

Brown-purple trumpets of the cornucopia
Stand clear against the brilliance of the moss
Under a clump of beech-trees at Gay Head,
While vast fairy-rings, some centuries of age,
Manacle the cropped grass of the South Downs.

The wooden ships of England knew dry-rot,
Pepys gathering toadstools bigger than his fists,
So that ten oaks were cut for each one used,
And the white-rimmed tawniness rioted again
Among the bombed buildings that I sometime knew.

Fungi have made their share of history:
St Anthony's fire, from ergot in the rye,
Swept savagely through medieval France,
Rotting potatoes drove the Irishman abroad,
And French grapes grown on North American stock.

A mouldering cantaloup from a Peoria supermarket
Supplanted the culture Fleming kept for years,
And others now sample soil, remove and scan
The moulds that, in their destructiveness,
Aid ailing man by driving out his enemies.

But I, walking in fields or through the woods,
Welcome the vermilion russula, the sulphur
Polyporus, or inky shaggy-cap upon a heap of dung,
Without questioning their usefulness to me.
The ecology of my appreciation seems to need

Clavaria's coral branches on a damp dark bank,
Odorous stink-horns prodding through the grass,
And petalled dry geasters studding a sandy road.
These many-fangled fruits make bright
My sundry places where no flowers can bloom.

G. S. FRASER (1914–80)

Lean Street

Here, where the baby paddles in the gutter,
　　Here in the slaty greyness and the gas,
Here where the women wear dark shawls and mutter
　　A hasty word as other women pass,

Telling the secret, telling, clucking and tutting,
　　Sighing, or saying that it served her right,
The bitch! – the words and weather both are cutting
　　In Causewayend, on this November night.

At pavement's end and in the slaty weather
　　I stare with glazing eyes at meagre stone,
Rain and the gas are sputtering together
　　A dreary tune! O leave my heart alone,

O leave my heart alone, I tell my sorrows,
　　For I will soothe you in a softer bed
And I will numb your grief with fat to-morrows
　　Who break your milk teeth on this stony bread!

They do not hear. Thought stings me like an adder,
　　A doorway's sagging plumb-line squints at me,
The fat sky gurgles like a swollen bladder
　　With the foul rain than rains on poverty.

Home Town Elegy

For Aberdeen in Spring

Glitter of mica at the windy corners,
Tar in the nostrils, under blue lamps budding
Like bubbles of glass the blue buds of a tree,
Night-shining shopfronts, or the sleek sun flooding
The broad abundant dying sprawl of the Dee:
For these and for their like my thoughts are mourners

That yet shall stand, though I come home no more,
Gas-works, white ballroom, and the red brick baths
And salmon nets along a mile of shore,
Or beyond the municipal golf-course, the moorland
                                                                paths
And the country lying quiet and full of farms.
This is the shape of a land that outlasts a strategy
And is not to be taken with rhetoric or arms.
Or my own room, with a dozen books on the bed
(Too late, still musing what I mused, I lie
And read too lovingly what I have read),
Brantôme, Spinoza, Yeats, the bawdy and wise,
Continuing their interminable debate,
With no conclusion, they conclude too late,
When their wisdom has fallen like a grey pall on my
                                                                eyes.

Syne we maun part, their sall be nane remeid –
Unless my country is my pride, indeed,
Or I can make my town that homely fame
That Byron has, from boys in Carden Place,
Struggling home with books to midday dinner,
For whom he is not the romantic sinner,
The careless writer, the tormented face,
The hectoring bully or the noble fool,
But, just like Gordon or like Keith, a name:
A tall, proud statue at the Grammar School.

SYDNEY GOODSIR SMITH (1915–75)

from Armageddon in Albyn

I EL ALAMEIN

O, dearlie they deed
St Valery's vengers
kites   – The gleds dine weel
In the Libyan desert –
Dearlie they deed,
Aa the winds furthtell it.

Around El Alamein
Ranks o carrion
Faur frae their hame
lie stark   Ligg sterk in the sun,
In the rutted sand
Whaur the tanks has run.

burning dawn   Yon burnan daw
dead of night   Than dumb-deid blacker,
Whiter than snaw
bones   Will the bricht banes glitter;
Scotland   That this was for Alba
must we make sure   Maun we mak siccar!

It wasna for thraldom
Ye ligg there deid,
if   Gin we should fail ye
The rocks wad bleed!
– O, the gleds foregaither
Roun Alba's deid.

II THE MITHER'S LAMENT

Whit care I for the leagues o sand,
The prisoners an the gear theyve won?

Ma darlin liggs amang the dunes
Wi mony a mither's son.

Doutless he deed for Scotland's life;
do not lie Doutless the statesmen dinna lee;
lamented But och tis sair begrutten pride
sour An wersh the wine o victorie!

VII THE WAR IN FIFE

storm-growling/cold Gurlie an gray the snell Fife shore,
mist Frae the peat-green sea the cauld haar drives,
The weet wind sings on the wire, and war
Looks faur frae the land o Fife.

in every house tarnished In ilka house tashed by the faem
empty Tuim beds tell o anither life,
The windae's blind wi the scuddan rain,
While war taks toll o the land o Fife.

By the 'Crusoe', backs tae the rain-straikit waa,
Auld jersied men staun hauf the day,
The fishing killt by trawlers, nou
They drink the rents the tourists pay.

But anither race has come, the pits
a headstrong folk no trick beguiles Breed a raucle fowk nae geck beguiles,
earth Deep in the yerth nae haar affects
The second war in the land o Fife.

Thae are the banded future; here
waste away Dwine the auld defeated race;
Unseen throu the cauld an seepan haar
Destroyers slip at a snail's pace.

across A foghorn booms athort the Forth,
troubled Drumlie lament for a sundered life,
The root an flouer that aince were kith
Made strangers in the land o Fife.

to the shore
The haar is chill, near in til the shore,
gulls/over the yellow firth
Nae maws screich owre the yalla freith,
swinging
The wireless frae a sweyan door
Ennobles horror, fire, an daith.

The foreign war tuims mony a bed
But yet seems faur awa –
Twa hunner years o Union's bled
than any war
The veins mair white nor ony war.

old man and lad
A third war cracks; lyart an loon
plunder
Thegither curse the lang stouthrife,
gloom
Mirk ower Scotland hings its rule
bitter cold
Like the snell haar hings ower Fife.

The Grace of God and the Meth-Drinker

go
There ye gang, ye daft
raving half-wit
And doitit dotterel, ye saft
outcast* vagabond soul
Crazed outland skalrag saul
big-holed* clothes
In your bits and ends o winnockie duds
fouled and musty rags
Your fyled and fozie-fousome clouts
triple-plastered
As fou's a fish, crackt and craftie-drunk
Wi bleerit reid-rimmed
whingeing mouth
Ee and slaveran crozie mou
staggering over the street
Dwaiblan owre the causie like a ship
Storm-toss't i' the Bay of Biscay O
At-sea indeed and hauf-seas-owre
uvula
Up-til-the-thrapple's-pap
Or up-til-the-crosstrees-sunk –
  Wha kens? Wha racks?
cares
hither-and-thither tottering in a stupefied daydream
Hidderie-hetterie stouteran in a dozie dwaum
fiery red-biddy*
O' ramsh reid-biddie – Christ!
  The stink
O' jake ahint him, a mephitic
reek/unusually exotic
Rouk o miserie, like some unco exotic
put up with
Perfume o the Orient no juist sae easilie tholit

* *outland* lit., landless; *winnockie* i.e., 'windowed'; *reid-biddie* red wine spliced with methylated spirits or other alcohol, prob. Irish – 'biddie' = diminutive of 'Bridget'

By the bleak barbarians o the Wast

penetrating the nostrils   But subtil, acrid, jaggan the nebstrous

supremely horrible stench   Wi 'n owrehailan ugsome guff, maist delicat,

the piss of a ruffian tomcat   Like in scent til the streel o a randie gib . . .

         O-hone-a-ree!

red   His toothless gums, his lips, bricht cramasie

very-bright   A schere-bricht slash o bluid

a beauty [?] like the shining fire   A schene like the leaman gleid o rubies

Throu the gray-white stibble

unshaven cheeks   O' his blank unrazit chafts, a hangman's

Heid, droolie wi gob, the bricht een

unseeing, cautious, indifferent and sly   Sichtless, cannie, blythe, and slee –

unknowing   *Unkennan.*

Ay,

poor outcast   Puir gangrel!

         There

incomprehensible   – But for the undeemous glorie and grace

O' a mercifu omnipotent majestic God

Superne eterne and sceptred in the firmament

where to/of the faithful   Whartil the praises o the leal rise

Like incense aye about Your throne,

everlasting   Ayebydan, thochtless, and eternallie hauf-drunk

Wi nectar, Athole-brose,* ambrosia – nae jake for

     You –

         God there! –

the aforementioned   But for the 'bunesaid unsocht grace, unprayed-for,

Undeserved

        Gangs,

           Unregenerate,

             Me.

Time Be Brief

Time be brief
My fair luve far –
Time be brief

* *Athole-brose* whisky, with honey and/or oatmeal

partings's hurtful

Our twynin's sair
This wearie week
I wad be whar
Titania sleeps
Amang her hair.

Time be brief
My witch is far
these   Lang thir nichts
And langer mair
The wearie days
everywhere   Her face aawhar
Her voice that speaks
In aa I hear.

Time be brief
The hert is sair
quick   Days be rathe
Nichts, draw her near –
swift   Time time be swith
My constant prayer
This wearie week
lacking   Wantan my dear.

Time be brief
My true-luve far
Rin on auld week
And bring me whar
She bydes for me
And I for her –
Time be brief
My true-luve far.

Omens

The lane hills and the mune
at night   (Nichtertale in Yarrow
Under the Gray Mear's Tail)*

* *Gray Mear's Tail* a waterfall near Moffat, NE Dumfriesshire

lament   — By me the white coronach
roaring waterfall   O' rairan linn
mountain torrent   Skriddan and cataract
         White i the wan
         Licht o the sickle mune.

         Throu the blae gulph
and gloom   O' mune and mirk
across   Athort my vision suddenlie
lone   A lane white bird
         — The screich o the linn
         At my back, and abune
         The far and numenous mune —
         Silent, the bird, and was gane.

         O, my hert, and I kent nocht
         The gods' intent
         Nor kent their omens'
         Truth or this
if I had   — But what gin I had then
knowledge   The kennin I hae nou?
         — Maybe's as weill our een
         See little, and far less
         Can understand.

all   ## Aa My Life

lover   Aa my life, my leman said,
livelong   Aa my life leelang
         Thou sall be my luve alane
          Aa my life leelang.

         And sae sall be, my dearest luve,
          I'll nane but thee belang,
         Till daith sall see us beddit doun
          As in life leelang.

         Aa my life, my leman said,
          This be our ainlie sang —

We'se gie auld Dis a kyndlie kiss
　　When time it is to gang.

love

But here we've aa our life to loe
　　Aa our life leelang
　— We'se sleep hereafter, lou me nou
　　And aa my life leelang
　　　　　　　　　　　Leelang —
　Aa my life leelang.

from Under the Eildon Tree

V SLUGABED

here I lie　　Here I ligg, Sydney Slugabed Godless Smith,
and poet　　The Smith, the Faber, ποιητής and Makar,
And Oblomov has nocht to learn me,
Auld Oblomov has nocht on me
alone　　Liggan my lane in bed at nune
gaping/mist　　Gantan at gray December haar,
A cauld, scummie, hauf-drunk cup o' tea
　　At my bed-side,
smoking　　　　Luntan Virginian fags
　— The New World thus I haud in fief
And levie kyndlie tribute. Black men slave
Aneath a distant sun to mak for me
Cheroots at hauf-a-croun the box.
ash/pillow　　Wi ase on the sheets, ase on the cod,
And crumbs of toast under my bum,
elegy　　Scrievan the last great coronach
O' the westren flickeran bourgeois world.
　　Eheu fugaces!
　　　　　　　　Lacrimæ rerum!
Nil nisi et cætera ex cathedra
　　　　　　　Requiescat up your jumper.

O, michtie Stalin in the Aist!
Could ye but see me nou,

The type, endpynt and final blume

servitude O' decadent capitalistical thirldom
   – It took five hunder year to produce me –
Och, could ye but see me nou
What a sermon could ye gie
   Further frae the Hailie Kremlin
bustling Bummlan and thunderan owre the Steppes,
humming Athort the mountains o' Europe humman
Till Swack! at my front door, the great *Schloss*
                                    Schmidt
That's *Numéro Cinquante* (ПЯТЬДЕСЯТ* ye ken)
former In the umquhile pairk o' Craigmillar House
complexion Whar Mariè Stewart o the snawie blee
Aince plantit ane o' a thousand treen.
   Losh, what a sermon yon wad be!
For Knox has nocht on Uncle Joe
And Oblomov has nocht on Smith
   And sae we come by a route maist devious
   Til the far-famed Aist-West Synthesis!
   Beluved by Hugh that's beluved by me
love/whisky And the baith o' us loe the barley-bree –
But wha can afford to drink the stuff?
   Certies no auld Oblomov!
   – And yet he does! Whiles!
not as much But no as muckle as Uncle Joe – I've smaa dout!
НА ЗГОРОВЬЕ* then, auld Muscovite!

Thus are the michtie faaen,
Thus the end o' a michtie line,
Dunbar til Smith the Slugabed
whose love burns no less bright Whas luve burns brichter nor them aa
than anyone's
fall from respectability And whas dounfaain is nae less,
   Deid for a ducat deid
By the crueltie o' his ain maistress.

piat' desiat fifty; *Na zdorovye* good health

DEORSA CAIMBEUL HAY/GEORGE CAMPBELL HAY (1915–84)

Bisearta

Chi mi rè geàrd na h-oidhche
dreòs air chrith 'na fhroidhneas thall air fàire,
a' clapail le a sgiathaibh,
a' sgapadh 's a' ciaradh rionnagan na h-àird' ud.

Shaoileadh tu gun cluinnte,
ge cian, o 'bhuillsgein ochanaich no caoineadh,
ràn corruich no gàir fuatha,
comhart chon cuthaich uaidh no ulfhairt fhaolchon,
gun ruigeadh drannd an fhòirneirt
o'n fhùirneis òmair iomall fhéin an t-saoghail;
ach sud a' dol an leud e
ri oir an speur an tosdachd olc is aognaidh.

C' ainm nochd a th' orra,
na sràidean bochda anns an sgeith gach uinneag
a lasraichean 's a deatach,
a sradagan is sgreadail a luchd thuinidh,
is taigh air thaigh 'ga reubadh
am broinn a chéile am brùchdadh toit a' tuiteam?
Is có an nochd tha 'g atach
am Bàs a theachd gu grad 'nan cainntibh uile,
no a' spàirn measg chlach is shailthean
air bhàinidh a' gairm air cobhair, is nach cluinnear?
Cò an nochd a phàidheas
sean chìs àbhaisteach na fala cumant?

Uair dearg mar lod na h-àraich,
uair bàn mar ghile thràighte an eagail éitigh,
a' dìreadh 's uair a' teàrnadh,
a' sìneadh le sitheadh àrd 's a' call a mheudachd,
a' fannachadh car aitil
's ag at mar anail dhiabhail air dhéinead,
an t-Olc 'na chridhe 's 'na chuisle,
chì mi 'na bhuillean a' sìoladh 's a' leum e.

Tha 'n dreòs 'na oillt air fàire,
'na fhàinne ròis is òir am bun nan speuran,
a' breugnachadh 's ag àicheadh
le shoillse sèimhe àrsaidh àrd nan reultan.

Bizerta

I see during the night guard
a blaze flickering, fringing the skyline over yonder,
beating with its wings
and scattering and dimming the stars of that airt.

You would think that there would be heard
from its midst, though far away, wailing and
                                        lamentation,
the roar of rage and the yell of hate,
the barking of the dogs from it or the howling of
                                        wolves,
that the snarl of violence would reach
from yon amber furnace the very edge of the world;
but yonder it spreads
along the rim of the sky in evil ghastly silence.

What is their name tonight,
the poor streets where every window spews
its flame and smoke,
its sparks and the screaming of its inmates,
while house upon house is rent
and collapses in a gust of smoke?
And who tonight are beseeching
Death to come quickly in all their tongues,
or are struggling among stones and beams,
crying in frenzy for help, and are not heard?
Who tonight is paying
the old accustomed tax of common blood?

Now red like a battlefield puddle,
now pale like the drained whiteness of foul fear,
climbing and sinking,

reaching and darting up and shrinking in size,
growing faint for a moment
and swelling like the breath of a devil in intensity,
I see Evil as a pulse
and a heart declining and leaping in throbs.
The blaze, a horror on the skyline,
a ring of rose and gold at the foot of the sky,
belies and denies
with its light the ancient high tranquillity of the stars.

Atman

Rinn thu goid 'nad éiginn,
dh'fheuch thu breug gu faotainn as;
dhìt iad, chàin is chuip iad thu,
is chuir iad thu fo ghlais.

Bha 'm beul onorach a dhìt thu
pladach, bìdeach 'sa ghnùis ghlais;
bha Ceartas sreamshùileach o sgrùdadh
a leabhar cunntais 's iad sìor phailt.

Ach am beul a dhearbhadh breugach,
bha e modhail, éibhinn, binn;
fhuair mi eirmseachd is sgeòil uaith
's gun e ro eòlach air tràth bìdh.

Thogte do shùil o'n obair
á cruth an t-saoghail a dheoghal tlachd;
mhol thu Debel Iussuf dhomh,
a cumadh is a dath.

Is aithne dhomh thu, Atmain,
bean do thaighe 's do chóignear òg,
do bhaidnein ghobhar is t' asail,
do ghoirtein seagail is do bhó.

Is aithne dhomh thu, Atmain:
is fear thu 's tha thu beò,

dà nì nach eil am breitheamh,
's a chaill e 'chothrom gu bhith fòs.

Chan ainmig t' fhallus 'na do shùilean;
is eòl duit sùgradh agus fearg;
bhlais is bhlais thu'n difir
eadar milis agus searbh.

Dh'fheuch thu gràin is bròn is gàire;
dh'fheuch thu ànradh agus grian;
dh'fhairich thu a' bheatha
is cha do mheath thu roimpe riamh.

Na'n robh thu beairteach, is do chaolan
garbh le caoile t' airein sgìth,
cha bhiodh tu 'chuideachd air na mìolan
an dubh phrìosan Mhondovì.

Nuair gheibh breitheamh còir na cùirte
làn a shùla de mo dhruim,
thig mi a thaobh gu d'fhàilteachadh
trasd an t-sràid ma chì mi thu.

Sidna Aissa, chaidh a cheusadh
mar ri mèirlich air bàrr sléibh,
is b'e 'n toibheum, Atmain, àicheadh
gur bràthair dhomh thu fhéin.

Atman

You thieved in your need,
and you tried a lie to get off;
they condemned you, reviled you and whipped you,
and they put you under lock and key.

The honourable mouth that condemned you
was blubberish and tiny in the grey face;
and Justice was blear-eyed from scrutinising
its account-books, that ever showed abundance.

But the mouth which was found lying
was mannerly, cheerful and melodious;
I got sharp repartee and tales from it,
though it was not too well acquainted with a meal.

Your eye would be raised from your work
to draw pleasure from the shape of the world;
you praised Jebel Yussuf to me,
its form and its colour.

I know you, Atman,
the woman of your house and your five youngsters,
your little clump of goats and your ass,
your plot of rye and your cow.

I know you, Atman:
you are a man, and you are alive;
two things the judge is not,
and that he has lost his chance of being ever.

Your sweat is not seldom in your eyes;
you know what sporting and anger are;
you have tasted and tasted the difference
between sweet and bitter.

You have tried hatred and grief and laughter;
you have tried tempest and sun;
you have experienced life
and never shrunk before it.

Had you been wealthy, and your gut
thick with the leanness of your tired ploughmen,
you would not be keeping company with the lice
in the black prison of Mondovi.

When the decent judge of the court
gets the fill of his eye of my back,
I will come aside to welcome you
across the street if I see you.

Our Lord Jesus was crucified
along with thieves on the top of a hill,
and it would be blasphemy, Atman, to deny
that you are a brother of mine.

To a Loch Fyne Fisherman

yonder

Calum thonder, long's the night to your thinking,
night long till dawn and the sun set at the tiller,
age and the cares of four and a boat to keep you
high in the stern, alone for the winds to weary.

A pillar set in the shifting moss, a beacon
fixed on the wandering seas and changing waters,
bright on the midnight waves and the hidden terrors;
the ancient yew of the glen, not heeding the ages.

Set among men that waver like leaves on the
                                    branches,
still among minds that flicker like light on the water.
Those are the shadows of clouds, the speckled and
                                    fleeting;
you are the hill that stands through shadow and
                                    sunlight.

Little you heed, or care to change with changes,
to go like a broken branch in the grip of a torrent;
you are your judge and master, your sentence
                                    unshaken,
a man with a boat of his own and a mind to guide
                                    her.

W. S. GRAHAM (1918–86)

The Children of Greenock

Local I'll bright my tale on, how
She rose up white on a Greenock day
Like the one first-of-all morning
On earth, and heard children singing.

She in a listening shape stood still
In a high tenement at Spring's sill
Over the street and chalked lawland
hopscotched*   Peevered and lined and fancymanned

On a pavement shouting games and faces.
She saw them children of all cries
With everyone's name against them bled
In already the helpless world's bed.

Already above the early town
The smoky government was blown
To cover April. The local orient's
Donkeymen, winches and steel giants

Wound on the sugar docks. Clydeside,
Webbed in its foundries and loud blood,
Binds up the children's cries alive.
Her own red door kept its young native.

Her own window by several sights
Wept and became the shouting streets.
And her window by several sights
Adored the even louder seedbeats.

She leaned at the bright mantle brass
Fairly a mirror of surrounding sorrows,

*peever the stone used in the game

The sown outcome of always war
Against the wordperfect, public tear.

Brighter drifted upon her the sweet sun
High already over all the children
So chained and happy in Cartsburn Street
Barefoot on authority's alphabet.

Her window watched the woven care
Hang webbed within the branched and heavy
Body. It watched the blind unborn
Copy book after book of sudden

Elements within the morning of her
Own man-locked womb. It saw the neighbour
Fear them housed in her walls of blood.
It saw two towns, but a common brood.

Her window watched the shipyards sail
Their men away. The sparrow sill
Bent grey over the struck town clocks
Striking two towns, and fed its flocks.

from Seven Letters

LETTER II

Burned in this element
To the bare bone, I am
Trusted on the language.
I am to walk to you
Through the night and through
Each word you make between
Each word I burn bright in
On this wide reach. And you,
Within what arms you lie,
Hear my burning ways
Across these darknesses

That move and merge like foam.
Lie in the world's room,
My dear, and contribute
Here where all dialogues write.

Younger in the towered
Tenement of night he heard
The shipyards with nightshifts
Of lathes turning their shafts.
His voice was a humble ear
Hardly turned to her.
Then in a welding flash
He found his poetry arm
And turned the coat of his trade.
From where I am I hear
Clearly his heart beat over
Clydeside's far hammers
And the nightshipping firth.
What's he to me? Only
Myself I died from into
These present words that move.
In that high tenement
I got a great grave.

Tonight in sadly need
Of you I move inhuman
Across this space of dread
And silence in my mind.
I walk the dead water
Burning language towards
You where you lie in the dark
Ascension of all words.
Yet where? Where do you lie
Lost to my cry and hidden
Away from the world's downfall?
O offer some way tonight
To make your love take place
In every word. Reply.
Time's branches burn to hear.
Take heed. Reply. Here

I am driven burning on
This loneliest element. Break
Break me out of this night,
This silence where you are not,
Nor any within earshot.
Break break me from this high
Helmet of idiocy.

Water water wallflower
Growing up so high
We are all children
We all must die.
Except Willie Graham
The fairest of them all.
He can dance and he can sing
And he can turn his face to the wall.
Fie, fie, fie for shame
Turn your face to the wall again.

Yes laugh then cloudily laugh
Though he sat there as deaf
And worn to a stop
As the word had given him up.
Stay still. That was the sounding
Sea he moved on burning
His still unending cry.
That night hammered and waved
Its starry shipyard arms,
And it came to inherit
His death where these words merge.
This is his night writ large.
In Greenock the bright breath
Of night's array shone forth
On the nightshifting town.
Thus younger burning in
The best of his puny gear
He early set out
To write him to his death
And to that great breath
Taking of the sea,

The graith of Poetry.
My musing love lie down
Within his arms. He dies
Word by each word into

Myself now at this last
Word I die in. This last.

LETTER VI

A day the wind was hardly
Shaking the youngest frond
Of April I went on
The high moor we know.
I put my childhood out
Into a cocked hat
And you moving the myrtle
Walked slowly over.
A sweet clearness became.
The Clyde sleeved in its firth
Reached and dazzled me.
I moved and caught the sweet
Courtesy of your mouth.
My breath to your breath.
And as you lay fondly
In the crushed smell of the moor
The courageous and just sun
Opened its door.
And there we lay halfway
Your body and my body
On the high moor. Without
A word then we went
Our ways. I heard the moor
Curling its cries far
Across the still loch.

The great verbs of the sea
Come down on us in a roar.
What shall I answer for?

Baldy Bane

Shrill the fife, kettle the drum,
   My Queens my Sluts my Beauties
Show me your rich attention
   Among the shower of empties.
And quiet be as it was once
   It fell on a night late
The muse has felled·me in this bed
   That in the wall is set.
Lie over to me from the wall or else
   Get up and clean the grate.

On such a night as this behind
   McKellar's Tanworks' wall
It seems I put my hand in hers
   As we played at the ball.
So began a folly that
   I hope will linger late,
Though I am of the kitchen bed
   And of the flannel sheet.
Lie over to me from the wall or else
   Get up and clean the grate.

Now pay her no attention now,
   Nor that we keep our bed.
hooded crow   It is yon hoodie on the gate
   Would speak me to the dead.
And though I am embedded here
   The creature to forget
I ask you one and all to come.
   Let us communicate.
Lie over to me from the wall or else
   Get up and clean the grate.

Make yourself at home here.
   My words you move within.
I made them all by hand for you
   To use as your own.

Yet I'll not have it said that they
   Leave my intention out,
Else I, an old man, I will up
   And at that yella-yite.*
Lie over to me from the wall or else
   Get up and clean the grate.

You're free to jig your fiddle or let
   It dally on the bow.
Who's he that bums his chat there,
   Drunk as a wheelbarrow?
Hey, you who visit an old man
   That a young wife has got,
Mind your brain on the beam there
   And watch the lentil pot.
Lie over to me from the wall or else
   Get up and clean the grate.

Now pay her no attention.
   I am the big bowbender.
These words shall lie the way I want
   Or she'll blacklead the fender.

[i.e. shilp] pale, sickly girl

No shallop she, her length and depth
   Is Clyde and clinker built.
When I have that one shafted I
   Allow my best to out.
Lie over to me from the wall or else
   Get up and clean the grate.

Full as a whelk, full as a whelk
   And sad when all is done.
The children cry me Baldy Bane
   And the great catches are gone.
But do you know my mother's tune,
   For it is very sweet?
I split my thumb upon the barb
   The last time I heard it.

---

* *yella-yite* yellow-hammer, but here probably rhyming slang meaning excrement personified, a worthless person

Lie over to me from the wall or else
  Get up and clean the grate.

Squeeze the box upon the tune
  They call Kate Dalrymple O.
Cock your ears upon it and
  To cock your legs is simple O.
Full as a whelk, full as a whelk
  And all my hooks to bait.
Is that the nightshift knocking off?
  I hear men in the street.
Lie over to me from the wall or else
  Get up and clean the grate.

twirl   Move to me as you birl, Meg.
  Your mother was a great whore.
I have not seen such pas de bas
  Since up in Kirriemuir.
I waded in your shallows once,
  Now drink up to that.
It makes the blood go up and down
latch   And lifts the sneck a bit.
Lie over to me from the wall or else
  Get up and clean the grate.

Through the word and through the word,
  And all is sad and done,
Who are you that these words
  Make this fall upon?
Fair's fair, upon my word,
  And that you shall admit,
Or I will blow your face in glass
  And then I'll shatter it.
Lie over to me from the wall or else
  Get up and clean the grate.

If there's a joke between us
  Let it lie where it fell.
The exact word escapes me
  And that's just as well.

I always have the tune by ear.
  You are an afterthought.
But when the joke and the grief strike
  Your heart beats on the note.
Lie over to me from the wall or else
  Get up and clean the grate.

Full as a whelk, full as a whelk
  My brain is blanketstitched.
It is the drink has floored us
  And Meg lies unlatched.
Lie over to me, my own muse.
  The bed is our estate.
Here's a drink to caulk your seams
  Against the birling spate.
Lie over to me from the wall or else
  Get up and clean the grate.

Now pay her no attention, you.
  Your gears do not engage.
By and large it's meet you should
  Keep to your gelded cage.
My ooze, my merry-making muse,
  You're nothing to look at.
But prow is proud and rudder rude
  Is the long and short of that.
Lie over to me from the wall or else
  Get up and clean the grate.

Think of a word and double it.
  Admit my metaphor.
But leave the muscle in the verse,
  It is the Skerry Vore.
Can you wash a sailor's shirt
  And can you wash it white?
O can you wash a sailor's shirt
  The whitest in the fleet?
Lie over to me from the wall or else
  Get up and clean the grate.

Full as a whelk and ending,
  Surprise me to my lot.
The glint of the great catches
  Shall not again be caught.
But the window is catching
  The slow mend of light.
Who crossed these words before me
  Crossed my meaning out.
Lie over to me from the wall or else
  Get up and clean the grate.

Cry me Baldy Bane but cry
  The hoodie off the gate,
And before you turn away
  Turn to her last estate.
She lies to fell me on the field
  Of silence I wrote.
By whose endeavour do we fare?
  By the word in her throat.
Lie over to me from the wall or else
  Get up and clean the grate.

She lies to fell me on the field
  That is between us here.
I have but to lift the sneck
  With a few words more.
Take kindly to Baldy Bane, then
  And go your ways about.
Tell it in the Causewayside
  And in Cartsburn Street,
Lie over to me from the wall or else
  Get up and clean the grate.

Love me near, love me far.
  Lie over from the wall.
You have had the best of me
  Since we played at the ball.
I cross the Fingal of my stride
  With you at beauty heat.
And I burn my words behind me.

Silence is shouted out.
Lie over to me from the wall or else
Get up and clean the grate.

Malcolm Mooney's Land

1

Today, Tuesday, I decided to move on
Although the wind was veering. Better to move
Than have them at my heels, poor friends
I buried earlier under the printed snow.
From wherever it is I urge these words
To find their subtle vents, the northern dazzle
Of silence cranes to watch. Footprint on foot
Print, word on word and each on a fool's errand.
Malcolm Mooney's Land. Elizabeth
Was in my thoughts all morning and the boy.
Wherever I speak from or in what particular
Voice, this is always a record of me in you.
I can record at least out there to the west
The grinding bergs and, listen, further off
Where we are going, the glacier calves
Making its sudden momentary thunder.
This is as good a night, a place as any.

2

From the rimed bag of sleep, Wednesday,
My words crackle in the early air.
Thistles of ice about my chin,
My dreams, my breath a ruff of crystals.
The new ice falls from canvas walls.
O benign creature with the small ear-hole,
Submerger under silence, lead
Me where the unblubbered monster goes
Listening and makes his play.
Make my impediment mean no ill
And be itself a way.

A fox was here last night (Maybe Nansen's,
Reading my instruments.) the prints
All round the tent and not a sound.
Not that I'd have him call my name.
Anyhow how should he know? Enough
Voices are with me here and more
The further I go. Yesterday
I heard the telephone ringing deep
Down in a blue crevasse.
I did not answer it and could
Hardly bear to pass.

Landlice, always my good bedfellows,
Ride with me in my sweaty seams.
Come bonny friendly beasts, brother
To the grammarsow and the word-louse,
Bite me your presence, keep me awake
In the cold with work to do, to remember
To put down something to take back.
I have reached the edge of earshot here
And by the laws of distance
My words go through the smoking air
Changing their tune on silence.

3

My friend who loves owls
Has been with me all day
Walking at my ear
And speaking of old summers
When to speak was easy.
His eyes are almost gone
Which made him hear well.
Under our feet the great
Glacier drove its keel.
What is to read there
Scored out in the dark?
Later the north-west distance
Thickened towards us.
The blizzard grew and proved

Too filled with other voices
High and desperate
For me to hear him more.
I turned to see him go
Becoming shapeless into
The shrill swerving snow.

4

Today, Friday, holds the white
Paper up too close to see
Me here in a white-out in this tent of a place
And why is it there has to be
Some place to find, however momentarily
To speak from, some distance to listen to?

Out at the far-off edge I hear
Colliding voices, drifted, yes
To find me through the slowly opening leads.
Tomorrow I'll try the rafted ice.
Have I not been trying to use the obstacle
Of language well? It freezes round us all.

5

Why did you choose this place
For us to meet? Sit
With me between this word
And this, my furry queen.
Yet not mistake this
For the real thing. Here
In Malcolm Mooney's Land
I have heard many
Approachers in the distance
Shouting. Early hunters
Skittering across the ice
Full of enthusiasm
And making fly and,
Within the ear, the yelling
Spear steepening to

The real prey, the right
Prey of the moment.
The honking choir in fear
Leave the tilting floe
And enter the sliding water.
Above the bergs the foolish
Voices are lighting lamps
And all their sounds make
This diary of a place
Writing us both in.

Come and sit. Or is
It right to stay here
While, outside the tent
The bearded blinded go
Calming their children
Into the ovens of frost?
And what's the news? What
Brought you here through
The spring leads opening?

Elizabeth, you and the boy
Have been with me often
Especially on those last
Stages. Tell him a story.
Tell him I came across
An old sulphur bear
Sawing his log of sleep
Loud beneath the snow.
He puffed the powdered light
Up on to this page
And here his reek fell
In splinters among
These words. He snored well.
Elizabeth, my furry
Pelted queen of Malcolm
Mooney's Land, I made
You here beside me
For a moment out
Of the correct fatigue.

I have made myself alone now.
Outside the tent endless
Drifting hummock crests.
Words drifting on words.
The real unabstract snow.

The Lying Dear

At entrance cried out but not
For me (Should I have needed it?)
Her bitching eyes under
My pressing down shoulder
Looked up to meet the face
In cracks on the flaking ceiling
Descending. The map of damp
Behind me, up, formed
Itself to catch the look
Under the closed (now)
Lids of my lying dear.

Under my pinning arm
I suddenly saw between
The acting flutters, a look
Catch on some image not me.

With a hand across her eyes
I changed my weight of all
Knowledge of her before.
And like a belly sledge
I steered us on the run
Mounting the curves to almost
The high verge. Her breath
Flew out like smoke. Her beauty
Twisted into another
Beauty and we went down
Into the little village
Of a new language.

The Night City

Unmet at Euston in a dream
Of London under Turner's steam
Misting the iron gantries, I
Found myself running away
From Scotland into the golden city.

I ran down Gray's Inn Road and ran
Till I was under a black bridge.
This was me at nineteen
Late at night arriving between
The buildings of the City of London.

And then I (O I have fallen down)
Fell in my dream beside the Bank
Of England's wall to bed, me
With my money belt of Northern ice.
I found Eliot and he said yes

And sprang into a Holmes cab.
Boswell passed me in the fog
Going to visit Whistler who
Was with John Donne who had just seen
Paul Potts shouting on Soho Green.

Midnight. I hear the moon
Light chiming on St Paul's.

The City is empty. Night
Watchmen are drinking their tea.

The Fire had burnt out.
The Plague's pits had closed
And gone into literature.

Between the big buildings
I sat like a flea crouched
In the stopped works of a watch.

Johann Joachim Quantz's Five Lessons

THE FIRST LESSON

So that each person may quickly find that
Which particularly concerns him, certain metaphors
Convenient to us within the compass of this
Lesson are to be allowed. It is best I sit
Here where I am to speak on the other side
Of language. You, of course, in your own time
And incident (I speak in the small hours.)
Will listen from your side. I am very pleased
We have sought us out. No doubt you have read
My Flute Book. Come. The Guild clock's iron men
Are striking out their few deserted hours
And here from my high window Brueghel's winter
Locks the canal below. I blow my fingers.

THE SECOND LESSON

Good morning, Karl. Sit down. I have been thinking
About your progress and my progress as one
Who teaches you, a young man with talent
And the rarer gift of application. I think
You must now be becoming a musician
Of a certain calibre. It is right maybe
That in our lessons now I should expect
Slight and very polite impatiences
To show in you. Karl, I think it is true,
You are now nearly able to play the flute.

Now we must try higher, aware of the terrible
Shapes of silence sitting outside your ear
Anxious to define you and really love you.
Remember silence is curious about its opposite
Element which you shall learn to represent.

Enough of that. Now stand in the correct position
So that the wood of the floor will come up through
                                                    you.
Stand, but not too stiff. Keep your elbows down.
Now take a simple breath and make me a shape
Of clear unchained started and finished tones.
Karl, as well as you are able, stop
Your fingers into the breathing apertures
And speak and make the cylinder delight us.

THE THIRD LESSON

Karl, you are late. The traverse flute is not
A study to take lightly. I am cold waiting.
Put one piece of coal in the stove. This lesson
Shall not be prolonged. Right. Stand in your place.

Ready? Blow me a little ladder of sound
From a good stance so that you feel the heavy
Press of the floor coming up through you and
Keeping your pitch and tone in character.

Now that is something, Karl. You are getting on.
Unswell your head. One more piece of coal.
Go on now but remember it must be always
Easy and flowing. Light and shadow must
Be varied but be varied in your mind
Before you hear the eventual return sound.

Play me the dance you made for the barge-master.
Stop stop Karl. Play it as you first thought
Of it in the hot boat-kitchen. That is a pleasure
For me. I can see I am making you good.
Keep the stove red. Hand me the matches. Now
We can see better. Give me a shot at the pipe.
Karl, I can still put on a good flute-mouth
And show you in this high cold room something
You will be famous to have said you heard.

THE FOURTH LESSON

You are early this morning. What we have to do
Today is think of you as a little creator
After the big creator. And it can be argued
You are as necessary, even a composer
Composing in the flesh an attitude
To slay the ears of the gentry. Karl,
I know you find great joy in the great
Composers. But now you can put your lips to
The messages and blow them into sound
And enter and be there as well. You must
Be faithful to who you are speaking from
And yet it is all right. You will be there.

Take your coat off. Sit down. A glass of Bols
Will help us both. I think you are good enough
To not need me anymore. I think you know
You are not only an interpreter.
What you will do is always something else
And they will hear you simultaneously with
The Art you have been given to read. Karl,

I think the Spring is really coming at last.
I see the canal boys working. I realise
I have not asked you to play the flute today.
Come and look. Are the barges not moving?
You must forgive me. I am not myself today.
Be here on Thursday. When you come, bring
Me five herrings. Watch your fingers. Spring
Is apparent but it is still chilblain weather.

THE LAST LESSON

Dear Karl, this morning is our last lesson.
I have been given the opportunity to
Live in a certain person's house and tutor
Him and his daughters on the traverse flute.
Karl, you will be all right. In those recent
Lessons my heart lifted to your playing.

I know. I see you doing well, invited
In a great chamber in front of the gentry. I
Can see them with their dresses settling in
And bored mouths beneath moustaches sizing
You up as you are, a lout from the canal
With big ears but an angel's tread on the flute.

But you will be all right. Stand in your place
Before them. Remember Johann. Begin with good
Nerve and decision. Do not intrude too much
Into the message you carry and put out.

One last thing, Karl, remember when you enter
The joy of those quick high archipelagoes,
To make to keep your finger-stops as light
As feathers but definite. What can I say more?
Do not be sentimental or in your Art.
I will miss you. Do not expect applause.

The Stepping Stones

I have my yellow boots on to walk
Across the shires where I hide
Away from my true people and all
I can't put easily into my life.

So you will see I am stepping on
The stones between the runnels getting
Nowhere nowhere. It is almost
Embarrassing to be alive alone.

Take my hand and pull me over from
The last stone on to the moss and
The three celandines. Now my dear
Let us go home across the shires.

TOM SCOTT (b. 1918)

The Mankind Toun

For Shirley Bridges

Hou lang we've socht
I dinna ken
For a toun that micht
Be fit for men.
Ten thousant year
Or mair or less
But yond or here
Wi smaa success.

We've fled mirk Thebes
Wi Ikhnaton,
startled   Fleggit the grebes
By Babylon
And sat in quorum,
Man til man
In Karakorum
Wi Jenghis Khan.

Seen Nineveh,
Byzantium,
Sidon, Troy,
Cartaga, Rome;
Corinth, wi its
Wreathit touers,
Damascan streets
Wi Asterte's whures;
Been amang the tents
Round Samarkan
bent-grass   And alang the bents
By Trebizon.

Frae Nippur, Tyre,
Jerusalem,
Athens, Palmyra,

Pergamum
Til Florence, Venice,
The toun on Thames,
Imperial Vienna's
Waltzan dames,
Braw touns we've seen,
And will again,
But nane that hes been
Fit for men.

Shall we never find
The toun whaur love
Rules mankind?
Whaur the hawk, the dove,
owl   And houlet form
A trinitie
That keeps frae hairm
each   Ilk chimney tree?
Whaur first is laist
And ilk and ane
Gie free their best
Til brither-men?

Whiles it seems
It canna be,
unless   Binna in dreams;
Or till we see
The minarets,
The spires that rise
above the gates Abuin the yetts
O paradise.

But na, we'll find
Midnicht or noon,
journey's   Our vaigin's end,
The mankind toun:
Yet bidan true
Til the Sender's aims
Seek further new
Jerusalems.

MURIEL SPARK (b. 1918)

Going up to Sotheby's

This was the wine. It stained the top of the page
when she knocked over the glass accidentally. A pity,
                                          she said,
to lose that drop. For the wine was a treat.
Here's a coffee-cup ring, and another. He preferred
                                          coffee to tea.
Some pages re-written entirely, scored through,
                                  cancelled over and over
on this, his most important manuscript.

That winter they took a croft in Perthshire,
living on oats and rabbits bought for a few pence
                                          from the madman.
The children thrived, and she got them to school
                                  daily, mostly by trudge.
He was glad to get the children out of the way, but
                                          always felt cold
while working on his book. This
is his most important manuscript, completed 1929.
'Children, go and play outside. Your father's trying
                                          to work.
But keep away from the madman's house.'
He looked up from his book. 'There's nothing
wrong with the madman.' Which was true.

She typed out the chapters in the afternoons. He
                                  looked happily at her.
He worked best late at night.
'Aren't you ever coming to bed? I often wonder,
are you married to me or to your bloody book?'
A smudge on the page, still sticky after all these

                                          years.
Something greasy on the last page.
This is that manuscript, finished in the late spring,
crossed-out, dog-eared; this, the original,

passed through several literary hands while
the pages she had typed were at the publishers'.
One personage has marked a passage with red ink,
has written in the margin, 'Are you *sure*?'

Five publishers rejected it in spite of
                                    recommendations.
The sixth decided to risk his pounds sterling down
                                    the drain
for the sake of prestige. The author was a difficult
                                    customer. However,
they got the book published at last.
Her parents looked after the children while the
                                    couple went to France
for a short trip. This bundle of paper, the original
                                    manuscript,
went into a fibre trunk, got damp into it, got mouldy
                                    and furled.
It took fifteen more years for him to make his
                                    reputation,
by which time the children had grown up, Agnes as a
secretary at the BBC, Leo as a teacher.

The author died in '48, his wife in '68.
Agnes and Leo married and begat.
And now the grandchildren are selling the
                                    manuscript.
Bound and proud, documented and glossed
by scholars of the land, smoothed out
and precious, these leaves of paper
are going up to Sotheby's. The wine-stained,
stew-stained and mould-smelly papers are
going up to Sotheby's. They occupy the front seat
of the Renault, beside the driver.
They are a national event. They are going up
to make their fortune at last,
which once were so humble, tattered, and so truly
                                    working class.

Against the Transcendentalists

There are more visionaries
Than poets and less
Poets than missionaries,
Poets are a meagre species.

There is more vanity, more charity,
There is more of everything than poetry
Which, for personal purposes,
I wish may preserve
Identity from any other commodity
Also from Delphic insanity,
Drunkenness and discrepancy
Of which there's already a great plenty.
And so I reserve
The right not to try to
Fulfil the wilderness or fly to
Empyreal vacuity with an eye to
Publication, for what am I to
Byzantium or Byzantium
To me? I live in Kensington
And walk about, and work in Kensington
And do not foresee departing from Kensington.
So if there's no law in Kensington
Adaptable to verse without contravening
The letter to prove
The law, I'll make one.

The first text is
The word. The next is
(Since morals prevent quarrels
And writers make poor fighters)
Love your neighbour, meaning
Your neighbour, let him love
His neighbour, and he his.
Who is Everyman, what is he
That he should stand in lieu of
A poem? What is Truth true of?

And what good's a God's-eye-view of
Anyone to anyone
But God? In the Abstraction
Many angels make sweet moan
But never write a stanza down.
Poets are few and they are better
Equipped to love and animate the letter.

I therefore resign
The seven-league line
In footwear of super-cosmic design
To the global hops
Of wizards and wops;
Hoping that if Byzantium
Should appear in Kensington
The city will fit the size
Of the perimeter of my eyes
And of the span of my hand:
Hands and eyes that understand
This law of which the third
Text is the thing defined,
The flesh made word.

Elegy in a Kensington Churchyard

Lady who lies beneath this stone,
Pupil of Time pragmatical,
Though in a lifetime's cultivation
You did not blossom, summer shall.

The fierce activity of grass
Assaults a century's constraint.
Vigour survives the vigorous,
Meek as you were, or proud as paint.

And bares its fist for insurrection
Clenched in the bud; lady who lies
Those leaves will spend in disaffection
Your fond estate and purposes.

Death's a contagion: spring's a bright
Green fit; the blight will overcome
The plague that overcame the blight
That laid this lady low and dumb,

And laid a parish on its back
So soon amazed, so long enticed
Into an earthy almanack,
And musters now the spring attack;
Which render passive, latent Christ.

Litany of Time Past

What's today?
  Hoops today.
What's yesterday?
  Tops yesterday.
What's tomorrow?
  Diabolo.

Moons and planets come out to play,
The Bear bowled, the Sun spun.
See the Devil-on-sticks run
Today, tomorrow, and yesterday.

What's Hope?
  Skipping rope.
What's Clarity?
  Salty peppery.
What's Faith?
  Edinburgh, Leith,
  Portobello, Musselburgh,
  and Dalkeith.

Out you are.
  In you are.
Mustard.
  Vinegar.

ELMA MITCHELL (b. 1919)

Thoughts after Ruskin

Women reminded him of lilies and roses.
Me they remind rather of blood and soap,
Armed with a warm rag, assaulting noses,
Ears, neck, mouth and all the secret places:

Armed with a sharp knife, cutting up liver,
Holding hearts to bleed under a running tap,
Gutting and stuffing, pickling and preserving,
Scalding, blanching, broiling, pulverising,
– All the terrible chemistry of their kitchens.

Their distant husbands lean across mahogany
And delicately manipulate the market,
While safe at home, the tender and the gentle
Are killing tiny mice, dead snap by the neck,
Asphyxiating flies, evicting spiders,
Scrubbing, scouring aloud, disturbing cupboards,
Committing things to dustbins, twisting, wringing,
Wrists red and knuckles white and fingers puckered,
Pulpy, tepid. Steering screaming cleaners
Around the snags of furniture, they straighten
And haul out sheets from under the incontinent
And heavy old, stoop to importunate young,
Tugging, folding, tucking, zipping, buttoning,
Spooning in food, encouraging excretion,
Mopping up vomit, stabbing cloth with needles,
Contorting wool around their knitting needles,
Creating snug and comfy on their needles.

Their huge hands! their everywhere eyes! their voices
Raised to convey across the hullabaloo,
Their massive thighs and breasts dispensing comfort,
Their bloody passages and hairy crannies,
Their wombs that pocket a man upside down!

And when all's over, off with overalls,
Quickly consulting clocks, they go upstairs,
Sit and sigh a little, brushing hair,
And somehow find, in mirrors, colours, odours,
Their essences of lilies and of roses.

HAMISH HENDERSON (b. 1919)

Seventh Elegy

SEVEN GOOD GERMANS

*The track running between Mekili and Tmimi was at one time a
kind of no-man's-land. British patrolling was energetic, and there
were numerous brushes with German and Italian elements. El
Eleba lies about half-way along this track.*

Of the swaddies

who came to the desert with Rommel

there were few who had heard (or would hear) of El

Eleba.

They recce'd,

or acted as medical orderlies

or patched up their tanks in the camouflaged

workshops

and never gave a thought to a place like El Eleba.

To get there, you drive into the blue, take a bearing

and head for damn-all. Then you're there. And where

are you?

– Still, of some few who did cross our path at El

Eleba

there are seven who bide under their standing crosses.

The first a Lieutenant.

When the medicos passed him

for service overseas, he had jotted in a note-book

*to the day and the hour   keep me steadfast   there

is only the decision and the will

the rest has no importance*

The second a Corporal.
      He had been in the Legion
and had got one more chance to redeem his lost
           honour.
What he said was
Listen here, I'm fed up with your griping –
If you want extra rations, go get 'em from Tommy!
You're green, that's your trouble. Dodge the column,
        pass the buck
and scrounge all you can – that's our law in the
        Legion.
You know Tommy's got 'em. . . . He's got mineral
        waters,
and beer, and fresh fruit in that white crinkly paper
and God knows what all! Well, what's holding you
        back?
Are you windy or what?
      Christ, you 'old Afrikaners'!
If you're wanting the eats, go and get 'em from
        Tommy!

The third had been a farm-hand in the March of
        Silesia
and had come to the desert as fresh fodder for
        machine guns.
His dates are inscribed on the files, and on the cross-
        piece.

The fourth was a lance-jack.
      He had trusted in Adolf
while working as a chemist in the suburb of Spandau.
His loves were his 'cello, and the woman who had
        borne him
two daughters and a son. He had faith in the
        Endsieg.
THAT THE NEW REICH MAY LIVE prayed the flyleaf
        of his Bible.

The fifth a mechanic.
                           All the honour and glory,
the siege of Tobruk and the conquest of Cairo
meant as much to that Boche as the Synod of
                                         Whitby.
Being wise to all this, he had one single headache,
which was, how to get back to his sweetheart (called
                                           Ilse).
– He had said
                   Can't the Tommy wake up and get
                                        weaving?
          If he tried, he could put our whole Corps in the bag.
          May God damn this Libya and both of its palm-trees!

The sixth was a Pole
                   – or to you, a Volksdeutscher –
who had put off his nation to serve in the
                                      Wehrmacht.
He siegheiled, and talked of 'the dirty Polacken,'
and said what he'd do if let loose among Russkis.
His mates thought that, though 'just a polnischer
                                  Schweinhund',
he was not a bad bloke.
                           On the morning concerned
he was driving a truck with mail, petrol and rations.
The MP on duty shouted five words of warning.
He nodded
             laughed
                        revved
                           and drove straight for El
                                           Eleba
not having quite got the chap's Styrian lingo.

The seventh a young swaddy.
                           Riding cramped in a lorry
to death along the road which winds eastward to
                                        Halfaya
he had written three verses in appeal against his
                                        sentence
which soften for an hour the anger of Lenin.

Seven poor bastards
dead in African deadland
(tawny tousled hair under the issue blanket)
wie einst Lili
dead in African deadland
einst Lili Marlene

ALEXANDER SCOTT (1920–89)

<table>
<tr><td>lament</td><td>Coronach</td></tr>
</table>

For the dead of the 5/7th Battalion, The Gordon Highlanders

lament	Waement the deid
	I never did,
one of the remainder	Owre gled I was ane o the lave
stayed	That somewey baid alive
trouble my spiritless	To trauchle my thowless hert
	Wi ithers' hurt.
	But nou that I'm far
from the fighting's fear	Frae the fechtin's fear,
	Nou I hae won awa frae aa thon pain
back to my books	Back til my beuks and my pen,
	They croud aroun me out o the grave
longing	Whaur love and langourie sae lanesome grieve.
	Cryan the cauld words:
endured our fates	'We hae dree'd our weirds,
remain behind	But you that byde ahin,
beyond/haven	Ayont our awesome hyne,
	You are the flesh we aince had been,
brittle broken bone	We that are bruckle brokken bane.'
dull speech	Cryan a drumlie speak:
	'You hae the words we spak,
	You hae the sang
	We canna sing,
must disperse	Sen death maun skail
poet's	The makar's skill.
	'Makar, frae nou ye maun
	Be singan for us deid men,
to the world we loved	Sing til the warld we loo'd
lied	(For aa that its brichtness lee'd)

And tell hou the sudden nicht

nothing   Cam doun and made us nocht.'

Waement the deid
I never did,
But nou I am safe awa
I hear their wae

weeping/dawn   Greetan greetan dark and daw,
their death yesterday my work   Their death the-streen my darg the-day.
today

EDWIN MORGAN (b. 1920)

The Starlings in George Square

I

Sundown on the high stonefields!
The darkening roofscape stirs –
thick – alive with starlings
gathered singing in the square –
like a shower of arrows they cross
the flash of a western window,
they bead the wires with jet,
they nestle preening by the lamps
and shine, sidling by the lamps
and sing, shining, they stir
the homeward hurrying crowds.
A man looks up and points
smiling to his son beside him
wide-eyed at the clamour on those cliffs –
it sinks, shrills out in waves,
levels to a happy murmur,
scatters in swooping arcs,
a stab of confused sweetness
that pierces the boy like a story,
a story more than a song.
He will never forget that evening,
the silhouette of the roofs,
the starlings by the lamps.

II

The City Chambers are hopping mad.
Councillors with rubber plugs in their ears!
Secretaries closing windows!
Window-cleaners want protection and danger money.
The Lord Provost can't hear herself think, man.
What's that?
Lord Provost, can't hear herself think.

At the General Post Office
the clerks write Three Pounds Starling in the savings-
                                                    books.
Each telephone-booth is like an aviary.
I tried to send a parcel to County Kerry but –

tangled   The cables to Cairo got fankled, sir.
What's that?
I said the cables to Cairo got fankled.

And as for the City Information Bureau –
I'm sorry I can't quite chirrup did you twit –
No I wanted to twee but perhaps you can't cheep –
Would you try once again, that's better, I – sweet –
When's the last boat to Milngavie? Tweet?
What's that?
I said when's the last boat to Milngavie?

III

There is nothing for it now but scaffolding:
clamp it together, send for the bird-men,
Scarecrow Strip for the window-ledge landings,
Cameron's Repellent on the overhead wires.
Armour our pediments against eavesdroppers.
This is a human outpost. Save our statues.
Send back the jungle. And think of the joke:
as it says in the papers, It is very comical
to watch them alight on the plastic rollers
and take a tumble. So it doesn't kill them?
All right, so who's complaining? This isn't Peking
where they shoot the sparrows for hygiene and cash.
So we're all humanitarians, locked in our cliff-
                                                    dwellings
encased in our repellent, guano-free and guilt-free.
The Lord Provost sings in her marble hacienda.
The Postmaster-General licks an audible stamp.
Sir Walter is vexed that his column's deserted.
I wonder if we really deserve starlings?
There is something to be said for these joyous
                                        messengers

that we repel in our indignant orderliness.
They lift up the eyes, they lighten the heart,
and some day we'll decipher that sweet frenzied
                                        whistling
as they wheel and settle along our hard roofs
and take those grey buttresses for home.
One thing we know they say, after their fashion.
They like the warm cliffs of man.

The Second Life

But does every man feel like this at forty –
I mean it's like Thomas Wolfe's New York, his
heady light, the stunning plunging canyons, beauty –
pale stars winking hazy downtown quitting-time,
and the winter moon flooding the skyscrapers,
                                        northern –
an aspiring place, glory of the bridges, foghorns
are enormous messages, a looming mastery
that lays its hand on the young man's bowels
until he feels in that air, that rising spirit
all things are possible, he rises with it
until he feels that he can never die –
Can it be like this, and is this what it means
in Glasgow now, writing as the aircraft roar
over building sites, in this warm west light
by the daffodil banks that were never so crowded and
                                        lavish –
green May, and the slow great blocks rising
under yellow tower cranes, concrete and glass and
                                        steel
out of a dour rubble it was and barefoot children
                                        gone –
Is it only the slow stirring, a city's renewed life
that stirs me, could it stir me so deeply
as May, but could May have stirred
what I feel of desire and strength
like an arm saluting a sun?

All January, all February the skaters
enjoyed Bingham's pond, the crisp cold evenings,
they swung and flashed among car headlights,
the drivers parked round the unlit pond
to watch them, and give them light, what laughter
and pleasure rose in the rare lulls
of the yards-away stream of wheels along Great
                                        Western Road!
The ice broke up, but the boats came out.
The painted boats are ready for pleasure.
The long light needs no headlamps.

Black oar cuts a glitter: it is heaven on earth.

Is it true that we come alive
not once, but many times?
We are drawn back to the image
of the seed in darkness, or the greying skin
of the snake that hides a shining one –
it will push that used-up matter off
and even the film of the eye is sloughed –
That the world may be the same, and we are not
and so the world is not the same,
the second eye is making again
this place, these waters and these towers,
they are rising again
as the eye stands up to the sun,
as the eye salutes the sun.

Many things are unspoken
in the life of a man, and with a place
there is an unspoken love also
in undercurrents, drifting, waiting its time.
A great place and its people are not renewed lightly.
The caked layers of grime
grow warm, like homely coats.
But yet they will be dislodged
and men will still be warm.
The old coats are discarded.

The old ice is loosed.
The old seeds are awake.

Slip out of darkness, it is time.

Glasgow Sonnets

I

A mean wind wanders through the backcourt trash.
Hackles on puddles rise, old mattresses
puff briefly and subside. Play-fortresses
of brick and bric-a-brac spill out some ash.
Four storeys have no windows left to smash,
but in the fifth a chipped sill buttresses
mother and daughter the last mistresses
of that black block condemned to stand, not crash.
Around them the cracks deepen, the rats crawl.
The kettle whimpers on a crazy hob.
Roses of mould grow from ceiling to wall.
The man lies late since he has lost his job,
smokes on one elbow, letting his coughs fall
thinly into an air too poor to rob.

II

puny

A shilpit dog fucks grimly by the close.
Late shadows lengthen slowly, slogans fade.
The YY PARTICK TOI grins from its shade
like the last strains of some lost *libera nos
a malo*. No deliverer ever rose
from these stone tombs to get the hell they made
children   unmade. The same weans never make the grade.
The same grey street sends back the ball it throws.
Under the darkness of a twisted pram
a cat's eyes glitter. Glittering stars press
between the silent chimney-cowls and cram
the higher spaces with their SOS.

Don't shine a torch on the ragwoman's dram.
Coats keep the evil cold out less and less.

III

'See a tenement due for demolition?
I can get ye rooms in it, two, okay?
Seven hundred and nothin legal to pay
for it's no legal, see? That's my proposition,
ye can take it or leave it but. The position
is simple, you want a hoose, I say
for eight hundred pounds it's yours.' And they,
trailing five bairns, accepted his omission
of the foul crumbling stairwell, windows wired
not glazed, the damp from the canal, the cooker
without pipes, packs of rats that never tired –
any more than the vandals bored with snooker
who stripped the neighbouring houses, howled, and
                                                    fired
their aerosols – of squeaking 'Filthy lucre!'

IV

Down by the brickworks you get warm at least.
Surely soup-kitchens have gone out? It's not
the Thirties now. Hugh MacDiarmid forgot
in 'Glasgow 1960' that the feast
of reason and the flow of soul have ceased
to matter to the long unfinished plot
of heating frozen hands. We never got
an abstruse song that charmed the raging beast.
So you have nothing to lose but your chains,
dear Seventies. Dalmarnock, Maryhill,
Blackhill and Govan, better sticks and stanes
should break your banes, for poets' words are ill
to hurt ye. On the wrecker's ball the rains
weeping   of greeting cities drop and drink their fill.

V

'Let them eat cake' made no bones about it.
But we say let them eat the hope deferred
and that will sicken them. We have preferred
silent slipways to the riveters' wit.
And don't deny it – that's the ugly bit.
Ministers' tears might well have launched a herd
of bucking tankers if they'd been transferred
from Whitehall to the Clyde. And smiles don't fit
either. 'There'll be no bevvying' said Reid
at the work-in. But all the dignity you muster
can only give you back a mouth to feed
and rent to pay if what you lose in bluster
is no more than win patience with 'I need'
while distant blackboards use you as their duster.

VI

The North Sea oil-strike tilts east Scotland up,
and the great sick Clyde shivers in its bed.
But elegists can't hang themselves on fled-
from trees or poison a recycled cup –
If only a less faint, shaky sunup
glimmered through the skeletal shop and shed
and men washed round the piers like gold and spread
golder in soul than Mitsubishi or Krupp –
The images are ageless but the thing
is now. Without my images the men
ration their cigarettes, their children cling
to broken toys, their women wonder when
the doors will bang on laughter and a wing
over the firth be simply joy again.

VII

Environmentalists, ecologists
and conservationists are fine no doubt.
Pedestrianization will come out
fighting, riverside walks march off the lists,

pigeons and starlings be somnambulists
in far-off suburbs, the sandblaster's grout
multiply pink piebald facades to pout
at sticky-fingered mock-Venetianists.
Prop up's the motto. Splint the dying age.
Never displease the watchers from the grave.
Great when fake architecture was the rage,
but greater still to see what you can save.
The gutted double fake meets the adage:
a wig's the thing to beat both beard and shave.

VIII

Meanwhile the flyovers breed loops of light
in curves that would have ravished tragic Toshy –
clean and unpompous, nothing wishy-washy.
Vistas swim out from the bulldozer's bite
by day, and banks of earthbound stars at night
begin. In Madame Emé's Sauchie Haugh, she
could never gain in leaves or larks or sploshy
lanes what's lost in a dead boarded site –
the life that overspill is overkill to.
Less is not more, and garden cities are
the flimsiest oxymoron to distil to.
And who wants to distil? Let bus and car
and hurrying umbrellas keep their skill to
feed ukiyo-e beyond Lochnagar.

IX

It groans and shakes, contracts and grows again.
Its giant broken shoulders shrug off rain.

shuffling It digs its pits to a shauchling refrain.
bold Roadworks and graveyards like their gallus men.
It fattens fires and murders in a pen
and lets them out in flaps and squalls of pain.
It sometimes tears its smoky counterpane
to hoist a bleary fist at nothing, then
at everything, you never know. The west
could still be laid with no one's tears like dust

and barricaded windows be the best
to see from till the shops, the ships, the trust
return like thunder. Give the Clyde the rest.
Man and the sea make cities as they must.

   x

From thirtieth floor windows at Red Road
he can see choughs and samphires, dreadful trade –
the schoolboy reading *Lear* has that scene made.
A multi is a sonnet stretched to ode
and some say that's no joke. The gentle load
of souls in clouds, vertiginously stayed
above the windy courts, is probed and weighed.
Each monolith stands patient, ah'd and oh'd.
And stalled lifts generating high-rise blues
can be set loose. But stalled lives never budge.
They linger in the single-ends that use
their spirit to the bone, and when they trudge
from closemouth to laundrette their steady shoes
carry a world that weighs us like a judge.

The First Men on Mercury

– We come in peace from the third planet.
Would you take us to your leader?

– Bawr stretter! Bawr. Bawr. Stretterhawl?

– This is a little plastic model
of the solar system, with working parts.
You are here and we are there and we
are now here with you, is this clear?

– Gawl horrop. Bawr. Abawrhannahanna!

– Where we come from is blue and white
with brown, you see we call the brown
here 'land', the blue is 'sea', and the white

is 'clouds' over land and sea, we live
on the surface of the brown land,
all round is sea and clouds. We are 'men'.
Men come –

– Glawp men! Gawrbenner menko. Menhawl?

– Men come in peace from the third planet
which we call 'earth'. We are earthmen.
Take us earthmen to your leader.

– Thmen? Thmen? Bawr. Bawrhossop.
Yuleeda tan hanna. Harrabost yuleeda.

– I am the yuleeda. You see my hands,
we carry no benner, we come in peace.
The spaceways are all stretterhawn.

– Glawn peacemen all horrabhanna tantko!
Tan come at'mstrossop. Glawp yuleeda!

– Atoms are peacegawl in our harraban.
Menbat worrabost from tan hannahanna.

– You men we know bawrhossoptant. Bawr.
We know yuleeda. Go strawg backspetter quick.

– We cantantabawr, tantingko backspetter now!

– Banghapper now! Yes, third planet back.
Yuleeda will go back blue, white, brown
nowhanna! There is no more talk.

– Gawl han fasthapper?

– No. You must go back to your planet.
Go back in peace, take what you have gained
but quickly.

– Stretterworra gawl, gawl . . .

– Of course, but nothing is ever the same,
now is it? You'll remember Mercury.

Cinquevalli

Cinquevalli is falling, falling.
The shining trapeze kicks and flirts free,
solo performer at last.
The sawdust puffs up with a thump,
settles on a tangle of broken limbs.
St Petersburg screams and leans.
His pulse flickers with the gas-jets. He lives.

Cinquevalli has a therapy.
In his hospital bed, in his hospital chair
he holds a ball, lightly, lets it roll round his hand,
or grips it tight, gauging its weight and resistance,
begins to balance it, to feel its life attached to his
by will and knowledge, invisible strings
that only he can see. He throws it
from hand to hand, always different,
always the same, always
different, always the
same.
His muscles learn to think, his arms grow very
                                                    strong.

Cinquevalli in sepia
looks at me from an old postcard: bundle of enigmas.
Half faun, half military man; almond eyes, curly hair,
conventional moustache; tights, and a tunic loaded
with embroideries, tassels, chains, fringes; hand on
                                                    hip
with a large signet-ring winking at the camera
but a bull neck and shoulders and a cannon-ball
at his elbow as he stands by the posing pedestal;
half reluctant, half truculent,
half handsome, half absurd,
but let me see you forget him: not to be done.

Cinquevalli is a juggler.
In a thousand theatres, in every continent,
he is the best, the greatest. After eight years
                                  perfecting
he can balance one billiard ball on another billiard
                                         ball
on top of a cue on top of a third billiard ball
in a wine-glass held in his mouth. To those
who say the balls are waxed, or flattened,
he patiently explains the trick will only work
because the spheres are absolutely true.
There is no deception in him. He is true.

Cinquevalli is juggling with a bowler,
a walking-stick, a cigar, and a coin.
Who foresees? How to please.
The last time round, the bowler
flies to his head, the stick sticks in his hand,
the cigar jumps into his mouth, the coin
lands on his foot – ah, but
is kicked into his eye
and held there as the miraculous monocle
without which the portrait would be incomplete.

Cinquevalli is practising.
He sits in his dressing-room talking to some friends,
at the same time writing a letter with one hand
and with the other juggling four balls.
His friends think of demons, but
'You could do all this,' he says,
sealing the letter with a billiard ball.

Cinquevalli is on the high wire in Odessa.
The roof cracks, he is falling, falling
into the audience, a woman breaks his fall,
he cracks her like a flea, but lives.

Cinquevalli broods in his armchair in Brixton Road.
He reads in the paper about the shells whining
at Passchendaele, imagines the mud and the dead.

He goes to the window and wonders through that
                                   dark evening
what is happening in Poland where he was born.
His neighbours call him a German spy.
'Kestner, Paul Kestner, that's his name!'
'Keep Kestner out of the British music-hall!'
He frowns; it is cold; his fingers seem stiff and old.

Cinquevalli tosses up a plate of soup
and twirls it on his forefinger; not a drop spills.
He laughs, and well may he laugh
who can do that. The astonished table
breathe again, laugh too, think the world
a spinning thing that spills, for a moment, no drop.

Cinquevalli's coffin sways through Brixton
only a few months before the Armistice.
Like some trick they cannot get off the ground
it seems to burden the shuffling bearers, all their arms
cross-juggle that displaced person, that man
of balance, of strength, of delights and marvels,
in his unsteady box at last into the earth.

The Dowser

With my forked branch of Lebanese cedar
I quarter the dunes like downs and guide
an invisible plough far over the sand.
But how to quarter such shifting acres
when the wind melts their shapes, and shadows
mass where all was bright before,
and landmarks walk like wraiths at noon?
All I know is that underneath,
how many miles no one can say,
an unbroken water-table waits
like a lake; it has seen no bird or sail
in its long darkness, and no man;
not even pharaohs dug so far
for all their thirst, or thirst of glory,

or thrust-power of ten thousand slaves.
I tell you I can smell it though,
that water. I am old and black
and I know the manners of the sun
which makes me bend, not break. I lose
my ghostly footprints without complaint.
I put every mirage in its place.
I watch the lizard make its lace.
Like one not quite blind I go
feeling for the sunken face.
So hot the days, the nights so cold,
I gather my white rags and sigh
but sighing step so steadily
that any vibrance in so deep
a lake would never fail to rise
towards the snowy cedar's bait.
Great desert, let your sweetness wake.

from Sonnets from Scotland

PILATE AT FORTINGALL

A Latin harsh with Aramaicisms
poured from his lips incessantly; it made
no sense, for surely he was mad. The glade
of birches shamed his rags, in paroxysms
he stumbled, toga'd, furred, blear, brittle, grey.
They told us he sat here beneath the yew
even in downpours; ate dog-scraps. Crows flew
from prehistoric stone to stone all day.
'See him now.' He crawled to the cattle-trough
at dusk, jumbled the water till it sloshed
and spilled into the hoof-mush in blue strands,
slapped with useless despair each sodden cuff,
and washed his hands, and watched his hands, and
washed
his hands, and watched his hands, and washed his
hands.

DE QUINCEY IN GLASGOW

Twelve thousand drops of laudanum a day
kept him from shrieking. Wrapped in a duffle
buttoned to the neck, he made his shuffle,
door, table, window, table, door, bed, lay
on bed, sighed, groaned, jumped from bed, sat and
wrote
till the table was white with pages, rang
for his landlady, ordered mutton, sang
to himself with pharmacies in his throat.
When afternoons grew late, he feared and longed
for dusk. In that high room in Rottenrow
he looks out east to the Necropolis.
Its crowded tombs rise jostling, living, thronged
with shadows, and the granite-bloodying glow
flares on the dripping bronze of a used kris.

POST-REFERENDUM

'No no, it will not do, it will not be.
I tell you you must leave your land alone.
Who do you think is poised to ring the phone?
Fish your straitjacket packet from the sea
you threw it in, get your headphones mended.
You don't want the world now, do you? Come on,
you're pegged out on your heathery futon,
take the matches from your lids, it's ended.'
We watched the strong sick dirkless Angel groan,
shiver, half-rise, batter with a shrunk wing
the space the Tempter was no longer in.
He tried to hear feet, calls, car-doors, shouts, drone
of engines, hooters, hear a meeting sing.
A coin clattered at the end of its spin.

AFTER A DEATH

A writer needs nothing but a table.
His pencil races, pauses, crosses out.

Five years ago he lost his friend, without
him he struggles through a different fable.
The one who died, he is the better one.
The other one is selfish, ruthless, he
uses people, floats in an obscure sea
of passions, half-drowns as the livid sun
goes down, calls out for help he will not give.
Examine yourself! He is afraid to.
But that is not quite true, I saw him look
into that terrible place, let him live
at least with what is eternally due
to love that lies in earth in cold Carluke.

THE COIN

We brushed the dirt off, held it to the light.
The obverse showed us *Scotland*, and the head
of a red deer; the antler-glint had fled
but the fine cut could still be felt. All right:
we turned it over, read easily *One Pound*,
but then the shock of Latin, like a gloss,
Respublica Scotorum, sent across
such ages as we guessed but never found
at the worn edge where once the date had been
and where as many fingers had gripped hard
as hopes their silent race had lost or gained.
The marshy scurf crept up to our machine,
sucked at our boots. Yet nothing seemed ill-starred.
And least of all the realm the coin contained.

RUARAIDH MACTHOMAIS/DERICK THOMSON (b. 1921)

Dà Thaibhse

Anns an dìg dhomhainn aig ceann na buaile,
bhiodh na cailleachan ag ràdh chaidh murt a
                                        dhèanamh;
bu tric a chunncas taibhse a' gluasad
air oir an rathaid, ri fèath 's ri siantan.

Is iomadh feasgar a ghabh mi seachad
air oir na h-iomagain is mi 'nam bhalach,
eadar coiseachd 's ruith, air eagal sealladh
fhaotainn a chaoidh den taibhs' gun anail.

'S ged ruiginn ceann na buaile an dràsda
tha fhios gu bheil tannasg truagh a' tàmh ann,
ach dhèanainn an diugh am barrachd dàlach
ri taibhse a' bhalaich a chaidh a bhàthadh.

Two Ghosts

In the deep ditch at the field end
the old women said there had been a murder;
often a ghost was seen moving
at the edge of the road, in calm or storm.

Many an evening I passed the place,
on edge and anxious when I was a boy,
half running, for fear of catching
a glimpse of the ghost with no breath in its body.

Though I were to reach the field-end now
I'm sure there's a poor ghost staying there,
but today I'd wait a little longer
for the ghost of the boy who has been drowned.

An Tobar

Tha tobar beag am meadhon a' bhaile
's am feur ga fhalach,
am feur gorm sùghor ga dhlùth thughadh,
fhuair mi brath air bho sheann chaillich,
ach thuirt i, 'Tha 'm frith-rathad fo raineach
far am minig a choisich mi le'm chogan,
's tha'n cogan fhèin air dèabhadh.'
Nuair sheall mi 'na h-aodann preasach
chunnaic mi 'n raineach a' fàs mu thobar a sùilean
's ga fhalach bho shireadh 's bho rùintean,
's ga dhùnadh 's ga dhùnadh.

'Cha teid duine an diugh don tobar tha sin'
thuirt a' chailleach, 'mar a chaidh sinne
nuair a bha sinn òg,
ged tha 'm bùrn ann cho brèagh 's cho geal.'
'S nuair sheall mi troimhn raineach 'na sùilean
chunnaic mi lainnir a' bhùirn ud
a ni slàn gach ciùrradh
gu ruig ciùrradh cridhe.

'Is feuch an tadhail thu dhòmhsa,'
thuirt a' chailleach, 'ga b'ann le meòirean,
's thoir thugam boinne den uisge chruaidh sin
a bheir rudhadh gu m' ghruaidhean.'
Lorg mi an tobar air èiginn
's ged nach b'ise bu mhotha feum air
'sann thuice a thug mi 'n eudail.

Dh' fhaodadh nach eil anns an tobar
ach nì a chunnaic mi 'm bruadar,
oir nuair chaidh mi an diugh ga shireadh
cha d'fhuair mi ach raineach is luachair,
's tha sùilean na caillich dùinte
's tha lì air tighinn air an luathghair.

The Well

Right in the village there's a little well
and the grass hides it,
green grass in sap closely thatching it.
I heard of it from an old woman
but she said: 'The path is overgrown with bracken
pail   where I often walked with my cogie,
and the cogie itself is warped.'
When I looked in her lined face
I saw the bracken growing round the well of her
                                                    eyes,

and hiding it from seeking and from desires,
and closing it, closing it.

'Nobody goes to that well now,'
said the old woman, 'as we once went,
when we were young,
though its water is lovely and white.'
And when I looked in her eyes through the bracken
I saw the sparkle of that water
that makes whole every hurt
till the hurt of the heart.

'And will you go there for me,'
said the old woman, 'even with a thimble,
and bring me a drop of that hard water
that will bring colour to my cheeks.'
I found the well at last,
and though her need was not the greatest
it was to her I brought the treasure.

It may be that the well
is something I saw in a dream,
for today when I went to seek it
I found only bracken and rushes,
and the old woman's eyes are closed
and a film has come over their merriment.

Srath Nabhair

Anns an adhar dhubh-ghorm ud,
àirde na sìorraidheachd os ar cionn,
bha rionnag a' priobadh ruinn
's i freagairt mireadh an teine
ann an cabair taigh m' athar
a' bhlianna thugh sinn an taigh le bleideagan
                                        sneachda.

Agus siud a' bhlianna cuideachd
a shlaod iad a' chailleach don t-sitig,
a shealltainn cho eòlach 's a bha iad air an Fhìrinn,
oir bha nid aig eunlaith an adhair
(agus cròthan aig na caoraich)
ged nach robh àit aice-se anns an cuireadh i a ceann
                                        fòidhpe.

A Shrath Nabhair 's a Shrath Chill Donnain,
is beag an t-iongnadh ged a chinneadh am fraoch
                                        àlainn oirbh,
a' falach nan lotan a dh' fhàg Pàdraig Sellar 's a
                                        sheòrsa,
mar a chunnaic mi uair is uair boireannach cràbhaidh
a dh' fhiosraich dòrainn an t-saoghail-sa
is sìth Dhè 'na sùilean.

Strathnaver

In that blue-black sky,
as high above us as eternity,
a star was winking at us,
answering the leaping flames of fire
in the rafters of my father's house,
that year we thatched the house with snowflakes.

And that too was the year
they hauled the old woman out on to the dung-heap,

to demonstrate how knowledgeable they were in
                                    Scripture,
for the birds of the air had nests
(and the sheep had folds)
though she had no place in which to lay down her
                                    head.

O Strathnaver and Strath of Kildonan,
it is little wonder that the heather should bloom on
                                    your slopes,
hiding the wounds that Patrick Sellar, and such as he,
                                    made,
just as time and time again I have seen a pious
                                    woman
who has suffered the sorrow of this world,
with the peace of God shining from her eyes.

Eilean Chaluim Chille an Loch Eiriosort, Leòdhas

Chaidh sinn air chuairt don eilean air là samhraidh, an 1955, là teth bruthainneach, is na pèileagan a' cluiche anns an loch, far am minig a dh' fhairich Murchadh Mòr Mac Mhic Mhurchaidh 'sadadh nan tonn' mu shròin na Làir Dhuinn

Fàs, fàs an grian-shruth bruthainneach trath-nòin,
sliosan do chnuic dathte le raineach 's fraoch,
còinteach is riasg do ghleannain, feur do lòin,
gort agus iodhlann shaidhbhir gheal nan naomh.

'S torrach an deanntag mu do chlachan lom,
i frasadh sìol as t-fhoghar thar nan leac;
far an robh gillean dìreach thogadh fonn
tha 'n seileasdair gun lùbadh nise streap.

Mhùch gnùsdaich chaorach seirm nan salm o chian,
tha guth na fidhle balbh 's am bogha brist,
tha fodair na *Làir Dhuinn* am brù nan sian,
is Murchadh Mòr aig neoni anns a' chist.

Bho abhal-ghort gu goirt, bho ghorm gu bàn,
fàsach ath-nuadhaicht' far 'n robh ionad Dhè,
bu leis an fhaoileig thu aig toiseach tràth'
's tha 'n fhaoileag fhathast crochte air a' sgèith.

St Columba's Isle, Loch Erisort, Lewis

Deserted in the noon-time's shimmering, pouring sun,
your hillsides stained with heather and with fern,
the moss and peat-mould of your glen, your meadow
                              grass,
the rich bright field and corn-yard of the saints.

The nettles multiply beside your rain-washed stones,
showering their autumn seeds over the slabs;
where once upstanding lads joined in the song,
the never-bending iris now grows tall.

The grunting sheep have drowned the chanted psalms
long since; the fiddle's still, broken its bow;
the Brown Mare's fodder eaten by the winds,

chest [coffin]   *and Murchadh Mòr* a cypher in his kist.*

The orchard starved, the green field fallow now,
a re-created desert in God's place,
you were the seagull's land when time began,
and still the seagull hangs from its own wings.

Clann-Nighean an Sgadain

An gàire mar chraiteachan salainn
ga fhroiseadh bho 'm beul,
an sàl 's am picil air an teanga,
's na miaran cruinne, goirid a dheanadh giullachd,

---

* *Murchadh Mòr, or Murdoch Mackenzie, seventeenth century Factor to the Earl of Seaforth in Lewis, chief of the Mackenzies of Achilty, and poet, lived on St Columba's Isle. He composed a poem entitled An Làir Dhonn, 'The Brown Mare'. He thinks of his own boat as a mare that needs no feeding other than the thudding of the waves against her prow.*

no a thogadh leanabh gu socair, cuimir,
seasgair, fallain,
gun mhearachd,
's na sùilean cho domhainn ri fèath.

B'e bun-os-cionn na h-eachdraidh a dh' fhàg iad
'nan tràillean aig ciùrairean cutach,
thall 's a-bhos air Galldachd 's an Sasainn.
Bu shaillte an duais a thàrr iad
ás na mìltean bharaillean ud,
gaoth na mara geur air an craiceann,
is eallach a' bhochdainn 'nan ciste,
is mara b'e an gàire
shaoileadh tu gu robh an teud briste.

Ach bha craiteachan uaille air an cridhe,
ga chumail fallain,
is bheireadh cutag an teanga
slisinn á fanaid nan Gall –
agus bha obair rompa fhathast
nuair gheibheadh iad dhachaigh,
ged nach biodh maoin ac':
air oidhche robach gheamhraidh,
ma bha siud an dàn dhaibh,
dheanadh iad daoine.

The Herring Girls

Their laughter like a sprinkling of salt
showered from their lips,
brine and pickle on their tongues,
and the stubby short fingers that could handle fish,
or lift a child gently, neatly,
safely, wholesomely,
unerringly,
and the eyes that were as deep as a calm.

The topsy-turvy of history had made them
slaves to short-arsed curers,

here and there in the Lowlands, in England.
Salt the reward they won
from those thousands of barrels,
the sea-wind sharp on their skins,
and the burden of poverty in their kists,
and were it not for their laughter
you might think the harp-string was broken.

But there was a sprinkling of pride on their hearts,
keeping them sound,
and their tongues' gutting-knife
would tear a strip from the Lowlanders' mockery –
and there was work awaiting them
when they got home,
though they had no wealth:
on a wild winter's night,
if that were their lot,
they would make men.

Dun Nan Gall

Far a bheil a' Ghàidhlig sgrìobht air na creagan
an sin dh' fhan i,
is pàisdean luideagach ga caitheamh,
a stiallan sgaoilte air na rubhachan an iar,
os cionn na mara
far a bheil grian na h-Eireann a' dol sìos,
is grian Ameireagaidh ag èirigh le èigheachd 's
                        caithream.

Cha bheathaich feur a' chànain seo,
chan fhàs i sultmhor an guirt no 'n iodhlainn;
fòghnaidh dhi beagan coirce 's eòrna,
cuirear grad fhuadachadh oirr' leis a' chruithneachd;
chan iarr i ach, cleas nan gobhar, a bhith sporghail
os cionn muir gorm, air na bideanan biorach.

Gus an tog a' chlann luideagach leoth' i
air bàta-smùid a Shasainn,

no a Ghlaschu, far a faigh i bàs,
an achlais a peathar –
Gàidhlig rìoghail na h-Albann 's na h-Eireann
'na h-ìobairt-rèite air altair beairteis.

Donegal

Where Gaelic is written on the rocks
there it has lived,
and ragged children use it;
its shreds are scattered on the western headlands,
above the sea,
where the sun of Ireland goes down
and the sun of America rises with exultant clamour.

Grass does not nourish this language,
it does not grow fat in fields or cornyards;
a little oats and barley suffices it,
wheat quickly frightens it away;
all it asks is to clamber, like the goats,
on sharp rocky pinnacles, above the blue sea,

Until the ragged children carry it away with them
on the steamer to England,
or to Glasgow, where it dies
in its sister's arms –
the royal language of Scotland and of Ireland
become a sacrifice of atonement on the altar of
riches.

Cisteachan-Laighe

Duin' àrd, tana
's fiasag bheag air,
's locair 'na làimh:
gach uair theid mi seachad
air bùth-shaoirsneachd sa' bhaile,
's a thig gu mo chuinnlean fàileadh na min-sàibh,

thig gu mo chuimhne cuimhne an àit ud,
le na cisteachan-laighe,
na h-ùird 's na tairgean,
na sàibh 's na sgeilbean,
is mo sheanair crom,
is sliseag bho shliseag ga locradh
bhon bhòrd thana lom.

Mus robh fhios agam dè bh' ann bàs;
beachd, bloigh fios, boillsgeadh
den dorchadas, fathann den t-sàmhchair.
'S nuair a sheas mi aig uaigh,
là fuar Earraich, cha dainig smuain
thugam air na cisteachan-laighe
a rinn esan do chàch:
'sann a bha mi 'g iarraidh dhachaigh,
far am biodh còmhradh, is tea, is blàths.

Is anns an sgoil eile cuideachd,
san robh saoir na h-inntinn a' locradh,
cha tug mi 'n aire do na cisteachan-laighe,
ged a bha iad 'nan suidhe mun cuairt orm;
cha do dh' aithnich mi 'm brèid Beurla,
an lìomh Gallda bha dol air an fhiodh,
cha do leugh mi na facail air a' phràis,
cha do thuig mi gu robh mo chinneadh a' dol bàs.
Gus an dainig gaoth fhuar an Earraich-sa
a locradh a' chridhe;
gus na dh' fhairich mi na tairgean a' dol tromham,
's cha shlànaich tea no còmhradh an cràdh.

Coffins

A tall thin man
with a short beard,
and a plane in his hand:
whenever I pass
a joiner's shop in the city,
and the scent of sawdust comes to my nostrils,

memories return of that place,
with the coffins,
the hammers and nails,
saws and chisels,
and my grandfather, bent,
planing shavings
from a thin, bare plank.

Before I knew what death was;
or had any notion, a glimmering
of the darkness, a whisper of the stillness.
And when I stood at his grave,
on a cold Spring day, not a thought
came to me of the coffins
he made for others:
I merely wanted home
where there would be talk, and tea, and warmth.

And in the other school also,
where the joiners of the mind were planing,
I never noticed the coffins,
though they were sitting all round me;
I did not recognise the English braid,
the Lowland varnish being applied to the wood,
I did not read the words on the brass,
I did not understand that my race was dying.
Until the cold wind of this Spring came
to plane the heart;
until I felt the nails piercing me,
and neither tea nor talk will heal the pain.

An Dàrna Eilean

Nuair a ràinig sinn an t-eilean
bha feasgar ann
's bha sinn aig fois,
a' ghrian a' dol a laighe
fo chuibhrig cuain
's am bruadar a' tòiseachadh ás ùr.

Ach anns a' mhadainn
shad sinn dhinn a' chuibhrig
's anns an t-solas gheal sin
chunnaic sinn loch anns an eilean
is eilean anns an loch,
is chunnaic sinn
gun do theich am bruadar pìos eile bhuainn.

Tha an staran cugallach
chon an dàrna eilein,
tha a' chlach air uideil
tha a' dion nan dearcag,
tha chraobh chaorainn a' crìonadh,
fàileadh na h-iadhshlait a' faileachdainn oirnn a-nis.

The Second Island

When we reached the island
it was evening
and we were at peace,
the sun lying down
under the sea's quilt
and the dream beginning anew.

But in the morning
we tossed the cover aside
and in that white light
saw a loch in the island,
and an island in the loch,
and we recognised
that the dream had moved away from us again.

The stepping-stones are chancy
to the second island,
the stone totters
that guards the berries,
the rowan withers,
we have lost now the scent of the honeysuckle.

GEORGE MACKAY BROWN (b. 1921)

The Funeral of Ally Flett

Because of his long pilgrimage
　　From pub to alehouse
　　　　And all the liquor laws he'd flout,
Being under age
　　　　And wringing peatbog spirit from a clout
Into a secret kettle,
　　And making every Sabbath a carouse,
Mansie brought a twelve-year bottle.

Because his shy foot turned aside
　　From Merran's door,
　　　　And Olga's coat with the red button
And Inga's side
　　　　Naked as snow or swan or wild bog cotton
Made him laugh loud
　　　　And after, spit with scunner on the floor,
Marget sewed a long chaste shroud.

disgust

Because the scythe was in the oats
　　When he lay flat,
　　　　And Jean Macdonald's best March ale
Cooled the long throats
　　　　(At noon the reapers drank from the common
　　　　　　　　　　　　　　　　　　　　　　pail)
And Sanders said
　　'Corn enough here for every tramp and rat',
Sigrid baked her lightest bread.

Although the fleet from Hamnavoe
　　Drew heavy nets
　　　　Off Noup Head, in a squall of rain,
Turning in slow
　　　　Gull-haunted circles near the three-mile line,
And mouthing cod

Went iced and salted into slippery crates,
One skipper heard and bowed his head.

Because at Dounby and the fair
    Twelve tearaways
        Brought every copper in the islands
Round their uproar
        And this one made a sweet and sudden silence
Like that white bird
    That broke the tempest with a twig of praise,
The preacher spoke the holy word.

Because the hour of grass is brief
    And the red rose
        Is a bare thorn in the east wind
And a strong life
        Runs out and spends itself like barren sand
And the dove dies
    And every loveliest lilt must have a close,
Old Betsy came with bitter cries.

Because his dance was gathered now
    And parish feet
        Went blundering their separate roads
After the plough
        And after net and peat and harvest loads,
Yet from the cradle
    Their fated steps with a fixed passion beat,
Tammas brought his Swedish fiddle.

Old Fisherman with Guitar

A formal exercise for withered fingers.
    The head is bent,
        The eyes half closed, the tune
Lingers
        And beats, a gentle wing the west had thrown
        Against his breakwater wall with salt savage
                                        lament.

So fierce and sweet the song on the plucked string,
   Know now for truth
      Those hands have cut from the net
The strong
      Crag-eaten corpse of Jock washed from a boat
      One old winter, and gathered the mouth of Thora
                           to his mouth.

Trout Fisher

Semphill, his hat stuck full of hooks
   Sits drinking ale
      Among the English fishing visitors,
      Probes in detail
         Their faults in casting, reeling, selection of
                              flies.
'Never', he urges, 'do what it says in the books'.
     Then they, obscurely wise,
        Abandon by the loch their dripping oars
      And hang their throttled tarnish on the scale.

'Forgive me, every speckled trout',
    Says Semphill then,
      'And every swan and eider on these waters.
    Certain strange men
       Taking advantage of my poverty
Have wheedled all my subtle loch-craft out
      So that their butchery
       Seem fine technique in the ear of wives and
                         daughters.
     And I betray the loch for a white coin.'

Hamnavoe Market

They drove to the Market with ringing pockets.

Folster found a girl
Who put wounds on his face and throat,
Small and diagonal, like red doves.

Johnston stood beside the barrel.
All day he stood there.
He woke in a ditch, his mouth full of ashes.

Grieve bought a balloon and a goldfish.
He swung through the air.
He fired shotguns, rolled pennies, ate sweet fog from
                                                  a stick.

Heddle was at the Market also.
I know nothing of his activities.
He is and always was a quiet man.

Garson fought three rounds with a negro boxer,
And received thirty shillings,
Much applause, and an eye loaded with thunder.

Where did they find Flett?
They found him in a brazen circle,
All flame and blood, a new Salvationist.

A gypsy saw in the hand of Halcro
Great strolling herds, harvests, a proud woman.
He wintered in the poorhouse.

They drove home from the Market under the stars
Except for Johnston
Who lay in a ditch, his mouth full of dying fires.

The Five Voyages of Arnor

I, Arnor the red poet, made
Four voyages out of Orkney.

The first was to Ireland.
That was a viking cruise.
Thorleif came home with one leg.
We left Guthorm in Ulster,
His blood growing cold by the saint's well.
Rounding Cape Wrath, I made my first poem.

Norway hung fogs about me.
I won the girl Ragnhild
From Paul her brother, after
I beat him at draughts, three games to two.
Out of Bergen, the waves made her sick.
She was uglier than I expected, still
I made five poems about her
That men sing round the benches at Yule.
She filled my quiet house with words.

'The cousin Sweyn is howe-laid in Iceland
After his man-slaying' . . .
They put an axe in my hand, the edge turned north.
Women in black stood all about me.
We sailed no further than Unst in Shetland.
We bade there a month.
We drank the ale and discussed new metres.
For the women, I reddened the axe at a whale
                                        wound.

I went the blue road to Jerusalem
With fifteen ships in a brawling company
Of poets, warriors, and holy men.
A hundred swords were broken that voyage.
Prayer on a hundred white wings
Rose every morning. The Mediterranean
Was richer by a hundred love songs.

We saw the hills where God walked
And the last hill where his feet were broken.
At Rome, the earl left us. His hooves beat north.

Three Fridays sick of the black cough
Tomorrow I make my last voyage.
I should have endured this thing,
A bright sword in the storm of swords,
At Dublin, Micklegarth, Narbonne.
But here, at Hamnavoe, a pillow is under my head.
May all things be done in order.
The priest has given me oil and bread, a sweet cargo.
Ragnhild my daughter will cross my hands.
The boy Ljot must ring the bell.
I have said to Erling Saltfingers, *Drop my harp*
Through a green wave, off Yesnaby,
Next time you row to the lobsters.

Kirkyard

A silent conquering army,
The island dead,
Column on column, each with a stone banner
Raised over his head.

A green wave full of fish
Drifted far
In wavering westering ebb-drawn shoals beyond
Sinker or star.

A labyrinth of celled
And waxen pain.
Yet I come to the honeycomb often, to sip the
                                             finished
Fragrance of men.

Taxman

Seven scythes leaned at the wall.
Beard upon golden beard
The last barley load
Swayed through the yard.
The girls uncorked the ale.
Fiddle and feet moved together.
Then between stubble and heather
A horseman rode.

from Runes from a Holy Island

Press-Gang
    A man-of-war enchanted
    Three boys away.
    Pinleg, Windbag, Lord Rum returned.

Hierarchy
    A claret laird,
    Seven fishermen with ploughs,
    Women, beasts, corn, fish, stones.

Harpoonist
    He once riveted boat to whale.
    Frail-fingered now
    He weaves crab prisons.

Books
    No more ballads in Eynhallow.
    The schoolmaster
    Opens a box of grammars.

Ruined Chapel
    Among scattered Christ stones
    Devoutly leave
    Torn nets, toothache, winter wombs.

Saint

> A starved island, Cormack
> With crossed hands,
> Stones become haddock and loaf.

Fish and Corn

> Our isle is oyster-gray,
> That patched coat
> Is the Island of Horses.

Beachcomber

Monday I found a boot –
Rust and salt leather.
I gave it back to the sea, to dance in.

Tuesday a spar of timber worth thirty bob.
Next winter
It will be a chair, a coffin, a bed.

Wednesday a half can of Swedish spirits.
I tilted my head.
The shore was cold with mermaids and angels.

Thursday I got nothing, seaweed,
A whale bone,
Wet feet and a bad cough.

Friday I held a seaman's skull,
Sand spilling from it
The way time is told on kirkyard stones.

Saturday a barrel of sodden oranges.
A Spanish ship
Was wrecked last month at The Kame.

Sunday, for fear of the elders,
I smoke on the stone.
What's heaven? A sea chest with a thousand gold
                                        coins.

Island School

A boy leaves a small house
   Of sea light. He leaves
      The sea smells, creel
      And limpet and cod.

The boy walks between steep
   Stone houses, echoing
      Gull cries, the all-around
      Choirs of the sea,

Ship noises, shop noises, clamours
   Of bellman and milkcart.
      The boy comes at last
      To a tower with a tall desk

And a globe and a blackboard
   And a stern chalk-
      smelling lady. A bell
      Nods and summons.

A girl comes, cornlight
   In the eyes, smelling
      Of peat and cows
      And the rich midden.

Running she comes, late,
   Reeling in under the last
      Bronze brimmings. She sits
      Among twenty whispers.

WILLIAM NEILL (b. 1922)

Map Makers

When Irongray grew out of *Earran Reidh*
the culture could not stand on level ground.
schoolmasters Grey dominies of unmalleable will
invented newer legends of their own
to satisfy the blacksmith and his children.

After *Cill Osbran* closed up to Closeburn
more books were shut than Osbran's psalter.
Seeking to baptize the new born name
the pedants hurried to the nearest water
which wasn't even warm.

When *Seann Bhaile* swelled to Shambelly
the old steading became a glutton's belch.
Every tourist pointed a magic finger
padding lean Fingal to a flabby Falstaff.

The cold men in the city
who circumscribe all latitude
wiped their bullseye glasses
laid down the stabbing pens
that had dealt the mortal wounds
slaying the history of a thousand years
in the hour between lunch and catching the evening
train.

De A Thug Ort Sgriobhadh Ghaidhlig?

Theirinn gum bu dual domh sin . . .
docha Bhaltair Mòr is coireach,

Earran Reidh, the level ground; *Cill Osbran*, the Church of Osbran (or Osbern); *Seann Bhaile*, the Old Steading.
These are all Gaelic place names in south-west Scotland, where Gaelic survived until c.1700. (See Journal of Scottish
Studies Vol 17.) Our modern map makers have anglicized and bastardized these, and many others. W.N.

sgeadaichte gu leir 'sa bhreacan:
ged nach spiocach e mu bhriogais
b'e gluntow wi giltin hippis,
ag eubhadh 'Suas leis a'Ghàidhlig'
mus robh An Comann idir againn
's a'Bheurla Mhòr a tighinn 'san fhasan
sa Chathair cheòthach mhòir Dhuneideinn,
bu chaomh an àite sin le Uilleam
is e ag radh *ane lawland ers*
wad mak a better noyis, ma tha.

Greitand doun in Gallowa
mar bu dual don *gallow breid*
a' dranndail is ag cainntearachd
le *my trechour tung,* gun teagamh
that *hes tane ane heland strynd.*

A' siùbhal dùthaich Chinneide
bho 'Carrick tae the Cruives o Cree'
mur eil luchd-labhairt eile ann
o horo nach bithinn sùgrach
bruidhinn ris gach craobh a th'innte.

Nach b'fheàrrde mi mo neart a chur
gu sgriobhadh Beurla Lunnainn slàn,
gu faighinn leabhar bàrdachd beag
is e le còmhdach cruaidh glan
na bhithinn a' toirt *the Carrick clay*
to Edinburgh Cors a' ghràidh.

Chan abrainn gu robh daoin' agam
cho uasal ris na Cinneadaich,
ach luchd-na-speàla an Culshian
Moireasdan, Ceallach, Nèill, is Odhar
a' glaodh gu h-àrd nam chuislean-sa
b'e *hungert helant ghaists a bh'annta;*
mus robh Albais nar measg-ne
Gàidhlig aig gach fear is tè dhiubh,
is mairg gun do dh'fhairtlich sin
air Raibeart san aon dùthaich seo.

O horo nach mi tha bàigheil
bhith nam fhuigheal nan Gaidheal deasaich;
Gaidhlig bhlasda Bhaltair Cinneide
eadar Rachrainn agus Manainn
eadar Dalruigh is Cinntire,
is Creag Ealasaid mar usgar
chnapa 'r thargaid dùthaich Ualraig,
Bruis is Aonghais is na Dughallaich,
dùthaich Bhluchbard agus Cian,
Rabbie is The Helant Captain,
is ma bhios feadhainn a' gearann
gun do sgriobh mi cùs 'sa Ghàidhlig,
b'e Cinneide a nochd an ròd dhomh;
le *sic eloquence*, mo thruaighe,
as they in Erschry use, mo thogair
is set my thraward appetyte.

Ro-fhadalach a nis bhith toinneadh
teanga borb gu bhlaschainnt Lunnainn,
but blabberand wi my Carrick lippis
Ersche and brybour I maun bide,
sawsy in saffron back and side.

What Compelled You to Write in Gaelic?

I would say that was my right,
probably Walter Mor's to blame
dressed up in the Gaelic fashion;
though not mean about the breeches
he went bare-kneed with saffron hippings
shouting 'Up with the Gaelic'
before An Comann was with us at all,
and posh English coming into fashion
in the big smoky city of Edinburgh
a place that William (Dunbar) much liked
and he saying that one lowland arse
would make a better noise, indeed.

Grumbling down in Galloway
the habit of yon gallows breed,
muttering and deedling (like a piper)
with my traitor tongue; doubtless,
that has taken a Highland twist.

Travelling in Kennedy's country
from 'Carrick to the Cruives o Cree'
if I find no other speakers (of Gaelic)
o horo won't I be joyful
speaking to each tree that's there.

Would it not have been better to spend my powers
writing faultless London English,
so I could get a little poetry book
with clean hard covers on it,
than that I should bring the Carrick clay
to Edinburgh Cross, my dear.

I would not say I came from people
as lordly as the Kennedies,
but farmhands in Culzean
Morrison, Kellie, Neill and Orr
crying aloud in my veins,
hungry highland ghosts they were,
before braid Scots came in among us
every man and woman had Gaelic
a pity that it was denied
to Robert (Burns) in that same country.

O horo am I not joyful
to be a relic of the Southern Gaels;
warm Gaelic of Walter Kennedy
between Rathlinn and the Isle of Man
between (St John's Town of) Dalry and Kintyre,
and Ailsa Craig like the jewel
on the boss of the shield of the land of Kennedy
of Bruce, of Angus (of Islay) and of the MacDowalls,
the land of the Bluchbard and Cian
Rabbie and the Highland Captain,

and if some should complain
that I write too much in Gaelic
it was Kennedy that pointed the way;
with some eloquence, (Gaelic exclamation)
as Gaelic poets use, (Gaelic exclamation)
is set my capricious (literary) taste.

Too late now to be twisting
a rough tongue to the accents of London,
but blabbering with my Carrick lips
Gaelic and villain I must bide,
impudent in saffron back and side.

IVOR CUTLER (b. 1923)

The Purposeful Culinary Implements

Open,
You patent-leather canteen!
Lift your
Fresh-cheeked faces,
Electro-plated nickle silver cutlery!
Run twinkling to the
Damask tablecover
And lay down flat
Into a pattern
To stimulate
My salivaries.
Complement the chinaware,
The fresh sausage rolls,
Crisply succulent,
The roundels of boiled beetroot
Each a crimson chariot-wheel
Fit to speed Mars,
The God of War.
Green lettuce leaves
Stroked with white
With,
Coyly esconced in their troughs,
Boiled shrimps,
Pink as cherubs.

O knives
Forks
And spoons!
Fulfil yourselves.
Then lay
In the washing-up bowl,
To emerge
Radiant
And be set
By a soft loving hand

Back in your
Patent-leather canteen
To sleep
And drowsily wait
Another purposeful waking.

The Darkness

The darkness
is in the tunnel.
When you walk through
you are dark.
As you near the exit
your front lightens,
the dark fades off.
And when you are out,
all the darkness is
back in the tunnel.
Just at the exit,
a faint shadow sits gently
on your shoulders
before sliding
away regretfully.

Now, at night –

The Railway Sleepers

The railway sleepers
heavy and dry
from old workingwomen's bones.

Trains press over like stout husbands.

Jacket vest and trousers
smelling of cloth and husband
lay black on a chair
not responding to light.

My nose on the pillow.
Breath flows along the cotton hollows.

A bare bulb
yellow in the signal box.

The heavy sleepers lie dark.
Creak under the frost.

A starving bush
perched on the verge
shrieks at dense air out the tunnel
tearing its twigs.
Ends of roots
suck cinders for organic compounds.

The signalman
is noticing his painted tea-flask
on the sill.
He picks his nose without knowing.
Snot drops about his feet.

Dawn
gleams like mercury
afraid to come up.

G. F. DUTTON (b. 1924)

street

this is a street,
paved and flat, saying
it leads somewhere.

I shall take it
but not seriously.
it will lose itself

in courts, piazzas
a haggle
of other streets, will end

in some smoking crater.
I shall take it
as if at my pleasure

as if I could choose
Kirkton Cross
or Ballymet

or Gorton Feus,
with this map in my head
this blood in my shoes.

clach eanchainn

that great stone
the shape of a brain
twisted and left there

out on the moor,
crystals and fire
fisted within it,

often has seen
forests go down
their soil squandered,

seeds blown in
blown out again,
ashes and iron

beneath it surrendered.
it was begun
with the first star

is now a stone
sheltering foxes
out on the moor.

often have men
marched through the dawn
to give it a name.

ALASTAIR MACKIE (b. 1925)

from Back-Green Odyssey

1

ablaze

The sun's oot. I sit, my pipe alunt and puff.
The claes-line's pegged wi washin. They could be
reach and thresh sails. (Let them) Hou they rax and thraw, and yet
drive nothing forward caa naething forrit. Gress growes on my deck.

Thro the wheep-cracks o my sails the blue
wine o the sea is blinkin to the bouwl rim
o the horizon whaur my classic tap
the Berwick Law hides oor nothrin Athens.

Nae watters for an odyssey ye'll think
whaur jist tankers, coasters, seine-netters ply.
Still ablow this blue roof and burst o sun

my mind moves amon islands. Ulysses –
master/moorings rope dominie, I cast aff the tether-tow
backside and steer my boat sittin on my doup-end.

2

The central belt unbuckles on the sands.
The only reek here is the cloods; the croods
waves are swaws that brakkin, skyte quicksiller baas.
The view is bigger nor Glesga toun.

throwing down The air is cowpin pints and nips for free;
than the sun's a bargain, cheaper nor Majorca.
pallid Fowks swap a peely-wally white for broun,
like chips, wi troosers or bikinis on.

They tak a dander oot at nichts, or jig
on the Folly; hing aff the pier for fish;
odds and ends sheet at targets for Hongkong trok. But still

fowk hae a duty to enjoy theirsels.
Aulder nor the thrum o the transistors
thudding   the sea is duntin cymbals to the moon.

3

I saw ye Penelope hingin oot claes;
woman/as if   a lang deem, lookin as gin ye didna
ken ye were lookt at; your brou frouned runkles
and your mou set like a dour horizon

far away   like the times ye tell me I'm hyne awa.
eyes   Then, naething steers me to the stars o your een
simmering   and the silence is hotterin wi the bile
o auld wars (twice as lang as dung doun Troy)

home to   You are the lang island I come hame till
in the beddit dark when I see your een,
intense darkness   the only starns the pit-mirk hisna dowsed.

The herbour crooks its airms. Tethert I lie
at last. I listen. The soond o the sea!
breath   I smell its tides forgaither in your souch.

4

prow   My main deck is a green. Near the foreheid
the kitchen plot. I am weel stockit wi
vittles. On the starboard gunnels, flouers
wrangle   and bushes whaur the birds tulzie and skriech.

I sit here, the captain and the haill crew
sun-scorched
day-dreaming   and keep my sun-birsled watches dwaumin.
scribble   Whiles I scour the sky-line, whiles I scart a line
voyage   in the log-book o my tethert vaigin;

the sea has a blue doze; a raggit skirlin
o bairns rises frae the beach; a sea gull
whines   peenges like a wean and oars air back.

I canna read my Homer in this sun.
I feel the reid meat of my body plot.

a dozing off   My odyssey is jist a doverin.

*

7

stretched out behind   Streekit ahint the winbreak I let

pricks my eyes   Homer drap. The print jobs my een. Instead
                         I watch a sma green-like beastie craalin

snowstorm   owre the blindrift of summer sun on the page,
                     that sang o him blattered by Poseidon

lightning   owre the levin and whirlypeels o the sea.
                     I watch this sudden drappin frae the air on till
                     the hexameters. Whaur was his Ithaca?

earth-shaker   I felt like the yird-shakker himsel then,
non-entity   heich abeen this nochtie o a cratur.
                      I let him streetch his pins a bit. A god

choose   can byde his time and wyle it tae, whit's mair.
itchy   Atween ennui and yokey fingers
sent him flying/then   I skytit him aff the page. Yaawned syne.

ALASTAIR REID (b. 1926)

A Lesson for Beautiful Women

Gazing and gazing in the glass,
she might have noticed slow cotillions pass
and might have seen
a blur of others in the antique green.
Transfixed instead,
she learned the inclinations of her neat small head
and, startling her own surprise,
wondered at the wonder in her jewelled eyes.

Gardens of rainbow and russet might have caught her
but, leaning over goldfish water,
she watched the red carp emphasise her mouth,
saw underneath
the long green weeds lace in
through a transparency of face and skin,
smiled at herself smiling reflectively,
lending a new complexion to the sky.

In service to her beauty
long mornings lengthened to a duty
patiently served before the triple mirror
whose six eyes sent her many a time in terror
to hide in rows of whispering dresses;
but her glass soul her own three goddesses
pursued, and if she turned away,
the same three mouths would breathe 'Obey, obey!'

And in procession, young men princely came,
ambassadors to her cool perfect kingdom.
Set at a distance by their praise,
she watched their unspeaking eyes adore her face.
Inside, her still self waited. Nothing moved.
Finally, by three husbands richly loved
(none of them young), she drifted into death,
the glass clouding with her last moist breath.

Changed into legend, she was given rest;
and, left alone at last,
the small mim servant shuttered in her being
peeped mousily out; and seeing
the imperious mirrors glazed and still,
whimpered forlornly down the dark hall
'Oh, grieve for my body, who would not let me be.
She, not I, was a most beautiful lady.'

Scotland

It was a day peculiar to this piece of the planet,
when larks rose on long thin strings of singing
and the air shifted with the shimmer of actual angels.
Greenness entered the body. The grasses
shivered with presences, and sunlight
stayed like a halo on hair and heather and hills.
Walking into town, I saw, in a radiant raincoat,
the woman from the fish-shop. 'What a day it is!'
cried I, like a sunstruck madman.
And what did she have to say for it?
Her brow grew bleak, her ancestors raged in their

graves

as she spoke with their ancient misery:
'We'll pay for it, we'll pay for it, we'll pay for it!'

Isle of Arran

Where no one was was where my world was stilled
into hills that hung behind the lasting water,
a quiet quilt of heather where bees slept,
and a single slow bird in circles winding
round the axis of my head.

Any wind being only my breath, the weather
stopped, and a woollen cloud smothered the sun.
Rust and a mist hung over the clock of the day.

A mountain dreamed in the light of the dark
and marsh mallows were yellow for ever.

Still as a fish in the secret loch alone
I was held in the water where my feet found ground
and the air where my head ended,
all thought a prisoner of the still sense –
till a butterfly drunkenly began the world.

James Bottle's Year

December finds him
outside, looking skyward.
The year gets a swearword.

His rage is never permanent.
By January he's out,
silent and plough-bent.

All white February,
he's in a fury
of wind-grief and ground-worry.

By March, he's back
scouring the ground for luck,
for rabbit-run and deer-track.

April is all sounds and smiles.
The hill is soft with animals.
His arms describe miles.

The local girls say
he's honeyed and bee-headed
at haytime in May.

In June,
he'll stay up late, he'll moon
and talk to children.

No one sees him in July.
At dawn, he'll ride away
with distance in his eye.

In August, you'd assume
yourself to be almost welcome.
He keeps open time.

But, on one September morning,
you'll see cloud-worries form.
His eyes flash storm warnings.

October is difficult.
He tries to puzzle out
if it's his or the season's fault.

In November, he keeps still
through hail and snowfall,
thinking through it all.

What's causing the odd weather?
Himself, or the capricious air?
Or the two together?

December, breathing hard,
he's back outside, hurling skyward
his same swearword.

Weathering

I am old enough now for a tree
once planted, knee high, to have grown to be
twenty times me,

and to have seen babies marry, and heroes grow deaf —
but that's enough meaning-of-life.
It's living through time we ought to be connoisseurs of.

From wearing a face all this time, I am made aware
of the maps faces are, of the inside wear and tear.
I take to faces that have come far.

In my father's carved face, the bright eye
he sometimes would look out of, seeing a long way
through all the tree-rings of his history.

I am awed by how things weather: an oak mantel
in the house in Spain, fingered to a sheen,
the marks of hands leaned into the lintel,

the tokens in the drawer I sometimes touch —
a crystal lived-in on a trip, the watch
my father's wrist wore to a thin gold sandwich.

It is an equilibrium
which breasts the cresting seasons but still stays calm
and keeps warm. It deserves a good name.

Weathering. Patina, gloss, and whorl.
The trunk of the almond tree, gnarled but still
                                              fruitful.
Weathering is what I would like to do well.

The Academy

I do not think of the academy
in the whirl of days. It does not change. I do.
The place hangs in my past like an engraving.
I went back once to lay a wreath on it,
and met discarded selves I scarcely knew.

It has a lingering aura, leather bindings,
a smell of varnish and formaldehyde,
a certain dusty holiness in the cloisters.
We used to race our horses on the sand
away from it, manes flying, breathing hard.

Trailing to the library of an afternoon,
we saw the ivy crawling underneath
the labyrinthine bars on the window ledges.
I remember the thin librarian's look of hate
as we left book holes in her shelves, like missing
                                              teeth.

On evenings doomed by bells, we felt the sea
creep up, we heard the temperamental gulls
wheeling in clouds about the kneeworn chapel.
They keened on the knifing wind like students souls.
Yet we would dent the stones with our own footfalls.

Students still populate the place, bright starlings,
their notebooks filled with scribbled parrot-answers
to questions they unravel every evening
in lamplit pools of spreading argument.
They slash the air with theory, like fencers.

Where is the small, damp-browed professor now?
Students have pushed him out to sea in a boat
of lecture-notes. Look, he bursts into flame!
How glorious a going for one whose words
had never struck a spark on the whale-road.

And you will find retainers at their posts,
wearing their suits of age, brass buttons, flannel,
patrolling lawns they crop with careful scissors.
They still will be in silver-haired attendance
to draw lines through our entries in the annals.

It is illusion, the academy.
In truth, the ideal talking-place to die.
Only the landscape keeps a sense of growing.
The towers are floating on a shifting sea.
You did not tell the truth there, nor did I.

Think of the process — moments becoming poems
which stiffen into books in the library,
and later, lectures, books about the books,

footnotes and dates, a stone obituary.
Do you wonder that I shun the academy?

It anticipates my dying, turns to stone
too quickly for my taste. It is a language
nobody speaks, refined to ritual:
the precise writing on the blackboard wall,
the drone of requiem in the lecture hall.

I do not think much of the academy
in the drift of days. It does not change. I do.
This poem will occupy the library
but I will not. I have not done with doing.
I did not know the truth there, nor did you.

Translator to Poet

For Pablo Neruda, 1904–1973

There are only the words left now. They lie like
                                        tombstones
or the stone Andes where the green scrub ends.
I do not have the heart to chip away
at your long lists of joy, which alternate
their iron and velvet, all the vegetation
and whalebone of your chosen stormy coast.
So much was written hope, with every line
extending life by saying, every meeting
ending in expectation of the next.
It was your slow intoning voice which counted,
bringing a living Chile into being
where poetry was bread, where books were banquets.
Now they are silent, stony on the shelf.
I cannot read them for the thunderous silence,
the grief of Chile's dying and your own,
death being the one definitive translation.

IAIN CRICHTON SMITH (b. 1928)

The Clearances

The thistles climb the thatch. Forever
this sharp scale in our poems,
as also the waste music of the sea.

The stars shine over Sutherland
in a cold ceilidh of their own,
as, in the morning, the silver cane

cropped among corn. We will remember this.
Though hate is evil we cannot
but hope your courtier's heels in hell

are burning: that to hear
the thatch sizzling in tanged smoke
your hot ears slowly learn.

Highlanders

They sailed away into the coloured prints
of Balaclava, or at tall Quebec
you'll see them climbing almost native rock
in search of French and not of cormorants.

Abroad, they fought the silks and bright coats
while to their homes the prancing dandies came
on horses like Napoleon's, in the calm
(but clouds of snuff) of all their ruined boats,

them high on Nelson's topmasts looking over
a coloured sea at evening coming up
with complex tackle and harmonious rope
from pictured oceans and a roaring fire.

Poem in March

Old cans sparkle. Tie slaps at the chin.
The mind puts on its sword.
This is the country of the daffodil
and the new flannels, radiant and belled.

The drawn cheeks and the spiky knees
are suddenly tulips, roses,
an England and the Low Countries.
A map of shadows passes

out on the sixteenth century sea,
Raleigh to sail and Drake
beyond the monks of eternity
reading a winter book.

The Law and the Grace

It's law they ask of me and not grace.
'Conform,' they say, 'your works are not enough.
Be what we say you should be,' even if
graceful hypocrisy obscures my face.

'We know no angels. If you say you do
that's blasphemy and devilry.' Yet I have
known some bright angels, of spontaneous love.
Should I deny them, be to falsehood true,

the squeeze of law which has invented torture
to bring the grace to a malignant head?
Do you want me, angels, to be wholly dead?
Do you need, black devils, steadfastly to cure

life of itself? And you to stand beside
the stone you set on me? No, I have angels. Mine
are free and perfect. They have no design
on anyone else, but only on my pride,

my insufficiency, imperfect works.
They often leave me but they sometimes come
to judge me to the core, till I am dumb.
Is this not law enough, you patriarchs?

from By the Sea

I

Sitting here by the foreshore day after day
on the Bed and Breakfast routine

I cower in green shelters, watch the sea
bubble in brown sea-pools, watch the sea

climb to the horizon and fall back
rich with its silver coins, its glittering.

Warmly scarfed, I almost remember how
beggars were, and in the thirties men

jumped from the wheel. I lock my will
on the National Health Service, will not fall

too deep for rescue but for the mind, the mind.
Two clouds loom together and are joined

as are two lovers in their nylon wings,
a yellow flutter on cramped bench. Thick rings

of routine save us, rings like marriage rings.
The yachts seem free in their majestic goings

and the great ships at rest. Helmeted girls
emerge from salons with their golden curls.

4

IN THE CAFE

The leaf-fringed fountain
with the grey Scots cherub
arches water
over the waterlogged pennies.

Mouths and moustaches move.
The sad-eyed waitress
hides her unringed hand.
Umbrellas stand at ease.

Outside, rain drips
soupily, 'the soup of the day.'
The sauce bottles are filled with old blood
above the off-white linen.

('Not that I didn't have
suitors', said the Edinburgh lady
seated in the shelter like a queen,
gloved hands on her worn sceptre.)

But the waitress meltingly watches
that white-haired three-year-old,
a huge bubble with wicked teeth,
combing his hair with his knife.

5

Milk jugs, cups,
pastries with pink ice,
menus rotating through one meal.
Most of what we do is refuel
then head for stations, lost in driving rain.

Waitresses with frilly aprons,
I can tell you
how the teeth rot under the pink ice,

and the sky-blue ashtrays contain
a little fire with lipstick, a little fire.

So few are beautiful,
so few outwear the rainy
sag of a dull air, so few ride
naturally as in woodland, the dream
of the eternally cantering proud horses.

Everything drips, drips, drips.
The water, blood, adulterated milk.
The stalls advertise 'Condensed Books'.
All week I have fed on cheap paper
turning like logged swing doors.

10

DUNOON AND THE HOLY LOCH

The huge sea widens from us, mile on mile.
Kenneth MacKellar sings from the domed pier.
A tinker piper plays a ragged tune
on ragged pipes. He tramps under a moon
which rises like the dollar. Think how here

missiles like sugar rocks are all incised
with Alabaman Homer. These defend
the clattering tills, the taxis, thin pale girls
who wear at evening their Woolworth pearls
and from dewed railings gaze at the world's end.

12

IN THE PARK

Over the shoes in pebbles I sit here.
Behind me, the silent bells of those red flowers.
Under that winged structure Greeks might wander,
retired Achilles in the varying shade

drifted from the Home, telling of wars,
and Helen's mouth open like that soft bloom
which turns to the sun softly in the dew
and busy orbit of the striped wasp.

On the smooth lawn a cat pursues a bird,
great Disney fool. The bird looks at him, flies,
lands and flies and this time doesn't stop.
The cat slouches back among the trees.

A lot of marble, messages in flowers –
this is Barnardo's Year – the door is open
to orphans ejected from our Welfare State,
that cosy bubble with few images.

The marble and carnations of Elysium.
Columns of lilies drink at the warm water.
All day the furious sun scans the lawns
and fat loud Ajax's waddling up to bowl.

from The White Air of March

I

This is the land God gave to Andy Stewart –
           we have our inheritance.
There shall be no ardour, there shall be indifference.
There shall not be excellence, there shall be the
                                average.
We shall be the intrepid hunters of golf balls.
Have you not known, have you not heard, has it not
                           been reported
that Mrs Macdonald has given an hour-long lecture
                         on Islay
and at the conclusion was presented with a bouquet
                         of flowers
by Marjory, aged five?
                Have you not noted
the photograph of the whist drive, skeleton hands,

rings on skeleton fingers?
                              Have you not seen
the glossy weddings in the glossy pages,
champagne and a 'shared joke'.
                                    Do you not see
the Music Hall's still alive here in the North? and on
                                        the stage
the yellow gorse is growing.
                    'Tragedy,' said Walpole, 'for those who feel.
For those who think, it's comic.'
                              Pity then those who feel
and, as for the Scottish Soldier, off to the wars!
The Cuillins stand and will forever stand.
Their streams scream in the moonlight.

        2

The Cuillins tower
clear and white.
In the crevices the Gaelic bluebells flower.

(Eastward
Culloden
where the sun shone
on the feeding raven.
Let it be forgotten!)

The Cuillins tower
scale on scale.
The music of the imagination must be restored,
upward.

(The little Highland dancer
in white shirt green kilt
regards her toe
arms akimbo.
Avoids the swords.)

To avoid the sword
is death.
      To walk the ward
of Dettol, loss of will,
where old men watch the wall,
eyes in a black wheel,
and the nurse in a starched dress
changes the air.

The Cuillins tower
tall and white.
March breeds white sails.

The eagle soars.
On the highest peaks
The sharpest axe.

8

The exiles have departed,
               leaving old houses.
The Wind wanders like an old man who has lost his
               mind.
'What do you want?' asks the wind. 'Why are you
               crying?
Are those your tears or the rain?'
I do not know. I touch my cheek. It is wet.
I think it must be the rain.

It is bitter
to be an exile in one's own land.
It is bitter
to walk among strangers
when the strangers are in one's own land.

It is bitter
to dip a pen in continuous water
to write poems of exile
in a verse without honour or style.

Gaelic Stories

Translated from Gaelic by the author

1

A fisherman in wellingtons
and his sweetheart
and his mother.

2

A story
about an old man
and a seal.

3

A woman
reading a Bible for seven years
waiting for a sailor.

4

A melodeon.
A peat stack.
An owl.

5

A croft.
Two brothers.
A plate with potatoes.

6

A girl from Glasgow
wearing a mini
in church.

7

The sea
and a drifter,
the Golden Rose.

8

A man who was in Australia
coming home
on a wedding night.

9

A romance
between cheese
and milk.

10

Glasgow
in a world of nylons
and of neon.

11

Two women
talking
in a black house.

12

A monster
rising from the sea,
'Will you take tea?'

13

A comedy
in a kitchen,
with jerseys.

14

A conversation
between a loaf and
cheese.

15

A conversation
between a wellington
and a herring.

16

A conversation
between fresh butter
and a cup.

17

A conversation
between Yarmouth
and Garrabost.

18

A moon
hard and high
above a marsh.

Shall Gaelic Die?

Translated by the author

1

A picture has no grammar. It has neither evil nor
good. It has only colour, say orange or mauve.
Can Picasso change a minister? Did he make a
sermon to a bull?

Did heaven rise from his brush? Who saw a church
that is orange?
In a world like a picture, a world without language,
would your mind go astray, lost among objects?

2

Advertisements in neon, lighting and going out, 'Shall
it . . . shall it . . . Shall Gaelic . . . shall it . . . shall
Gaelic . . . die?'

3

Words rise out of the country. They are around us. In
every month in the year we are surrounded by words.
Spring has its own dictionary, its leaves are turning in
the sharp wind of March, which opens the shops.
Autumn has its own dictionary, the brown words
lying on the bottom of the loch, asleep for a season.
Winter has its own dictionary, the words are a
blizzard building a tower of Babel. Its grammar is
like snow.
Between the words the wild-cat looks sharply across
a No-Man's-Land, artillery of the Imagination.

4

They built a house with stones. They put windows in
the house, and doors. They filled the room with
furniture and the beards of thistles.
They looked out of the house on a Highland world,
the flowers, the glens, distant Glasgow on fire.
They built a barometer of history.
Inch after inch, they suffered the stings of suffering.
Strangers entered the house, and they left.
But now, who is looking out with an altered gaze?
What does he see?
What has he got in his hands? A string of words.

5

He who loses his language loses his world. The
Highlander who loses his language loses his world.
The space ship that goes astray among planets loses
the world.
In an orange world how would you know orange? In
a world without evil how would you know good?
Wittgenstein is in the middle of his world. He is like
a spider.

sea and wood

The flies come to him. 'Cuan' and 'coill' rising.
When Wittgenstein dies, his world dies.
The thistle bends to the earth. The earth is tired of it.

6

I came with a 'sobhrach' in my mouth. He came with
a 'primrose'.
A 'primrose by the river's brim'. Between the two
languages, the word 'sobhrach' turned to 'primrose'.
Behind the two words, a Roman said 'prima rosa'.
The 'sobhrach' or the 'primrose' was in our hands. Its
reasons belonged to us.

Gaelic Songs

I listen to these songs
from a city studio.
They belong to a different country,
to a barer sky,
to a district of heather and stone.
They belong to the sailors
who kept their course
through nostalgia and moonlight.
They belong to the maidens
who carried the milk in pails
home in the twilight.
They belong to the barking of dogs,
to the midnight of stars,

to the sea's terrible force,
exile past the equator.
They belong to the sparse grass,
to the wrinkled faces,
to the houses sunk in the valleys,
to the mirrors
brought home from the fishing.

Now they are made of crystal
taking just a moment
between two programmes
elbowing them fiercely
between two darknesses.

Christmas 1971

There's no snow this Christmas . . . there was snow
when we received the small horses and small cart,
brothers together all those years ago.
There were small watches made of liquorice
surrealist as time hung over chairs.
I think perhaps that when we left the door
of the white cottage with its fraudulent icing
we were quite fixed as to our different ways.
Someone is waving with black liquorice hands
at the squashed windows as the soundless bells
and the soundless whips lash our dwarf horses
                                        forward.
We diverge at the road-end in the whirling snow
never to meet but singing, pulling gloves
over and over our disappearing hands.

The Glass of Water

My hand is blazing on the cold tumbler.
My eye looks through it to the other side.
If it were what is real, if it were heaven
how I corrupt it with my worn flesh.

How its neutrality is aggrandised
by fever and by empire. I constrain
and grasp this parish which is pastoral.

To be pure is not difficult, it's impossible.
How could the saint work to this poverty,
this unassumingness, this transparency?
How could his levels be so wholly calm?
The fact of water is unteachable.
It's less and more than honour standing up
invulnerable in its vulnerable glass.

How Often I Feel Like You

Ah, you Russians, how often I feel like you
full of ennui, hearing the cry of wolves
on frontiers of green glass.
In the evening
one dreams of white birches and of bears.
There are picnics in bright glades and someone
                                        talking
endlessly of verse as if mowing grass,
endlessly of philosophy round and round
like a red fair with figures of red soldiers
spinning forever at their 'Present Arms'.
How long it takes for a letter to arrive.
Postmen slog heavily over the steppes
and drop their dynamite through the letter-box.
For something is happening everywhere but here.
Here there are Hamlets and old generals.
Everyone sighs and says 'Ekh' and in the stream
a girl is swimming naked among gnats.
This space is far too much for us like time.
Even the clocks have asthma. There is honey,
herring and jam and an old samovar.
Help us, let something happen, even death.
God has forgotten us. We are like fishers
with leather leggings dreaming in a stream.

Chinese Poem

1

To Seumas Macdonald,
                              now resident in Edinburgh –
I am alone here, sacked from the Department
for alcoholic practices and disrespect.
A cold wind blows from Ben Cruachan.
There is nothing here but sheep and large boulders.
Do you remember the nights with *Reliquae Celticae*
and those odd translations by Calder?
Buzzards rest on the wires. There are many seagulls.
My trousers grow used to the dung.
What news from the frontier? Is Donald still
                                                        Colonel?
Are there more pupils than teachers in Scotland?
I send you this by a small boy with a pointed head.
Don't trust him. He is a Campbell.

2

The dog brought your letter today
from the red postbox on the stone gate
two miles away and a bit.
I read it carefully with tears in my eyes.
At night the moon is high over Cladach
and the big mansions of prosperous Englishmen.
I drank a half bottle thinking of Meg
and the involved affairs of Scotland.
When shall we two meet again
in thunder, lightning or in rain?
The carrots and turnips are healthy,
the *Farmers' Weekly* garrulous.
Please send me a *Radio Times* and a book
on cracking codes. I have much sorrow.
Mrs Macleod has a blue lion on her pants.
They make a queenly swish in a high wind.

3

There is a man here who has been building a house
for twenty years and a day.
He has a barrow in which he carries large stones.
He wears a canvas jacket.
I think I am going out of my mind.
When shall I see the city again,
its high towers and insurance offices,
its glare of unprincipled glass?
The hens peck at the grain.
The wind brings me pictures of exiles,
ghosts in tackety boots, lies,
adulteries in cornfields and draughty cottages.
I hear Donald is a brigadier now
and that there is fighting on the frontier.
The newspapers arrive late with strange signs on
them.
I go out and watch the road.

4

Today I read five books.
I watched Macleod weaving a fence
to keep the eagles from his potatoes.
A dull horse is cobwebbed in rain.
When shall our land consider itself safe
from the assurance of the third rate mind?
We lack I think nervous intelligence.
Tell them I shall serve in any capacity,
a field officer, even a private,
so long as I can see the future
through uncracked field glasses.

5

A woman arrived today
in a brown coat and a brown muff.
She says we are losing the war,
that the Emperor's troops are everywhere
in their blue armour and blue gloves.

She says there are men in a stupor
in the ditches among the marigolds
crying 'Alas, alas.'
I refuse to believe her.
She is, I think, an agent provocateur.
She pretends to breed thistles.

from A Life

LEWIS 1928–45

3

Our landmark is the island, complex thing.
A rock, a death, a house in which were made
our narrow global seaward-going wings,
the rings of blue, the cloth both fine and frayed.
It sails within us, as one poet said,
its empty shelves are resonant. A scant
religion drives us to our vague tremens.
We drag it at our heels, as iron chains.
A winsome boyhood among glens and bens
casts, later, double images and shades.
And ceilidhs in the cities are the lens
through which we see ourselves, unmade, remade,
by music and by grief. The island sails
within us and around us. Startled we
see it in Glasgow, hulk of the humming dead,
and of the girls in cornfields disarrayed.

10

Roses, I think there is salt on you,
and on the headland I hear the exiles' songs.

The thatched roofs, woven by dead hands,
are sunk among the superannuated school buses,

in a field of daisies and lush grasses.
The buzzard slants over the untilled ground.

Varying perfumes taunt me. In church I saw
the fifty-year-old girl I used to know,

her face curdled and gaunt. Bibles
are open in the churchyards, marbly white,

and the sea sighs towards the gravestones.
On the moors

the heather is wine-red and the lochs
teem with unhunted fish. The sky

is an eternal blue and God drowses
momently from his justice. Singing,

the drunk sways among poppies, missing
the rusty unused scythe. The boats are

a frieze on the far horizon, smoking gently,
and almost motionless. The cornfields were

a nest of snaky legs: and now it is
the butterfly that wafts there. This is not

a haunt of angels. The devils kneel at night
offering whisky in a bottle to

those who despise church windows in their reds.
Gaunt girl I walked with in the long ago,

sleep gently in the beams of the red moon,
whose claws are crablike in your drained breast.

OBAN 1955–82

        I

Oban in autumn, and reflective Mull
cast on the water. How the snowy gull

pecks at waste herring bones on the scaly quay.
The central glitter of the boundless sea.

Like pots that boil on Sundays, engines find
their drumming destination, and the mind

its fixed direction. By tall cliffs I see
the jackdaws playing. On green benches the

tourists repose at evening, while the tide
whispers and chuckles. O I see you, bride,

Gaelic, mysterious: and this radiance is
the extravagant presence of the sea's abyss

extending to Iona and its graves.
The very stones are green. The sea is sheaves

of endless blue on blue and lucid crowns
of jellyfish drift lazily. No one drowns

in this amazing light. The War Memorial burns.
One soldier helps another through the stone.

2

A Roman rector, measured gravitas,
a Gaelic scholar too. He knows each child.
Our own names honour us and each one salutes

us from his sparkling bicycle. The school hums,
directed engine. Black-winged he comes
along the shiny corridors. In the hall

appointing prefects he quotes from Paul.
The race is to the kind, not to the smart,
to Brutus not to Antony. The clear art

of human Homer is our constant aim:
whatever's comely. Casually he says,
'It was Housman taught me in my Cambridge days.'

And behind him Macintyre and William Ross.
Where's Eliot and Auden? Horace glows,
each marble phrase, the clarity of prose.

'Transposing Greek to Gaelic is no toil.
They had their clans, their sea terms. And the style
of the great *Odyssey* is what Gaelic knows.'

Easily he chats to the crofting man
who sucks a straw: as easily as he scans
those vast hexameters or the pibroch.

                          Does
what's comely and what's right by natural rule,
by Roman cheerfulness and harmonious Greek.
Propounds a human yet a rigorous school.

3

For Donalda

So I come home to you
as the one I didn't leave behind
as the quick diligent
drawer back of curtains,

lest the house should be seen
as too much slept in
when there is so much wind
among the sunlight:

so many rainbows
trembling among news
of the daft old glasses
twinkling together:

so many owls
sucking to their eyes
the moon-struck mice
in the leafy classroom,

and the world a skirt
turning a corner
altering pleat by pleat
its breezy sculpture.

Listen

Listen, I have flown through darkness towards joy,
I have put the mossy stones away from me,
and the thorns, the thistles, the brambles.
I have swum upward like a fish

through the black wet earth, the ancient roots
which insanely fight with each other
in a grave which creates a treasure house
of light upward-springing leaves.

Such joy, such joy! Such airy drama
the clouds compose in the heavens,
such interchange of comedies,
disguises, rhymes, denouements.

I had not believed that the stony heads
would change to actors and actresses,
and that the grooved armour of statues
would rise and walk away

into a resurrection of villages,
townspeople, citizens, dead exiles,
who sing with the salt in their mouths,
winged nightingales of brine.

BURNS SINGER (1928–64)

A Sort of Language

Who, when night nears, would answer for the
                                              patterns
Words will take on? emerging huge, far, shiny,
What unfrequented systems? Or like clouds
Unseen and hiding brightness, bringing rain,
Progressions that the wind drives on, drives after,
Who will say? I who have seen, seen many,
Imagining I scattered them abroad,
Starlight for Calvary and the immense equations
That drew to unity two who knew not either,
As to a hill at midnight, I have seen words,
Seen them with thanks too, shivering, become
Fragile and useless, pale as the steel sparks
Tramcars make waifs of when they round a corner.

Peterhead in May

Small lights pirouette
Among these brisk little boats.
A beam, cool as a butler,
Steps from the lighthouse.

Wheelroom windows are dark.
Reflections of light quickly
Skip over them tipsily like
A girl in silk.

One knows there is new paint
And somehow an intense
Suggestion of ornament
Comes into mind.

Imagine elephants here.
They'd settle, clumsily sure

Of themselves and of us and of four
Square meals and of water.

Then you will have it. This
Though a grey and quiet place
Finds nothing much amiss.
It keeps its stillness.

There is no wind. A thin
Mist fumbles above it and,
Doing its best to be gone,
Obscures the position.

This place is quiet or,
Better, impersonal. There
Now you have it. No verdict
Is asked for, no answer.

Yet nets will lie all morning,
Limp like stage scenery,
Unused but significant
Of something to come.

For Josef Herman

Nothing, nothing, nothing
Can never ever happen
To this man who sits here
Some distance from the river.

His plump and portly hands
Conjure the daylight out
Of the pits' blackness and
Absorb the sun of Spain.

The Hebrides are his,
The ghetto and the city.
His loneliness is such
That children love to share it.

Companionship is his
And wise frivolities.
I wonder, if you could look
Quietly into his eyes

And they laughed as confidently
As the humming wings of flies,
If it would seem to you
That you had never died.

SOS Lifescene

That plunging mast, nailed to a whirligig gale,
Shows its three sheer signs of drowning. Those
                              crewed wet boards
Drag at the spray. Oceans drip backwards and forth
From that tall steel prow, those seamen, crouched
                                        that sail.

Crouched to climb: cling of the white wetnesses.
Heave of the sea's deep sheets, wheezing like twenty
Conferences stacked round tables, pressing
Processions, quarrel of kingdoms: pitch salt centre.

Out of it, down from it, hangs the electric shout,
Nine gooseflesh sparks breathing white out on the
                                        rabble
Of sweaty and swaggering gales. Held hard to the
                                        squabbling
Waters, to Save Our Souls the sounds fade out.

Yet steered, here steered, and over the sea's salt dregs
Set climbing forth, is crewed by the conscious and
                                        steered.
Wheeled in two knotted hands through the callous
                                but prayer-
Breasting, heart-wresting hour, is ruddered with rags.

For the men, backed out to the bone, catch up on the
                                                    past
In a straight line, like winter . . . the trees. Burn back
The barren courses, confront the naked mistake,
The embezzled hours accounted, the fake blot erased.

Talk yourself out of it! Out of it! Talk yourself! Talk!
And a death's click closes those offices foaming with
                                                    grins.
That stoke-black lascar, damp and salt with work,
Looks through a lurch at the red wreck under his
                                                    skin.

That engineer who's thistle-eyed for sleep
Circles the clock through goaded hoops and trances
To where she departs . . . to where she hurries . . .
                                            she dances . . .
The damp cellar and whisky . . . the heart in a
                                                heap . . .

SOS it repeats, repeats, told, retold.
Small white far cry for help as they kindle close
Together or blaze in a curse. For the storm grows
To death for the captain and the boy blown blue by
                                                the cold.

Corked nets and clinging baits, those sodden boards
Muscled about by their men, drag deep at the shoals
And their hooked catchings draw blood. But bite to
                                                the core!
There are nine white pips crying 'help' in a black
                                                bowl.

Seeds of the storm, quick fish, the intense alone
Of their human cry, where the storm bleats down like
                                                a ram
And the waves whinny away; where the smooth sky's
                                                brown
Blacks out, and the stars are dead and don't matter a
                                                damn.

What matters is the cry, the cry like a screw,
Sharp-oiled to turning, clean-cutting fish-silver
                                        through
And through the teak air,
A makeshift repetitive batter to riveting prayer.

Like stitching sails this windfall patches men,
Question to answer, push and heave and tug,
Thick-fibred needlework, an electric plug,
Nine cock-crows savage the air and cry us all home.

ALASTAIR FOWLER (b. 1930)

Catacomb Suburb

Other burial places console more.
Torcello's reeds moan, blur in the wind,
Palliate: its green air steeps
And clarifies marble, immersed apostles merging
With reawakened stone. San Michele's door
Gives on water. Country headstones thrust
Lichen out, art's distracting slips.

But here nothing mitigates or changes.
Not the dull grids of cypress avenues;
Not guide-stops where we chose to queue
For the least alien Dante to underworlds
Down San Callisto's broken steps. Worn,
Sudden steps. Jokes about being found
Lost in the catacombs fixed our jaws.

Below, what waits beneath is not below,
But all about, not to be missed. Our guide
Goes with the torch to find why the power failed.
We are posted in darknesses that I clench
Avoiding others in close-tiered *niches*.
A Giant of cells condemned for miles around,
Crumbled, decayed, will bring conviction in,

At last. Lights and friends are nothing now.
Numbers have no safety in them, even,
In this close corridor, odd slice
Of tufa cake. I used to think the name
'Fly cemeteries' meant they both were black.
But five tiers of graves, a hundred miles,
Is what can swallow thought. *In pace; in pace;*

In pace; in pace; mansionem in pace.
Everywhere the signs of believers,
Who came here, first of dying men,

Against the law, all law and fear, to live.
Not to hide, rather set out in witness
These adverse cases. They laid out quite openly
That Severa lived nine days eleven hours.

Yet here resolve enlarges beyond surprise.
I think of working powers: fathers of later
Unsepulchral cities trying claims
Of love and space: housing priorities raised
With the dead. 'My dear Crome, as to your last,
We must make common cause in finding ways
Through time's mansions to keep the loved in phase.'

Relative

No Rembrandt's mother's face,
It changed in its possession.
I didn't want to sit in her dark, hated
Going to hear the blurring cataract
And see the same stories told again.
But the last times of all
She was too home-trained to blame neglect.
Gentled. She had a migratory look,
All steep eyes and fine glass bone.
Her knuckle tugged and clung to make quite sure:
Tell me I'm not to die.
(The old promise to stay young was broken.)
If you'd seen you would have wanted to keep her
                                        going
In spite of age: age that I might have kept
Coming some time more slowly. She was lucid,
                                        though.
To think that that could disconcert.
The senses fade and seem to leave quiet;
So that we feel relief when the fluttering stops.
Then a flame I thought was out blazed up
Again, like the bedroom fire she used to light
To make the harmless shadows, when I was ill.
Tell me I'm not to die.

Oh she is wonderful, they said, considering.
Only considering; not remembering, like me
(But unlike her), her former judgement. Have parts
Of all living been mislaid as far?
Knowing less of herself she similarly clung
To sameness. Her mind remained.
Then something much more fugitive would stray
Along old bridle-paths long overgrown,
Until the words were lost, and then their sound;
Even the stories. Visits anthologized
Only the most familiar recensions.
In longer episodes I might have told her
Apart from the tale. Tell me I still may.

GEORGE MACBETH (1932–92)

An Ode to English Food

O English Food! How I adore looking forward
to you, Scotch trifle at the North British Hotel,
Princes Street, Edinburgh. Yes, it is good, very good,
the best in Scotland.

Once I ate a large helping at your sister
establishment, the Carlton Hotel on Waverley Bridge
overlooking the cemetery on Carlton Hill. It was rich,
very rich and pleasant. O, duck, though,

roast, succulent duck of the Barque and Bite,
served with orange sauce, mouth-meltingly delicious!
You I salute. Fresh, tender and unbelievable English
duck. Such

luscious morsels of you! Heap high the
groaning platter with pink fillets, sucking pig and
thick gammon, celestial chef. Be generous with the
crackling. Let your hand slip with the gravy trough,
dispensing plenty. Yes, gravy, I give you your due,
too. O savoury and delightsome gravy, toothsome
over

the white soft backs of my English potatoes,
fragrant with steam. Brave King Edwards, rough-
backed in your dry scrubbed excellence, or with
butter, salty. Sweet

potatoes! Dear new knobbly ones, beside the
oiled sides of meaty carrots. Yes, carrots. Even you,
dumplings,

with indigestible honey, treacle-streaky things.
You tongue-burners. You stodgy darlings. Tumbled
out of the Marks and Spencer's tin or Mr Kipling

silver paper wrapper, warm and ready except in
summer. Cold strawberry sauce, cream and
raspberries. O sour gooseberry pie, dissemble
nothing, squeezed essence

of good juice. Joy in lieu of jelly at children's
parties, cow-heel that gives the horn a man seeing my
twelve-year-old buttocks oiled in hospital by a nurse
assured me, dirty

old bugger. I eat my six chosen slices of bread,
well buttered, remembering you and your successor
the tramp who stole a book for me. Cracked

coffee cup of the lucky day, betokening
mother-love, nostalgic. Fill with Nescafé and milk for
me. It is all great, sick-making allure of old food,
sentiment of the belly. I fill with aniseed's

parboiled scagliola, porphyry of the balls.
With, O with, licorice, thin straws of it in sherbert,
sucked up, nose-bursting explosives of white
powders! Yes,

montage of pre-European Turkish delights
obtained under the counter in wartime, or during
periods of crisis, and

O the English sickness of it. Food, I adore you.
Pink-faced and randy! Come to me, mutton chops.
Whiskers of raw chicken-bones, wishes

and plastic cups. Unpourable Tizer. Take me
before I salivate. I require your exotic fineness, taste

of the English people, sweep me off my feet
into whiteness, a new experience. With beer. And
with blue twists of salt in the chip packets. Grease of
newspaper. Vinegar of the winter nights holding
hands in lanes after *The Way to the Stars*. It

is all there. Such past and reticence! O such
untranslatable grief and growing pains of the delicate
halibut. The heavy cod, solid as gumboots. And the
wet haddock, North Sea lumber of a long Tuesday's
lunch. Fish and sauce. Nibbles and nutshells. Gulps
of draught ale, Guinness or cider made with steaks.
English food, you are all we have. Long may you
reign!

The Renewal

The need to find a place always returns.
In Richmond, where my eighteenth-century bricks
Fashioned an avenue to stable skin,

I built a proper house. At Holland Park,
That fleece and leather took their comfort from,
I tried another, in another way.

Both worked. And what the simple martyrdom
Of wanting some position broke for sticks,
And set in place, held back the creeping dark.

I turned there, in my darkness, on my beds.
In tiny rooms, alone, and with my wives,
Or girls who passed for wives. And all my burns

From being lonely, and unsatisfied,
Flared in the silence, like a sheen from tin.
I waited, and, while waiting, something died.

Then, in the heat of Norfolk, I found you.
You brought the sun, through darkness, to my hives,
The bolted iron to my crumbling sheds,

You changed the whole world's shape. Your power
                                        grew,
And I, in feeling that, wanted some place
More generous for it than those gentle homes.

I needed somewhere with a flirt of grace
To match your fervour for long acreage.
I found it, here at Oby. Naked space

Over the cornfields, and the next-door farm,
Contracts to an oasis with great trees
That north-east winds can ravage in their rage

And leave still rooted and serene. In these
I feel the sweep of beech-wood, like an arm,
And something deeper, in our copper beech.

That brings a birthright in its massive reach,
A sense of giant time. Seeing it blaze
In widespread feathering, I feel the past,

The creak of longships on the Caister shore,
The swing of mills beside the easy broads,
And something closer, groping slow, at last,

The pleasant rectors, knocking croquet balls.
I take their heritage, and what it pays,
And vow today to make its profits pour

Through founded channels, in my well-kept grounds,
As growth, and preservation. Nothing falls
Or sings, in this wide garden, but its sounds

Calm me, and make our full liaison rich.
So my dream-Scotland grief was noble in
Will drag its graves beneath these grounded urns,

And stake its base in watered Norfolk clay,
And Kinburn be reborn, as what it was,
And my grandfather, and our Springer bitch,

Both live, in their own way, and like it here,
And feel the rain and sunlight on their skin,
And no one tell apart, which one is which,

The dream of former grandeur, and the firm
Everyday presence of our daily lives.
This is my hope, and what these lines affirm.

Draft for an Ancestor

When I was young, and wrote about him first,
My Uncle Hugh was easier to hold.
        Now, in my age, at worst
    I take him by some outer fold
Of what was his. His Humber, by the door.
    That, at the least, if nothing more

Creates an image of his prosperous time
And thumbs in waistcoats to suggest their power.
        I hear tall glasses chime
    And clocks from walnut sound the hour
As they drive to Derby, where their horse will lose.
    At last, it seems, men have to choose

What traits in relatives they will to raise
To the height of models, awkward, fey, or strong,
        And there arrange as praise
    For the unhooked soul, keen to belong
To its family, some tree of love and grace
    In which there blossoms no mean face.

I feel this drive. As years go by, it grows
And I want an ancestry of heroic mould
        Fit for a world that knows
    How to accept the subtly bold
Who grasp at shields and leaves with a sprig of wit
    And honours their effrontery with it.

So Uncle Hugh, that self-made, stubborn man
I see in photographs, and hear in my head,
Provides a flash of élan
To the ranks of my more sombre dead
And, startling, floods their quarters with his brash
And flighty Scottish kind of dash.

ALASDAIR GRAY (b. 1934)

Awakening

I woke to find pain laid on a bare bed with me,
so near, his head, cut in pale stone, was my head,
his brain my brain,
and I could not resign my thoughts to that proximity.
He was so close a company he felt like loneliness.

I tried at length to know a door to make him leave
                                                    by,
                    a bribe to make him go,
but oh my dear, he grins
from everywhere I look, at everything I do.
I meet his image where I once met you.
He feeds at every meal, beckons down every street
and yet could not withstand
one pressure of your hand.

Come back to me soon. I am changing without you.
My mind turns cold and luminous like a moon.
Keys, coins, receipts accumulate in my pockets.
I grow calm and brutal on beer and thick meat.

CHRISTOPHER SALVESEN (b. 1935)

Ninian Winyet*

Ninian am I? Why, this is none of I . . .
My little dog is barking. What door is this,
Which gates have I gone through? Rain and the dark
Have soaked me – searched me, drawn me out and
                         home:
    Linlithgow my kindly town, where I taught
And, teaching, learnt to fasten in my mind
The restless gulls, the wildfowl on the loch.
Passand to the sea, when I tuik that name –

builder   The bringer – biggar of a bricht white cell –
Lytle I thocht on the onset and meaning
Of *nox*, my self to be banissit, deth
In a strangearis land. Luik, in yonder manger –

halls   Yule was aye the feast: the haas nou are bare,
The wintry fields excludit fra the warmth,
The palace, the haly palace, subvertit
To a stabil, levelling a fause wey out.

bones dashed violently   They cry it 'casting doun' – banes wappit furth
Of their sepulture, fruit-trees pluckit up
By the ruits, altars and images smashed
To the singing of psalms. Whattin a Scotland

much too close   Survives? Ower-near was it to the groves
hissing   Of Baal, bizzand in the beautie of summer –
Paradise lives its past thir present dayis.

gates   I knaw about yettis – expellit, shot out
from teaching
on to be a soldier caught
in the fight   Fra teching schule; on til a soldier, catcht
In the fecht: 'Och for mair papir or pennyis':
Exiled, wryting *in Germania res Scoticas*,
Orisons, epistilis, in Latin tongue.
Our auld plain Scottis, with Sotheron unacquaint,
Maks speech in me and music still fra hame –

locked   But aa for nocht, thae yettis are steikit fast.

*Ninian Winzet (or Winyet, as it would have been pronounced) wrote and spoke against John Knox and the Reformation in Scotland. He was appointed Abbot of the Benedictine Monastery of St James (a twelfth-century Scottish foundation) in Ratisbon (Regensburg) in 1577. He died 21 September 1592, aged 75. C.S.

away from my beginning
to a narrow street where

Driven furth of my setting-out, I carry
Back to a wynd whaur there's nae gaun back. *Janua*
Mordax, the door whaur the dog is chained, turns me
Awa to my business, with inward bite.
Banisht, dimmed – but furth of Europe, nae: nor
Furth of my unhurried citie, Hierusalem.
The pilgrims pass as years back once they did;
Voices lodge in cloisters their fathers founded,
Ruins I minister to and restore.
Others remain like rookeries, ancient, disbanded:
'The sure way to banish the rooks, pull down their
                                    nests' –
Those bundles of sticks, those notes in the living
                                 branches.

They will bury me here, a Scot; the gates
Of the motherland open through the night.
When I win back home to the glinting loch
My nation works abroad – who says I'm allowed it,
Dreams of ruin to come, rats' bones, a town in rain.

History of Strathclyde

How earth was made, I might have had it sung,
How life began – hushed rocking of the tide
Lapping the sleepy margins of the world.

But – searching back into almost unsearchable
Time (and yet, the waters have always stirred) –
Footprints tell a different order of fact:
Three-toed, Batrachian, printed in the rocks,
In the flaggy sandstone of Euchan Water
In the upper reaches of Nithsdale – early
Exploratory steps as the moment passed;
Petrified, along with suncracks and ripples,
Like those of any casual hen or dog
On a wet concrete path – the same sun shone.

Ah but the earth, this grassy land, has changed.
These pitted marks I long to think are raindrops

More properly interpreted as sea-spray:
No fossil bones or plants remain to help us
But – carcasses and all organic debris
Devoured by scavengers and scouring tides –
It was a coast, the glaring salty shore
Where bushy banks run now and the rowans sway.

A kingdom in the history of man,
A Dark Age kingdom and in that well named –
So little known of family and fighting,
Thus easily guessed at but so hard to grasp –
It was a border, and a middle ground,
As the power of Rome withdrew: other tides,
Less tied to the moon's control, carried on
The moves of life, washed over them as well.

Today in the bright afternoon I saw,
As I walked a drove-road towards the north,
The black-faced ewes cropping the heathery hills,
One, by the track, seeming asleep: except –
A neat dark-red pit in the bony face –
The crows had pecked its eyes out: for a moment,
As the sun went on with its mindless work,
In that wool hulk, a history of Strathclyde.

Among the Goths

Who *is* there to listen, who hears me? The wind
                                                while I walk
On the shore blows steadily colder, the cloud
All-covering shifts in itself, a white
Inhospitable sky, the sea – how I hate
The sea: if it tells me of rhythm, the beginning of life,
With equal insistence it tells me of no return,
Of the daytime of life unadapted to the unlit depths.
And yet, when I look to the dusty freezing plain
The lack of escape is what chills me even more.
Somewhere in summer on quiet days I can hear,
Enrolled in the landmass, music, an inland voice:

Theodora is dozing, the corn gathers the sun;
The cattle are sleek, the smell of the farm is health,
The bees are at work, later the village will dance.
Will I get there ever? What could a visitor give?
Confined to this strand I can wait for community,
                                                    wait
Just as well for the wings to carry me, soaring, alone,
To words of the upper air and the traveller's view.
How far that Forest, its Gothic cold how far
From blooming like the Golden world: and yet –
                                              where else?
That imperial island – remembered there: will it root,
Be held, my laurel buried, by this Pontic shore?
Illyrian, a castle – Princess, allow me place
By the swarming waves alone, all winter long
A prisoner of elegy, work, the denial of home:
But granted nevertheless unfettered time,
No terminus to strain for, nor any need
Save singing, spelling out the syllables of exile and
                                                    love.
Withdrawn, that dream: returned to barbarity, wild
Wind-cropped grass, where I dwell on my words and
                                                    fate,
Where I lie in longing, examined with diffident stare,
Approached with gifts and rough unmanageable
                                                  tongue.
I feel the frontier pressing towards an end –
A stone could be planted, those miles from the city's
                                                  heart;
But the land goes on, over the brackish lake,
To where mountains mass, and the clouds, and the
                                              blue beyond
Shows through: not understood, and captive, on the
                                                  edge,
Though I never get back, there is more to come, there
                                              is room.

KENNETH WHITE (b. 1936)

The House at the Head of the Tide

Five miles out of town
you come to a place called
the White Field

two wings and a whiteness
(ideogram for 'perseverance')

moorland, a rocky coast
and a hundred islands
the sea often green, gurly green
but every now and then
a sharp, breath-catching blue
with always breakers

peace, peace in the breakers

a place, this, of darkness and of light
darknesses and lights
in quick succession
the sun reveals, cloud conceals
and always a music
of wind on moor, tide on shore
and a silence

a fifth quartet

'we must be still
and still moving
for a further union
a deeper communion
through the dark cold
and the empty desolation
the wave cry, the wind cry
the vast waters
of the petrel and the porpoise'

a country lane lined with gorse
this house of stone
lined with a thousand books
that speak of ideas, islands
according to an order
as yet only dimly apprehended
vaguely sensed

chaoticism

where are we?
where are we going?
one who has thought his way
through the thicket
says it is a question of
moving into a new place
a clearing
we speak here in terms of
atlantica
a breathing and a breadth

pelagian space:
what was left out and behind
when the roads were built
and the codes of command
crammed into the mind
what was left out
becoming more and more
faintly articulate

still there in the gull cry
the wave clash
those darknesses, those lights
(but who hears? who sees?
who can say?)

another mindscape

moving out then
into the landscape

walking
in the white of the morning

walking and watching
listening

yellow flowers
tossing in the wind
a crow on a branch
caw-cawing
the rivulet
reflecting the sky
in blue-grey ripples
white beach, wrack
the high gait and snootiness
of oyster-catchers
a blue crab groping in a pool
bright shell

the notes accumulate

towards a writing
that has more in view
than the art of making verse
out of blunt generalities
and personal complaining

atlantic archipelago
and a sense of something
to be gathered in

the mind gropes
like a blue crab in a pool
tosses in the wind
reflects the sky in ripples
flies high
leaves signs in the sand
lies recklessly strewn
at the edge of the tide

comes back to the books
the many manuscripts

scriptorium
in candida casa
altus prosator

binoculars focused also
on the red-roofed
abandoned sardine-factory
at the tip of the promontory –
some kind of homology

a place to work from
(to work it all out)
a place in which to
house a strangeness

this strange activity
(philosophy? poetry?
practice? theory?)

from an accumulation of data
to the plural poem

beyond the generality

from Late August on the Coast

A SHORT INTRODUCTION TO WHITE POETICS

Consider first the Canada Goose
brown body, whitish breast
black head, long black neck
with a white patch from throat to cheek
bill and legs black
flies in regular chevron or line formation
flight note: *aa-honk*
(that's the one old Walt heard on Long Island)

Then there's the Barnacle Goose
black and white plumage
white face and forehead
(in German, it's *Weisswangengans*)
flight in close ragged packs
flight note
a rapidly repeated *gnuk:*
gnuk gnuk gnuk gnuk gnuk gnuk gnuk
(like an ecstatic Eskimo)

Look now at the Brent Goose
small and dark
black head, neck and breast
brillant white arse
more sea-going than other geese
feeds along the coast
by day or by night
rapid flight
seldom in formation
irregularly changing flocks
her cry:
a soft, throaty gut-bucket *rronk*

The Red-Breasted Goose
has a combination of
black, white and chestnut plumage
legs and bill blackish
quick and agile, this beauty
seldom flies in regular formation
cry:
a shrill *kee-kwa kee-kwa*
(who, what? who, what?)

The Greylag
pale grey forewings
thick orange bill
lives near the coastline
flies to grazing grounds at dawn
usually in regular formation
cry: *aahng ung-ung*

(like a Chinese poet
exiled in Mongolia)

As to the Bean Goose
she has a dark forewing
and a long black bill
talks a lot less than other geese
just a low, rich, laconic *ung-unk*

The Snow Goose
has a pure white plumage
with blacktipped wings
dark pink bill and legs
(in North America turns blue
a dusky blue-grey)
in Europe you might take her for a swan
or maybe a gannet
till she lets you know abruptly
with one harsh *kaank*
she's all goose

so
there they go
through the wind, the rain, the snow

wild spirits
knowing what they know

STEWART CONN (b. 1936)

Todd

My father's white uncle became
  Arthritic and testamental in
  Lyrical stages. He held cardinal sin
Was misuse of horses, then any game

Won on the sabbath. A Clydesdale
  To him was not bells and sugar or declension
  From paddock, but primal extension
Of rock and soil. Thundered nail

Turned to sacred bolt. And each night
  In the stable he would slaver and slave
  At cracked hooves, or else save
Bowls of porridge for just the right

Beast. I remember I lied
  To him once, about oats: then I felt
  The brand of his loving tongue, the belt
Of his own horsey breath. But he died,

When the mechanised tractor came to pass.
  Now I think of him neighing to some saint
  In a simple heaven or, beyond complaint,
Leaning across a fence and munching grass.

On Craigie Hill

The farmhouse seems centuries ago,
The steadings slouched under a sifting of snow
For weeks on end, lamps hissing, logs stacked
Like drums in the shed, the ice having to be cracked
To let the shaggy cats drink. Or
Back from the mart through steaming pastures
Men would come riding – their best

Boots gleaming, rough tweeds pressed
To a knife-edge, pockets stuffed with notes.

Before that even, I could visualise (from coloured
Prints) traps rattling, wheels spinning; furred
Figures posing like sepia dolls
In a waxen world of weddings and funerals.
When Todd died, last of the old-stagers,
Friends of seventy years followed the hearse.
Soon the farm went out of the family; the Cochranes
Going to earth or, like their cousins,
Deciding it was time to hit town.

The last link broken, the farm-buildings stand
In a clutter below the quarry. The land
Retains its richness – but in other hands.
Kilmarnock has encroached. It is hard to look
Back with any sense of belonging.
Too much has changed, is still changing.
This blustery afternoon on Craigie Hill
I regard remotely the muddy track
My father used to trudge along, to school.

The Yard

The yard is littered with scrap, with axles
And tyres, buckled hoops and springs, all rusting.
The wreckage of cars that have been dumped.

The hut is still there. In the doorway
Two men talk horses – but not as he did
In the days when the Clydesdales came

To be shod, the milk-wagons for repair.
The din of iron on iron brings it all back:
Rob beating the anvil, to a blue flame.

The beast straining, the bit biting in,
Horn burning, the sour tang of iron,
The sizzling, the perfect fit of the shoe.

In his mind's eye, the whole yard is teeming
With horses, ducking blackthorn, tails
Swishing, the gates behind them clanging . . .

The men have started to strip an old van.
In passing he takes a kick at the wing. No one
Notices. The dead metal does not ring at all.

Summer Afternoon

She spends the afternoon in a deckchair,
Not moving, a handkerchief over
Her head. From the end of the garden
Her eyes look gouged. The children stare,
Then return to their game. She used to take
Them on country walks, or swimming in the lake.
These days are gone, and will not come again.

Dazzling slats of sunlight on the lawn
Make her seem so vulnerable; her bombazine
Costume fading with each drifting beam.
As the children squall, she imagines
Other generations: Is that you, Tom,
Or Ian, is it? – forgetting one was blown
To bits at Ypres, the other on the Somme.

Momentarily in pain, she tightens
Her lips into something like a grin.
There comes the first rustle of rain.
Carrying her in, you avoid my eye
For fear of interception, as who should say
Shall we, nearing extremity,
Be equal objects of distaste and pity?

Yet desperate in the meantime to forbear
For the sake of the love this poor
Creature bore us, who was once so dear.

To My Father

One of my earliest memories (remember
Those Capone hats, the polka-dot ties)
Is of the late thirties: posing
With yourself and grandfather before
The park railings; me dribbling
Ice cream, you so spick and smiling
The congregation never imagined
How little you made. Three generations,
In the palm of a hand. A year later
Grandfather died. War was declared.

In '42 we motored to Kilmarnock
In Alec Martin's Terraplane Hudson.
We found a pond, and six goldfish
Blurred under ice. They survived
That winter, but a gull got them in the end.
Each year we picnicked on the lawn;
Mother crooking her finger
As she sipped her lime. When
They carried you out on a stretcher
She knew you'd never preach again.

Since you retired, we've seen more
Of each other. Yet I spend this forenoon
Typing, to bring you closer – when
We could have been together. Part of what
I dread is that clear mind nodding
Before its flickering screen. If we come over
Tonight, there will be the added irony
Of proving my visit isn't out of duty
When, to myself, I doubt the dignity
Of a love comprising so much guilt and pity.

Under the Ice

Like Coleridge, I waltz
on ice. And watch my shadow
on the water below. Knowing that
if the ice were not there
I'd drown. Half willing it.

In my cord jacket
and neat cravat, I keep
returning to the one spot.
How long, to cut
a perfect circle out?

Something in me
rejects the notion.
The arc is never complete.
My figures-of-eight
almost, not quite, meet.

Was Raeburn's skating parson
a man of God, poised
impeccably on the brink;
or his bland stare
no more than a decorous front?

If I could keep my cool
like that. Gazing straight ahead,
not at my feet. Giving
no sign of knowing
how deep the water, how thin the ice.

Behind that, the other
question: whether the real you
pirouettes in space,
or beckons from under the ice
for me to come through.

WILLIAM MCILVANNEY (b. 1936)

Bless This House

A sampler for Glasgow bedsits

Bless this house, wherever it is,
This house and this and this and this

Pitched shaky as small nomad tents
Within Victorian permanence,

Where no names stay long, no families meet
In Observatory Road and Clouston Street

Where Harry and Sally who want to be 'free'
And Morag who works in the BBC

And Andy the Artist and Mhairi and Fran
(Whose father will never understand)

And John from Kilmarnock and Jean from the Isles
And Michael who jogs every day for miles

And Elspeth are passing through this year:
Bless them the short time they are here.

Bless the cup left for a month or more
On the dust of the window-ledge, the door

That won't quite shut, the broken fan,
The snowscape of fat in the frying pan.

Bless each burnt chop, each unseen smile
That they may nourish their hopes a while.

Bless the persistence of their faith,
The gentle incense of their breath.

Bless the wild dreams that are seeded here,
The lover to come, the amazing career.

Bless such small truths as they may find
By the lonely night-light of the mind.

Bless these who camp out in the loss of the past
And scavenge their own from what others have lost,

Who have courage to reach for what they cannot see
And have gambled what was for what may never be.

So turn up the hi-fi, Michael and John.
What is to come may be already gone.

And pull up the covers, Jean and Mhairi.
The island is far and you've missed the ferry.

The Song Mickey Heard at the Bottom of his Pint in the Zodiac Bar

I am the man whose back you see
In any crowded bar.
The future never reaches me
Though they say it isn't far.

The mirror stores my quiet smiles,
The pillow hoards my sighs.
Nations have watched for centuries
And never seen my eyes.

Who baked the bread in Babylon?
Who swept the streets in Rome?
Who held the reins that held the horse
That brought the great men home?

Passing Through Petra

Places persist, time stays
Beyond the uses of itself,
The small insistent residue,
Ubiquity in nowhere,
Buttercup pollen on our shoes as children.

The wall the sunlight softened for no reason.
The room in sudden stasis,
The body-moulded jacket on a chair,
The heel of bread, a table and some dust.
The Maltese girl,
The way a hand touched forehead,
Half-lost face.

And this not for regretting
Nor forcibly retained. But just admitted.
An intractable,
A part of us beyond our purposes.

Places we have to go, need things to do,
Arrive, it seems, past our own destinations.

Always in each of us
The part that stays
Where nothing has a use beyond endurance,
Becalmed in ancient sunlight of our own,
Touching a braille of stone, sunk just in being,
Flowering in old clefts of our lives,
Passing through Petra.

ROBIN FULTON (b. 1937)

Remembering an Island

'Island
what shall I say of you, your peat-bogs,
your lochs, your moors and berries?' Strange words
to remember on a Stockholm street-crossing – it's like
a dream where you find a door in a solid wall.

North-east, east and south-east
a top-heavy pile of thunderclouds,
west over Kungsholmen a glassy fire:
between, the city is a Dutch masterpiece,
still-life with evening traffic-flow.

And not a dream. I know where the walls end
and begin again. I touch doors on time.
The highland roads in my mind have been
                                        redeveloped –
a few old curves still visible, like
the creases in my birth-certificate from the thirties.

Travelling Alone

The countless forests we pass hour after hour,
they are anonymous with such grace.
Would we feel safer
if all the dead came back and stood waiting?

The north train and the south train pass.
Sitting in one I see myself in the other.
Without much grace
I keep crossing my own invisible path.

A film suddenly stopping in a crowd-scene:
black holes in space, where the people were.
Each has stepped into
the outer darkness of his own company.

Museums and Journeys

An exhibition: a hundred years of Edinburgh life.
Coming out I move as heavily as a diver
on the ocean floor: one step, one breath
against the weight of the invisible dead. So many
yet the air is clear. And they've no time for me,
their view of the future blocked by giant headlines.

A journey: one I didn't want to take but took
shutting my eyes – a child again hoping the needle
wouldn't hurt. Lakes and forests, lakes and forests
pass with the weightless ease of delirium. So many.
My view of the past stays clear but hard to read
like a radio-map of a secret corner in the night sky.

Museums and journeys. We meet as strangers do
at the end of long ellipses over continents.
We exchange histories. Our view of the present is
                                              clear
but the landscapes go on sliding past. So many
memories, I try to say 'One at a time!'
They keep piling up like urgent unanswered letters.

Stopping by Shadows

High up, birches have a homely aspect,
small, like things we discover and recognise,
returning after an absence of many years.
Closer, they're almost transparent in the snow
and above, boulders big as cathedrals poise
– on the edge since prehistory.

Midday. I stop at the edge of the shadow
that has filled this space all winter,
the sun a white breath at the cliff-top,
a brief flame in the ice of a remote tree.
I turn and watch my own shadow dissolving
slowly in the luminous dark air

then take a cold step back to life,
skis hiss-hiss on snow-crystals
that spent all night quietly hardening.
Across the valley red and yellow figures
on a brilliant field jump into focus
like true events under a microscope.

Resolutions

All day the air got harder and harder.
I woke in the small hours, rooftops

frozen seas of tranquillity, while far
below the first flakes fell on the street.

The air of another planet come down to earth,
we breathe harshly between familiar stones.

No place for flesh. Spirit and bone
at odds, the nerves caught between, singing:

'Must it be?' It must be must be must be
bouncing like a ball in a small room without
                                        windows.

Remembering Walls

I once wanted these walls
to turn magically clear
as air and let me walk through.

Now that strangers have moved in
strange furniture I want
the house stone-solid and dour,

resisting the dank strath winds
and to the dry pine-descant
adding a worn ground-bass

angular, melancholy.
It follows me from winter to
winter. Safe in its lulls

voices that cannot last long,
that did not always please me,
will last as long as I shall.

No one watches the wet slates
dry and glisten again and dry.
My private music remembers me.

D. M. BLACK (b. 1941)

From the Privy Council

Delicacy was never enormously
My style. All my favourite girls
Walked at five miles an hour or ate haggis,
Or swam like punts. I myself,
Though not of primeval clumsiness, would often
Crack tumblers in my attention to their content
Or bruise with my embrace some tittering nymph.
It was accidental only – I have little
Sadistic enthusiasm – yet when the time came
And they sent me to the Consultant on Careers,
Executioner was the immediate decision.
My nature is a quiet, conforming thing,
I like to be advised, and am not arrogant:
I agreed:
They stripped me of my suit, shored off my hair
And shaved a gleaming scalp onto my skull;
Clad me in fitting hides,
Hid my poignant features with a black mask,
And led me the very first day to the public platform.
I had to assist only: the carriage of carcasses
Is a heavy job, and not for a spent headsman.
Later they let me handle the small hatchet
For cutting off hands and so forth – what is called
hackwork
Merely; but I earned the prize for proficiency
And the end of my first year brought total
promotion:
Hangman and headsman for the metropolitan burgh
Of Aberfinley. I had a black band
Printed on all my note-paper. Every morning
I hectored my hatchetmen into a spruce turn-out,
Insisted on a keen edge to all their axes.
My jurisdiction spilled
Over the county border – half Scotland's assassins
Dragged their victims into the benign realm

Where I held sway;
And the trade was gripped in the rigours of
                                        unemployment
Outside my scope. There was one solution:
The London parliament passed an urgent Act
Creating a new sinecure: Hangman
And headsman in the Royal Chamber – the post
To be of Cabinet rank, and in the Privy Council.
How many lepers and foundling-hospitals
Have cause to bless me now! On the Privy Council
My stately head is much admired, and the opulent
                                        grace
With which I swing my kindly turnip watch.
And here you will find the origin of the tired joke
About passing from executive to admin.

Kew Gardens

In memory of Ian A. Black, died January 1971

Distinguished scientist, to whom I greatly defer
(old man, moreover, whom I dearly love),
I walk today in Kew Gardens, in sunlight the colour
                                        of honey
which flows from the cold autumnal blue of the
                        heavens to light these tans and golds,
these ripe corn and leather and sunset colours of the
                                        East Asian liriodendrons,
of the beeches and maples and plum-trees and the
                        stubborn green banks of the holly hedges –
and you walk always beside me, you with your
                                        knowledge of names
and your clairvoyant gaze, in what for me is sheer
                                        panorama
seeing the net or web of connectedness. But today it
                                        is I who speak
(and you are long dead, but it is to you I say it):

'The leaves are green in summer because of
                                        chlorophyll

and the flowers are bright to lure the pollinators,
and without remainder (so you have often told me)
these marvellous things that shock the heart the head
                                    can account for;
but I want to sing an excess which is not so simply
                                    explainable,
to say that the beauty of the autumn is a redundant
                                    beauty,
that the sky had no need to be this particular shade
                                    of blue,
nor the maple to die in flames of this particular
                                    yellow,
nor the heart to respond with an ecstasy that does
                                    not beget children.
I want to say that I do not believe your science
although I believe every word of it, and intend to
                                    understand it
that although I rate that unwavering gaze higher than
                                    almost everything
there is another sense, a hearing, to which I more
                                    deeply attend.
Thus I withstand and contradict you, I, your child,
who have inherited from you the passion which
                                    causes me to oppose you.'

AONGHAS MACNEACAIL (b. 1942)

dol dhachaigh – 2

seall na geòidh
a' siubhal 's
na gobhlain-gaoithe

's fhad' o dh'fhalbh a' chuthag

seall na duilleagan dearg ag
éirigh air
sgiath sgairt-ghaoith
ag éirigh 's a' siubhal

tha'm bradan sgrìob mhór a-mach
air a shlighe

ghrian a' dol 'na sìneadh
ghealach ag éirigh
        'nam parabolathan caochlaideach eòlach

samhradh a' siubhal
foghar air a dhruim
        cleòc mór a' sgaoileadh as a dhéidh

null 's a-nall air cala
        fògarrach a-null 's a-nall
null 's a-nall
        null 's a-nall

going home – 2

see the geese
journeying and
the swallows

long since the cuckoo went

see the red leaves
rising on
the wing of a gust
rising and travelling

the salmon is a great way out
on his journey

the sun reclining
moon rising
*   in their familiar changing parabolas*

summer journeying
autumn on his back
*   a great cloak spreading behind*

back and forward on the wharf
*   an exile back and forward*
back and forward
*   back and forward*

gleann fadamach

plèan a' dol tarsainn
cho àrd 's nach cluinnear i
long a' dol sìos an cuan
ach fada mach air fàire

cuid dhen t-saoghal
a' siubhal 's a' siubhal

sa bhaile seo
chan eileas a' siubhal ach an aon uair
's na clachan a rinn ballaichean
a' dol 'nan càirn

glen remote

plane crossing
so high it can't be heard
ship going down the ocean
far out on the horizon

a part of the world
travelling travelling

in this village
people only travel once
and the stones that made walls
become cairns

from an cathadh mor

3

mìorbhail an t-sneachda
gach criostal àraid
gach criostal gun chàraid
meanbh-chlachaireachd
gach lóineag a' tàthadh
saoghal fo chidhis

sneachda fìorghlan
      (ìocshlaint nan galair
      fras chalman air iteal
      mealltach mesmearach)
sneachda gun lochd
      (cléireach ag ùrnaigh
      an cille stàilinn
      ghlas a chreideimh
      cléireach a' guidhe
      fhradharc 'na bhoisean
      ag àicheadh a bhruadar)

sneachda lainnireach
        (leanabh a' ruidhleadh aig uinneig
        sùilean a' dealradh)
sneachda grioglannach
        (speuran brùite   dùinte)
sneachda brìodalach
        snàigeach sniagach
sneachda lìonmhorachadh
        sàmhach sàmhach
sneachda càrnach
sneachda fillteach
sneachda casgrach

        6

sìneadh a h-éididh air
cathair   caisteal   clachan

sgaoileadh a còt' air
gach buaile   gach bealach
gach sgurr is gach rubha
h-uile sràid anns gach baile
geal   geal   geal

plangaid air saoghal
brat-sìth do threubhan domhain

an gilead gealltanach   gluasadach

        8

chan fhaic an t-iasgair ach cobhar
sgorran is sgeirean fo chobhar
sgaothan a' gluasad
                thar a' chala
                thar an raoin
                thar an t-sléibh
cha dhearc a shùil air cuan air cala
chan fhaic e ach cobhar nan sgaoth
a' traoghadh air raointean

an eathar 'na taibhse air teadhair
a lìn nan greasain gheal bhreòiteach
oillsginn gun anam a' crochadh is
     bòtainnean laighe mar chuirp

sluaghan a' chuain do-ruigsinn

from *the great snowbattle*

3

marvel of snow
every crystal unique
every crystal without peer
micro-masonry
every flake cementing
a world beneath its mask

virginal snow
    (balm for plagues
    flurry of flying doves
    deceptive, deadening)
faultless snow
    (a cleric prays
    in the steel cell
    of his credo
    cleric beseeches,
    his sight in his palms
    denying his dreams)

brilliant snow
    (child dancing at window
    eyes reflect glitter)
constellated snow
    (the skies are bruised   enclosed)
cajoling snow
    snaking sneaking
multiplying snow
    silent silent

mounding snow
pleating snow
slaughtering snow

6

stretching her raiment on
city   castle   clachan

spreading her coat on
each meadow   each pass
each peak and each reef
all the streets in each town
white   white   white

a blanket on the world
a flag of truce for
all the tribes in a universe

the whiteness promising   shifting

8

the fisher sees nothing but foam
summits and skerries are under the spray
shoals are moving
                    over harbours
                    across fields
                    across the moors
his eye cannot see ocean, anchorage
he sees only foaming shoals
subsiding on meadows

the boat is a tethered ghost
his nets white friable webs
his oilskins hang soulless while
     boots are outstretched corpses

ocean's multitudes are out of reach

ALAN BOLD (b. 1943)

June 1967 at Buchenwald

The stillness of death all around the camp was uncanny and
intolerable.
BRUNO APITZ, *Naked Among Wolves*

This is the way in. The words
Wrought in iron on the gate:
JEDEM DAS SEINE. Everybody
Gets what he deserves.

The bare drab rubble of the place.
The dull damp stone. The rain.
The emptiness. The human lack.
JEDEM DAS SEINE. JEDEM DAS SEINE.
Everybody gets what he deserves.

It all forms itself
Into one word: Buchenwald.
And those who know and those
Born after that war but living
In its shadow, shiver at the words.
Everybody gets what he deserves.

It is so quiet now. So
Still that it makes an absence.
At the silence of the metal loads
We can almost hear again the voices,
The moaning of the cattle that were men.
Ahead, acres of abandoned gravel.
Everybody gets what he deserves.

Wood, beech wood, song
Of birds. The sky, the usual sky.
A stretch of trees. A sumptuous sheet
Of colours dragging through the raindrops.
Drizzle loosening the small stones
We stand on. Stone buildings. Doors. Dark.

A dead tree leaning in the rain.
Everybody gets what he deserves.

Cold, numb cold. Despair
And no despair. The very worst
Of men against the very best.
A joy in brutality from lack
Of feeling for the other. The greatest
Evil, racialism. A man, the greatest good.
Much more than a biological beast.
An aggregate of atoms. Much more.
Everybody gets what he deserves.

And it could happen again
And they could hang like broken carcasses
And they could scream in terror without light
And they could count the strokes that split their skin
And they could smoulder under cigarettes
And they could suffer and bear every blow
And they could starve and live for death
And they could live for hope alone
And it could happen again.
Everybody gets what he deserves.

We must condemn our arrogant
Assumption that we are immune as well
As apathetic. We let it happen.
History is always more comfortable
Than the implications of the present.
We outrage our own advance as beings
By being merely men. The miracle
Is the miracle of matter. Mind
Knows this but sordid, cruel and ignorant
Tradition makes the world a verbal shell.
Everybody gets what he deserves.

Words are fallible. They cannot do
More than hint at torment. Let us
Do justice to words. No premiss is ever
Absolute; so certain that enormous wreckage

Of flesh follows it syllogistically
In the name of mere consistency. In the end
All means stand condemned. In a cosmic
Context human life is short. The future
Is not made, but waits to be created.
Everybody gets what he deserves.

There is the viciously vicarious in us
All. The pleasure in chance misfortune
That lets us patronise or helps to lose
Our limitations for an instant.
It is that, that struggle for survival
I accuse. Let us not forget
Buchenwald is not a word. Its
Meaning is defined with every day.
Everybody gets what he deserves.

Now it is newsprint and heavy headlines
And looking with a camera's eyes.
Now for many it is only irritating
While for others it is absolutely deadly.
No one is free while some are not free.
While the world is ruled by precedent
It remains a monstrous chance irrelevance.
Everybody gets what he deserves.

We turn away. We always do.
It's what we turn into that matters.
From the invisible barracks of Buchenwald
Where only an unsteady horizon
Remains. The dead cannot complain.
They never do. But we, we live.
Everybody gets what he deserves.

That which once united man
Now drives him apart. We are not helpless
Creatures crashing onwards irresistibly to doom.
There is time for everything and time to choose
For everything. We are that time, that choice.
Everybody gets what he deserves.

This happened near the core
Of a world's culture. This
Occurred among higher things.
This was a philosophical conclusion.
Everybody gets what he deserves.

The bare drab rubble of the place.
The dull damp stone. The rain.
The emptiness. The human lack.

Grass

Grass basks greedily in the sun
As light penetrates each vein
Saturating the stem in the sheath.

Grass contains every gradation of green:
Loves both fiery sun and drenching rain;
Tugs the watcher downwards, underneath

Grass to crushing earth and stone.
Still the watcher comes to watch again,
To see the grass caress the gravel path.

A Special Theory of Relativity

According to Einstein
There's no still centre of the universe:
Everything is moving
Relative to something else.
My love, I move myself towards you,
Measure my motion
In relation to yours.

According to Einstein
The mass of a moving body
Exceeds its mass
When standing still.

My love, *in moving*
Through you
I feel my mass increase.

According to Einstein
The length of a moving body
Diminishes
As speed increases.
My love, after accelerating
Inside you
I spectacularly shrink.

According to Einstein
Time slows down
As we approach
The speed of light.
My love, as we approach
The speed of light
Time is standing still.

Love-Lowe

fireside   Yer glowin' gowden by the guschach
                   Tho' the flames are red.
[fish] churning   Like water thresh'd wi' keethin'-sight
                   Ye mak me feel guid.

ill-gotten property As a thief wi' glender-gear
                   I keep ye close
passing sunbeam Ye gae through me as the sun-glaff glides
                   Straight through ma gless.

shine/brightly   Aye, ye gleet an' glitter glegly
small boat   A saft sunblink on a scow.
blundering   I'm aye blowthirin', but, lassie,
love-flame   It's the richt love-lowe,
                   The richt love-lowe.

The Auld Symie

raw-cold   Winter is deasie
                       An' ootside the snaw
                    Churns like a salmon
death-throe   In its deid-thraw.

                    White gettin' mair white
                       Piled on the stanes
                    Folk look stark naked
bones   Clad in their banes.

devil   But still the auld symie
hook-nose   Wi' bent kipper-nose
                    Maks for the kirk where
                       God alane goes.

ALISON FELL (b. 1944)

Desire

The wind is strong enough to move wasps.
This blowing branch is mine,
silvery thing, all mine,
my teethmarks swarm over it:
what sweet sap and small beetles racing.

Mother warns me I will get worms
from this zest
for chewing and digesting
fur buds and the satin
leaves of beech, from all this
testing and possessing.
'Stop that,' she says.
'Stop this minute. See the
wee eggs you'll swallow!'

My needle-bright eye is rash
and scans greedily,
sees pine-cones lose pollen
in yellow gusts;
the loch's rim has a
curd of it, the face of
the middle deeps is
skimmed with dust and wrinkles.

The birch trunk wears a
sleeve of paper, clear-layered,
like sunburned skin – a wrap.
It streams from my thumbnail
till the wind snatches it.

Pushing Forty

Just before winter
we see the trees show
their true colours:
the mad yellow of chestnuts
two maples like blood sisters
the orange beech
braver than lipstick

Pushing forty, we vow
that when the time comes
rather than wither
ladylike and white
we will henna our hair
like Colette, we too
will be gold and red
and go out
in a last wild blaze

Freeze-frame

*On my bedroom wall there's an old black-and-white snapshot of
two sisters in a snow-crusted garden. The wee one is caught in the
act of smashing a snowball at the big one, who stands knock-
kneed, unprotesting.*

1947. That winter they talk of.
A winter like fists or wizards,

one or the other. The frozen lawn
pitted with porridge and scraps,

soup-bone fat with marrow
that the crows brawl over,

big sister buttoned up
with her puppet gloves dangling.

For background, there's the gable
where old Jessie lived,

a black wedge, and her
the witch of a hundred cats,

reading
your mind's eye, your bad eye.

1947. Small birds dumb as dolls
on the winter wire. I saw

their hearts like peas
and pitied them

that they were never born with tongues
to tell us things. I emptied

my wishes up chimneys, insisted
on reindeer.

Click of the camera fixes
my mittened hand to a blur:

the snowball's invisible as anger
shuttered in the nick of time.

My sister is too patient,
with her face like Petrouchka

and her snow-drifted smile.
She has no tongue, she says

nothing, thinks of Jessie
with the soot under her skirts

and the cats
wicked on the wall.

IAN ABBOT (1944–89)

The Mechanisms of the Gin

Sixteen teeth, set
in a lurid, iron smile.
Chained to the earth, anchored
into black soil, nonetheless
its everyday, simple grin sustains itself.

Its mouth spills feathers.
White bones tumble from it
one upon another: numberless
but laid like runes across the ground.
The great jaw of the badger, skull of the grouse,
an endless filigree of weasels. Yearly
it raises cairns that honour
no more than its own eternal memory.

You tend it with utmost care. Intimately prime as
                                   your father did
its double jagged sickles and its tight-sprung mouth,
                                         arrange
its hidden ribbon of links. Then turn for home,
                                       moving
heavily downward into sleep.
Only to dream of iron laughter shouting in the
                                        wood
and the spare, insatiable gaze
that will see your own flesh folded in the earth
and then will sit back patient, waiting;
grinning till the wandered, bone-white stars begin to
                                       fall.

A Body of Work

Do you not see, finally,
how the earth is moving to inhabit me?

My teeth
are the white stones of the river-bed;
throughout the day
an otter dozes in the dank holt of my mouth.
The sinews of my legs
go down into the earth like roots, and knots of
                                         shifting clay
compose the muscles of my face.
My hair, my sex becoming
clumps of hoary winter grass.

Seasons are manifest in me:
I know their white, their green, their turning yellow.
Laughing, my voice is the fever of stags; the pure
transparency of leaves is in my speech. Constellations
sift their burning atoms through my veins.

But in singing, weeping,
waking in the night and crying out,
my language is a deer dismembered under pines,
bloody and netted with shadows.
An intricate labyrinth of entrails,
lit from within
and patiently transfigured to the lightning grin of
                                         bones.

TOM LEONARD (b. 1944)

Six Glasgow Poems

1

THE GOOD THIEF

heh jimmy
yawright ih
stull wayiz urryi
ih

heh jimmy
ma right insane yirra pape
ma right insane yirwanny us jimmy
see it nyir eyes
wanny uz

heh

heh jimmy
lookslik wirgonny miss thi gemm
gonny miss thi GEMM jimmy
nearly three a cloke thinoo

dork init
good jobe theyve gote thi lights

2
SIMPLE SIMON

thurteen bluddy years wi thim ih
no even a day aff
jiss gee im thi fuckin heave
weeks noatiss nur nuthin
gee im thi heave
thats aw

ahll tellyi sun
see if ah wiz Scot Symon
ahd tell him wherrty stuff thir team
thi hole fuckin lota thim
thats right

a bluddy skandal thats whit it iz
a bluddy skandal

sicken yi

3
COLD, ISN'T IT

wirraw init thigithir missyz
geezyir kross

4
A SCREAM

yi mist yirsell so yi did
we aw skiptwirr ferz njumptaffit thi lights
YIZIR AW PINE THEY FERZ THIMORRA
o it wizza scream
thaht big shite wiz dayniz nut

tellnyi jean
we wirraw shoutn backit im
rrose shoutit shi widny puhllit furra penshin
o yi shooda seeniz face
hi didny no wherrty look

thing iz tay
thirz nay skool thimorra
thi daft kunt wullny even getiz bluddy ferz

5
THE MIRACLE OF THE BURD AND THE FISHES

ach sun
jiss keepyir chin up
dizny day gonabootlika hawf shut knife
inaw jiss cozzy a burd

luvur day yi
ach well
gee it a wee while sun
thirz a loat merr fish in thi sea

6
GOOD STYLE

helluva hard tay read theez init
stull
if yi canny unnirston thim jiss clear aff then
gawn
get tay fuck ootma road

ahmaz goodiz thi lota yiz so ah um
ah no whit ahm dayn
tellnyi
jiss try enny a yir fly patir wi me
stick thi bootnyi good style
so ah wull ·

Poetry

the pee as in pulchritude,
oh pronounced ough
as in bough

the ee rather poised
(pronounced ih as in wit)
then a languid high tea . . .

pause: then the coda –
ray pronounced rih
with the left eyebrow raised
– what a gracious bouquet!

Poetry.
Poughit. rih.

That was my education
– and nothing to do with me.

Jist ti Let Yi No

from the American of Carlos Williams

ahv drank
thi speshlz
that wurrin
thi frij

n thit
yiwurr probbli
hodn back
furthi pahrti

awright
they wur great
thaht stroang
thaht cawld

Paroakial

thahts no whurrits aht
thahts no cool man
jiss paroakial

aw theez sporran heads
tahty scoan vibes
thi haggis trip

bad buzz man
dead seen

goahty learna new langwij
sumhm ihnturnashnl
Noah Glasgow hangup
bunnit husslin

gitinty elektroniks man
really blow yir mine
real good blast
no whuhta mean

mawn
turn yirself awn

Feed Ma Lamz

Amyir gaffirz Gaffir. Hark.

    nay fornirz ur communists
    nay langwij
    nay lip
    nay laffn ina sunday
    nay g.b.h. (septina wawr)
    nay nooky huntn
    nay tea-leaven
    nay chanty rasslin
    nay nooky huntn nix doar
    nur kuvitn their ox

Oaky doaky. Stick way it
– rahl burn thi lohta yiz.

from Unrelated Incidents

I

its thi lang-
wij a thi
guhtr thaht hi
said its thi
langwij a
thi guhtr

awright fur
funny stuff
ur
Stanley Bax-
ter ur but
luv n science
n thaht naw

thi langwij
a thi
intillect hi
said thi lang-
wij a thi intill-
ects Inglish

then whin thi
doors slid
oapn hi raised
his hat geen
mi a fare-
well nod flung
oot his right

fit boldly n
fell eight
storeys
doon thi

empty
lift-shaft

2

ifyi stull
huvny
wurkt oot
thi diff-
rince tween
yir eyes
n
yir ears;
— geez peace.
pal!

fyi stull
huvny
thoata lang-
wij izza
sound-system:
fyi huvny
hudda thingk
aboot thi dif-
frince tween
sound
n object n
symbol; well,
ma innocent
wee
friend — iz
god said ti
adam:

a doant kerr
fyi caw it
an apple
ur
an aippl —

jist leeit
alane!

3

this is thi
six a clock
news thi
man said n
thi reason
a talk wia
BBC accent
iz coz yi
widny wahnt
mi ti talk
aboot thi
trooth wia
voice lik
wanna yoo
scruff. if
a toktaboot
thi trooth
lik wanna yoo
scruff yi
widny thingk
it wuz troo.
jist wanna yoo
scruff tokn.
thirza right
way ti spell
ana right way
ti tok it. this
is me tokn yir
right way a
spellin. this
is ma trooth.
yooz doant no
thi trooth
yirsellz cawz
yi canny talk

right. this is
the six a clock
nyooz. belt up.

from Ghostie Men

right inuff
ma language is disgraceful

ma maw tellt mi
ma teacher tellt mi
thi doactir tellt mi
thi priest tellt mi

ma boss tellt mi
ma landlady in carrington street tellt mi
thi lassie ah tried tay get aff way in 1969 tellt mi
sum wee smout thit thoat ah hudny read chomsky
                                                    tellt mi
a calvinistic communist thit thoat ah wuz revisionist
                                                    tellt mi

po-faced literati grimly kerryin thi burden a thi past
                                                    tellt mi
po-faced literati grimly kerryin thi burden a thi future
                                                    tellt mi
ma wife tellt mi jist-tay-get-inty-this-poem tellt mi
ma wainz came hame fray school an tellt mi
jist aboot ivry book ah oapnd tellt mi
even thi introduction tay thi Scottish National
                                        Dictionary tellt mi

ach well
all livin language is sacred
fuck thi lohta thim

Fathers and Sons

I remember being ashamed of my father
when he whispered the words out loud
reading the newspaper.

'Don't you find
the use of phonetic urban dialect
rather constrictive?'
asks a member of the audience.

The poetry reading is over.
I will go home to my children.

JOHN DIXON (b. 1946)

The Secret Garden

When did gardens ever forget to have their springs?
Sometime back in January; but with me, and you,
it's as if they'd floated the world alongside us
in midwinter, so that those sticks we took for
trees turned out to be a laburnum. 'Now you'll see
where I was alone,' she declared, and led me there,

to a shrub that parted as soon as it was touched.
'I was only three at the time,' she said of this
miracle, that looked like a Red Sea crossing back
to the promised land she'd made of me, a space
we were far to big for now, gripping her there still
like a prisoner it didn't want to release.

It was all so calm and uncomplicated, but
might have been Antarctica so far away
did she seem. The middle of spring made more sense, as
did the light which towered up in front of us, as if
it had just arrived there from Greece that day, to say
nothing of a window the wrong way round its air;

everything in fact but those evergreens, a bare
patch of ground they sheltered, and some geraniums,
or the pots they'd been in. I can recall it now
in the broken brown light the compost heaped on us,
complementing murk from the leaves; and one last stalk
sticking out at me, like those skeletons you see.

No, we can't go back, not unless you count the earth
in, and think of it too, while forwards means decay,
so that we can stand here like models if we want
trying our romance on for size and saying, 'Love
never has to pay'. But it does, and for so much
more than it will ever have; let alone today.

VERONICA FORREST-THOMSON (1947–75)

Strike

For Bonnie, my first horse

I

Hail to thee, blithe horse, bird thou never wert!
And, breaking into a canter, I set off on the long road
                                                    south
Which was to take me to so many strange places,
That room in Cambridge, that room in Cambridge,
                                that room in Cambridge,
That room in Cambridge, this room in Cambridge,
The top of a castle in Provence and an aeroplane in
                                            mid-Atlantic.
Strange people, that lover, that lover, that lover, that
                                                    lover.
Eyes that last I saw in lecture-rooms
Or in the Reading Room of The British Museum
                                        reading, writing,
Reeling, writhing, and typing all night (it's cheaper
                                    than getting drunk),
Doing tour en diagonale in ballet class (that's cheaper
                                than getting drunk too).
But first I should describe my mount. His strange
                                                    colour;
He was lilac with deep purple points (he was really a
                                            siamese cat).
His strange toss and whinny which turned my
                                                    stomach
And nearly threw me out of the saddle. His eyes
His eyes his eyes his eyes his eyes
Eyes that last I saw in lecture rooms
His eyes were hazel brown and deceptively
                                            disingenuous.
I got to know those eyes very well.
Our journey through England was not made easier by
                                                the fact

That he would eat only strawberries and cream (at
                                         any season).
And he wanted a lot of that.
Nevertheless I got here and the first time I ever set
                                    foot in the place
I knew it was my home. The trouble was to convince
                                    the authorities.
Jobs were scarce and someone with a purple-point
                                    siamese to keep
In strawberries and cream has a certain standard of
                                         living.
When I sold my rings and stopped buying clothes I
                                         knew
It was the end. When I cut down on food it was clear
I was on some sort of quest.
There was an I-have-been-here-before kind of feeling
                                    about it.
That hateful cripple with the twisted grin. But
Dauntless the slughorn to my ear I set.

II

How many miles to Babylon?
Threescore and ten.
Can I get there by candlelight?
Yes. But back again?
From perfect leaf there need not be
Petals or even rosemary.
One thing then burnt rests on the tree:
The woodspurge has a cup of three,
One for you, and one for me,
And one for the one we cannot see.

III

What there is now to celebrate:
The only art where failure is renowned.
A local loss
Across and off the platform-ticket found
For the one journey we can tolerate:

To withered fantasy
From stale reality. Father, I cannot tell a lie;
I haven't got the time.
Mirth cannot move a soul in agony.
Stainless steel sintered and disowned;
Stars in the brittle distance just on loan.
The timetables of our anxiety glitter, grow
One in the alone. The cosmic ozones know
Our lease is running out.
Deserted now the house of fiction stands
Exams within and driving tests without,
Shading the purpose from the promised lands
No milk our honey.
And the train we catch can't take us yet
To the blind corner where he waits
Between the milk and honey gates:
The god we have not met.

LIZ LOCHHEAD (b. 1947)

Dreaming Frankenstein

For Lys Hansen, Jacki Parry and June Redfern

She said she
woke up with him in
her head, in her bed.
Her mother-tongue clung to her mouth's roof
in terror, dumbing her, and he came with a name
that was none of her making.

No maidservant ever
in her narrow attic, combing
out her hair in the midnight mirror
on Hallowe'en (having eaten
that egg with its yolk hollowed out
then filled with salt)
– oh never one had such success as this
she had not courted.
The amazed flesh of her
neck and shoulders nettled
at his apparition.

Later, stark staring awake to everything
(the room, the dark parquet, the white high Alps
                                        beyond)
all normal in the moonlight
and him gone, save a ton-weight sensation,
the marks fading visibly where
his buttons had bit into her and
the rough serge of his suiting had chafed her sex,
she knew – oh that was not how –
but he'd entered her utterly.

This was the penetration
of seven swallowed apple pips.
Or else he'd slipped like a silver dagger
between her ribs and healed her up secretly

again. Anyway
he was inside her
and getting him out again
would be agony fit to quarter her,
unstitching everything.

Eyes on those high peaks
in the reasonable sun of the morning,
she dressed in damped muslin
and sat down to quill and ink
and icy paper.

Heartbreak Hotel

Honeymooning alone
oh the food's
quite good (but it all needs salting).
Breadsticks admonish,
brittle fingers among formality – bishops' hats,
stiff skirts, white linen, silver implements.

This dining room
is all set for a funeral,
an anatomy lesson,
a celebration of communion
or a conjuring trick – maybe someone
will be sawn in half,
or a napkin could crumple
to an amazing dove.
Except
it's all empty
though I eat my helping
under a notice that says This Place
is Licensed for Singing and Dancing.

Go to your room.
What more lovely than to be alone
with a Teasmade a radio and a telephone?
Loose end? Well, this is what you find

when you take the time off to unwind.
Empty twinbeds
and the space all hanging heavy
above your neat spare shoes
in your wall-to-wall wardrobe
underneath the jangling wires.

Honeymooning alone
can't get to sleep without the lights on,
can't swallow all that darkness on my own.
Syrup from the radio's
synthetically soothing late night show
oh remember, remember
then I reach to pop one of those press-stud pills
I keep under the pillow so
my system will still tick next week
on the blink
a little crazily for you.
I can't sleep –
it's as livid as a scar
the white neon striplight
above my vanity bar.

Mirror, Mirror on the wall
does he love me enough,
does he love me at all?
Should I go back
with that celebrated shout?
Did my eyebrows offend you?
Well I've plucked them out.
Oh me and my mudpack,
I can't smile
my face will crack.
I'll come clean.
I've made good new resolutions
re my skincare routine.
Every day
there's a basket of blossomheads,
crumpled kleenex to throw away.
As if I found it easy to discard.

Think hard.
I've got a week to think it over
a shelf full of creams, sweet lotions
I can cover,
smother all my darkness in, smooth it over.
Oh it'll take more than this aerosol
to fix it all, to fix it all.

Mirror's Song

For Sally Potter

Smash me looking-glass glass
coffin, the one
that keeps your best black self on ice.
Smash me, she'll smash back –
without you she can't lift a finger.
Smash me she'll whirl out like Kali,
trashing the alligator mantrap handbags
with her righteous karate.
The ashcan for the stubbed lipsticks
and the lipsticked butts,
the wet lettuce of fivers.
She'll spill the Kleenex blossoms,
the tissues of lies, the matted
nests of hair from the brushes'
hedgehog spikes, she'll junk
the dead mice and the tampons
the twinking single eyes
of winkled out diamanté, the hatpins
the whalebone and lycra,
the appleblossom and the underwires,
the chafing iron that kept them maiden,
the Valium and initialled hankies,
the lovepulps and the Librium,
the permanents and panstick and
Coty and Tangee Indelible,
Thalidomide and junk jewellery.

Smash me for your daughters and dead
mothers, for the widowed
spinsters of the first and every war
let her
rip up the appointment cards for the
terrible clinics,
the Greenham summonses, that date
they've handed us. Let her rip.
She'll crumple all the
tracts and the adverts, shred
all the wedding dresses, snap
all the spike-heel icicles
in the cave she will claw out of –
a woman giving birth to herself.

The Grim Sisters

And for special things
(weddings, school-
concerts) the grown up girls next door
would do my hair.

Luxembourg announced *Amami Night*.

I sat at peace passing bobbipins
from a marshmallow pink cosmetic purse
embossed with jazzmen,
girls with pony tails and a November
topaz lucky birthstone.
They doused my cow's-lick, rollered
and skewered tightly.
I expected that to be lovely
would be worth the hurt.

They read my Stars,
tied chiffon scarves to doorhandles, tried
to teach me tight dancesteps
you'd no guarantee

any partner you might find would ever be able to
keep up with as far as I could see.

There were always things to burn
before the men came in.

For each disaster
you were meant to know the handy hint.
Soap at a pinch
but better nailvarnish (clear) for ladders.
For kisscurls, spit.
Those days womanhood was quite a sticky thing
and that was what these grim sisters came to mean.

'You'll know all about it soon enough.'
But when the clock struck they
stood still, stopped dead.
And they were left there
out in the cold with the wrong skirtlength
and bouffant hair,
dressed to kill,

who'd been
all the rage in fifty-eight,
a swish of Persianelle
a slosh of perfume.
In those big black mantrap handbags
they snapped shut at any hint of *that*
were hedgehog hairbrushes
cottonwool mice and barbed combs to tease.
Their heels spiked bubblegum, dead leaves.

Wasp waist and cone breast, I see them yet.
I hope, I hope
there's been a change of more than silhouette.

from The Furies

I: HARRIDAN

Mad Meg on my mantelpiece,
Dulle Griet by Brueghel, a Flemish masterpiece
in anybody's eyes. 'Well worth historical
                                    consideration'
was how I looked at it. The surrealist tradition
from Bosch to Magritte is such a Flemish thing!
Oh a work of great power, most interesting . . .
I chose it for my History of Art essay, took pains
to enumerate the monsters, reduce it all to picture
                                               planes.
I was scholarly, drew parallels
between Hieronymus Bosch's and Pieter Brueghel's
                                               Hells;
Compared and contrasted
Symbolism and Realism in the Flemish School;
discussed: Was Meg 'mad' or more the
                              Shakespearean Fool?

The fool I was! Mad Meg, Sour-Tongued Margot,
maddened slut in this mass of misery, a Virago,
at her wit's end, running past Hell's Mouth, all
                                       reason gone,
she has one mailed glove, one battered breastplate
                                               on.
Oh that kitchen knife, that helmet, that silent shout,
I know Meg from the inside out.
All she owns in one arm, that lost look in her eyes.
These days I more than sympathise.

Oh I am wild-eyed, unkempt, hellbent, a harridan.
My sharp tongue will shrivel any man.
Should our paths cross
I'll embarrass you with public tears, accuse you with
                                            my loss.

My Mother's Suitors

have come to court me
have come to call oh
yes with their wonderful world
war two moustaches their long
stem roses their cultivated
accents (they're English aren't they
at very least they're
educated-Scots).
They are absolutely
au fait with menu-French
they know the language of flowers
& oh they'd die
rather than send a dozen yellow
they always get them right & red.
Their handwriting on the florist's card
slants neither too much to the left or right.

They are good sorts.
They have the profile for it – note
the not too much nose
the plenty chin. The
stockings they bring have no strings
& their square
capable hands are forever
lifting your hair and gently
pushing your head away from them
to fumble endearingly at your nape
with the clasp of the pretty heirloom
little necklace they know their
grandmother would have wanted
you to have.
(Never opals – they know
that pearls mean tears).

They have come to call & we'll all
go walking under the black sky's
droning big bombers

among the ratatat of ack-ack.
We'll go dancing & tonight
shall I wear the lilac, or the
scarlet, or the white?

VALERIE GILLIES (b. 1948)

Fellow Passenger

Mister B. Rajan, diamond buyer,
crystallises from this travelling companion.
He goes by rail, it seems, by criss
and cross, Hyderabad to Bangalore
to Madras, Madras, Madras,
seeking the industrial diamond.

He brings new orient gems from hiding.
Himself, he wears goldwealthy rings
of ruby, and, for fortune,
another of God Venkateswaran.
His smile is a drillpoint diamond's,
incisive his kindness.

Sparrowboned, he walks unstable passageways,
living on boiled eggs and lady's-fingers
with noggins of whisky to follow.
He dreams of his house, the shrineroom picture
of Sai Baba, corkscrew-haired young saint.
And he has at home beautiful hidden daughters.

The Piano-tuner

Two hundred miles, he had come
　　　　to tune one piano, the last hereabouts.
Both of them were relics of imperial time:
　　　　the Anglo-Indian and the old upright
　　　　　　　　　　　　　　　　knockabout.

He peered, and peered again
　　　　into its monsoon-warped bowels.
From the flats of dead sound he'd beckon
　　　　a tune on the bones out to damp vowels.

His own sounds were pidgin.
    The shapeliness of his forearms
lent his body an English configuration,
    but still, sallow as any snakecharmer

he was altogether piebald.
    Far down the bridge of his nose
perched roundrimmed tortoiseshell spectacles;
    his hair, a salt-and-pepper, white foreclosed.

But he rings in the ear yet,
    his interminable tapping of jarring notes:
and, before he left,
    he gave point to those hours of discord.

With a smile heavenly
    because so out of place, cut off from any home
                        there,
he sat down quietly
    to play soft music: that tune of 'Beautiful
                      Dreamer',

a melody seized from yellowed ivories
    and rotting wood. A damper
muffled the pedal point of lost birthright. We eaves-
    dropped on an extinct creature.

Young Harper

Above Tweed Green levels
Maeve first raises the harp.

Prosper her hand that plucks
then clenches fist like a jockey.

Grip inside thighs
the colt with a cropped mane.

Turn blades on the curved neck
bristling with spigots.

Out from the rosewood forest
came this foal of strung nerve.

Stand in your grainy coat,
let her lift elbows over you.

Keep her thumbs bent
and fingers hard to do the playing.

Eight summers made them, clarsach,
I freely give you my elder daughter.

The Ericstane Brooch

The gold cross-bow brooch,
The Emperors' gift to an officer,
Was lost on the upland moor.
The pierced work and the inscription
Lay far from human habitation.

It worked on time and space
And they were at work on it.
What could withstand them?
But it was waiting for the human,
To address itself to a man or woman.

In the wilderness it meant nothing.
The great spaces dissolved its image,
Time obliterated its meaning.
Without being brought in,
It was less than the simplest safety-pin.

Now the brooch is transporting the past
To the present, the far to the near.
Between the two, its maker and wearer

And watcher live mysteriously.
Who is this who values it so seriously?

It exists, it has been seen by him.
If it speaks, it can only say
'He lost me.' And we reply, 'Who?
For he can also be our loss,
This moment floating face-down in the moss.'

Dumb replica: the original is in Los Angeles.
How is it, the man once destroyed,
His brooch continues boundlessly?
Our very existence is what it defies:
We no longer see what once we scrutinized.

RON BUTLIN (b. 1949)

This Evening

You placed yellow roses by the window, then,
leaning forwards, began combing your red hair;
perhaps you were crying.
To make the distance less I turned away
and faced you across the earth's circumference.

The window-pane turns black:
across its flawed glass suddenly your image
runs on mine.
I stare at the vase until yellow
is no longer a colour, nor the roses flowers.

Night-life

My nerves are stretched tight above the city:
a night-map of neon and sodium.

Hours earlier you wore darkness as love itself:
moonlight you ground more finely with each kiss,
starlight you scattered out of reach.

And now, what burning inside me?
what light trapped in a clenched sky?

Inheritance

   Although there are nettles here, and thorns,
you will not be stung. Trust me. I've something
to show you made from twigs, bird-spittle, down
and journeyings in all weathers.
   See how easily your hand covers
the nest and its eggs. How weightless they are.
Your fingernail, so very much smaller than mine,

can trace the delicate shell's blue veins
until they crack apart, letting silence
spill into your hand. There is a sense
of separation almost too great to bear
– and suddenly you long to crush all colour
from these pale blue eggs, for in their brief
fragility you recognise as grief
the overwhelming tenderness you feel.
    This is your inheritance:
your fist clenched on yolk and broken shell,
on fragments of an unfamiliar tense.

Claiming My Inheritance

I paused, then briefly tried to clear the mess
of yolk-slime and albumen. My distress
was private: I could not explain
what made me run home faster than
I ever ran before.

                    Since then I've taken pains
to learn the language of what's done and said
(in restaurants, in stations, on the beach, in bed)
to friends (observing gender, number, business/
                                                social),
my fellow-guests and God. For interpersonal
dynamics read *non-verbal empathy*: offence
or reinforcement at a glance. I'm quick to sense
unhappiness in others – that reassuring smile
(too well-timed), that altered tone of voice. My skill
at recognising joy is rather minimal,
however – seeming to suggest
the world is one vast Rorschach test.
I've learnt the words for things and feelings: how and
                                                when
to use them. In making conversation,
love and enemies I take especial care
no accent-lapse, no unfamiliar
tense construction, clumsy phrase

or hesitation (worst of all) betrays
I am a foreigner.

After I had crushed the eggs. A pause:

as if the colours of the earth and sky –

as if all laws affirming spontaneity –

As if the present tense were happening too soon
the fence I stood beside became a wooden thing,
the gate was iron-lengths – heated, hammered, bent
and riveted in place years earlier. I leant
against it. I struck it, but could not animate the dead
place to suffer for me. Instead,
the emptiness that stained
the empty sky above me blue,
gave definition to
my isolation.
Only this completed world remained.

The older I become the more
I am aware of exile, of longing for –

I clench my fist on nothing and hold on.

RAYMOND VETTESE (b. 1950)

Prologue

Ae nicht I sat by mysel at the fire
except   and thocht. Nae soond in the street forbyes
the wun blawin thro the telephone wire.
stars   A quarter-muin gied but sma licht, starns,
in clood, barely shone: a dour compromise
'twixt soond, silence, dairk, licht –
brains   the ootward cast o the state o my harns,
caught in a whirl, sometimes sure   catched in a swither, whiles shair o the richt,
wrung/troubled   whiles thrawed wi doot . . . this maitter's fasht me
                                      lang,
th' uprisin o Scots, och, I micht be wrang.

all this could but waste   Mebbe aa this cuid but connach braith.
many a fool pursued a choice   There's monie a gow gaed aifter a wile,
certain of it, yet found, dejected,   fu-shair o't, yet fun', disjaskit, sair daith,
sore death
pledge   no hecht o life. Ay, and sae it micht be
my trifling flowery style   wi mysel, and my foot'rin phraisie style:
petulant/worn-out   snashgab, nocht mair, a silly dashelt screed,
bummlin aboot, barmy on words, skinkin orra bree* –
ach, the thocht o the waste is whit I maist dreid,
a lifetime pursuing   waste o span hundin a deein cause,
my thick bluid dreepin clause by clause.

*doubtful**   Whit's the point in this dootsum endeavour
tae bring back whit's lang gane, whit purpose?
Mebbe the fowk wha say it's gane forever
are richt, and mebbe I should turn awa
bound to this   frae sic daft notions. Yet I'm thirlt til this,
I canna gie it owre, it's stuck in me
beyond reason.   like faith, ayont reason. It's my weird's caa,
destiny's summons
boast   or sae I blaw, tae shaw whit it micht be,
this language, used/whim   this leid, yased aricht. That's mebbe a fraik
challenge/path   but's the brag that sets me oot on this raik.

* *skinkin orra bree* pouring leftover liquor from one dish to another; *dootsum* also formidable

I hae a vision o Scotland set free
is one
and freedom and language tae me is ane.
I hae a vision that Scotland micht be
itsel again, its present and its past
united
souderet for the future's sake, tho the pain
o Freedom's no easy nor wantin doot
and whiles I dae nocht but staun aghast
seeping
at the thocht o't, feel the strength sypin oot
from assurance/half-night
frae sickerness, as I dae this hauf-nicht
fu o gloamin unease, an' dootsum licht.

The toon is quiet, only noo and then
nimble feet stamp in the empty
street beyond
swippert feet dunt in the tuim street ayont.
I sit and think on the likely again,
question
speir the chances o mendin, the chances
final/a downfall not lit
o hinmaist decline, a doonfaa no alunt
with a last flicker/dreary drizzle
wi ae laist leam, but dairk wi dreich smirr
lively hope
o lichtless silence. Nae gleg hope dances
on such a night when
on sic a nicht whaun nae sunk life can stir,
I must rise above the mire* of
disquiet
yet I maun rise abuin the lair o wanrufe
flounder/woe-scooping
an idle fool
or slutter in't, wae-gowpin, a slottery coof.

strange [foreign] direction
I set my compass tae a fremmit airt,
search/star
reenge aifter yon driven starn, let it lead
whaur it will, ayont stoundin fearfu hairt;
weary thoughts/strike out
fling aff my trauchelt thochts and stramp oot
on the lang traik til the truth in my heid
released
that winna be lowsèd save in words like these.
perhaps/floundering
It's aiblins daft, this ploiter o pursuit
owre bitter acres whaur the braith micht freeze,
but it's the ae gait, I doot, for me.
haven/must be
Somewhaur the bield and the green maun be.

* *lair* also lore, learning

My Carrion Words

In deep
o dairk sleep
I dreamt my words
gaithert like stairvin birds
on a bare tree
and skreiched owre me
cough   wi carrion hoast:
Lost! Lost!

and then   And syne
would lose   I ran, wad tine
sobbing   that greetin
forsaken   o things forleeten
intense darkness   i the muckle dairk,
anxiety   but aye the cark
murmured in the background souched ahent:
beware!   Tak tent! Tent!

Whaun I woke
the day spoke
wi anither voice
purred pleasant choice that croodled douce choice:
give up this nonsense,
this pretence;
what's gone is gone, here's
English for contemporary ears.

But ach, I doot
I'm no cut oot
for sic mense
(that's dowit leid for 'common sense');
weakened language the auld coorse Scotland's in me,
an' the bare tree
an' the stairvin birds:
frae sic as them, frae yon, my carrion words.

The Vieve Cry

living

sullenly	Dour-hunched in a drizzle
wearisome	o dreich November
enveloped in mist	or smoort in haar
	frae bitter North Sea
forlorn	this toon's forlane.

	Yet I've seen
	yon steeple-vane
shine above [and in good fettle]	skyre abuin
as if unafraid of anything it would crow	as gin unfleggit o ocht it wad craw
brazen-faced on everything	braisant on aa!

	In dourest season
near-extinct	o near-tint sun
cheerfulness	that crouseness vaunts
shadows	oot o shaddas,
chill wind-blasted narrow alleys	oot a snell-wun narra wynds,

beyond/into	an' ayont, intil nicht,
barren	whaur hirsty fields
	streetch cauld
embrace in toil [or darkness?]	yet hause in dairk
power	the starry maucht o seed.

sad [and infertile]	In dowf season,
dismal	dowie, deid still,
above	abuin frozen braith,
	I hear it:
death-grip distorts	the vieve cry nae daith-grupp thraws.

TOM POW (b. 1950)

part two of The Gift of Sight

SAINT MEDAN

That Medan was beautiful,
    there was no doubt.
Wherever she went,
    hearts were routed.

But, to her, these looks
    were but a costume
she couldn't cast off.
    She saw her fortune

not in the fancy
    of romantic play –
it was in inner things
    her interests lay.

Medan took a vow
    of chastity; her life
she bound to Christ.
    It was a sharp knife

in the hearts of men.
    But one noble knight
did not believe her.
    To quit his sight

she left Ireland
    for green Galloway.
To the Rhinns she came,
    to live in poverty.

The knight followed.
    He would die or wed

his heart's crusade.
    Pure Medan now fled

to a rock in the sea.
    With prayer, the rock
became a boat;
    the boat she took

thirty miles away.
    Still, he followed;
blindly obeying
    what the hollow

in his heart called for.
    He'd have been lost,
but a crowing cock –
    to both their costs –

told him the house
    where Medan lay.
Shaken, she climbed
    and she prayed

as she climbed
    into a thorn tree.
From there, she asked,
    'What do you see

in me to excite
    your passion?' 'Your face
and eyes,' he replied.
    She sighed, 'In which case . . .'

then impaled her eyes
    on two sharp thorns
and flung them at him.
    Desire was torn

forever from that knight.
    He looked at his feet,

where the eyes had rolled –
    lustrous jade, now meat

for ants. Horror-struck,
    he left – a penitent.
Medan washed her face,
    for a spring – heaven-sent –

gurgled from the dry earth.
    The rest of her days
were lived in poverty
    and sanctity. (*Praise*

the Lord, sang Ninian.)
    The proud cock half-lived,
but crowed no more.
    And sight became the gift

Saint Medan gave,
    so that all could suffer
in equal measure,
    beauty and terror.

BRIAN MCCABE (b. 1951)

Spring's Witch

I wait out winter plagued by your ghost –
impatient rains whisper, winds rumour you,
caressing the skins of my windows,
speaking into the ears of my chimneys:

She's coming, say the rains.
As before, wind says.

And you do, one dark March day:
loud and chaotic, incanting your 'ohs',
no prim Primavera, no flowers-in-toes,
but cackling as you cast off your clothes.

She's here, say the rains.
As before, wind says.

Your black hair is treacled by the rain.
You raise the wand and you conjure again
whatever love I have for living
from this world's rebirth in spring.

She's leaving, say the rains.
Gone, gone, wind says.

The Blind

The blind old men who come arm in arm
On good-smelling days to the park,
Grateful to the girl who brings them
Since they seldom have the chance
Of a slow, recollective game of bowls.
The sun that signs their faces
With smudge-like marks where eyes were
Suggests to their memories a notion

Of green, and summer days ago.
Taking pleasure from the silence of grass
And the weight of the wood in the hand,
They engross themselves in the game
They play by sound intuition:
The girl is young, sighted.
She stands at the far end of darkness
And claps her hands – once, twice –
And then the first bowler stoops,
As if about to kneel and be blessed,
Then throws to her clapping hands.
As the dark wood is travelling the green
She waits, motionless, and waits
As if by any slight move she might alter
The swing and slowing of the bowl.
When it halts, she bows, she measures,
Then calls its distance, its 'time':
'*Seven feet, at four o'clock.*'
Again she claps her hands.
Another player stoops, lets go . . .
This time it comes closer, close enough
To enter the young girl's shadow.
When it kisses the jack, there's a 'cloc'.

The old men smile.

This is Thursday

The key argues with the lock
before the ward door is opened
and a male nurse orders me in.
I note the military manner,
the clipped moustache, explain
I'm an old friend of hers
come to visit on impulse.
He nods, inspects my appearance
and suggests that I wait here.
'Here' is a windowless room
where television tells the news

to a range of empty chairs.
A chalked blackboard declares
that this is Thursday.
I wish it wasn't, aware
of the custard-yellow walls
and someone's hand over there –
waving to me, and to no one.
A pale plant starved of light
wilts in its own dim corner.
I ask myself: How could anyone
leap from a tenement window
and land in this dark asylum?
And I wait. Wait for the present
to step out of the past. Then,
across a wasteland of years,
through a fog of sedation,
my old friend looks at me again
with her violated eyes.

GERALD MANGAN (b. 1951)

Glasgow 1956

There's always a headscarf stooped
into a pram, nodding in time
with a plastic rattle, outside a shop
advertising a sale of wallpaper.

There's a queue facing another queue
like chessmen across the street;
a hearse standing at a petrol-pump
as the chauffeur tests the tyres,

the undertaker brushes ash off
his morning paper, and my mother,
looking down at me looking up,
is telling me not to point.

The background is a level site
where we recreate the war.
Calder Street is Calder Street,
level as far as the Clyde.

Without a tree to denote it,
the season is moot. That faint
thunder is the Cathcart tram,
and the sky is white as a trousseau

posed against blackened bricks.
A grey posy in her hands,
the bride stands smiling there
for decades, waiting for the click.

Heraclitus at Glasgow Cross

Where Gallowgate meets London Road
    and the world walks out with his wife,

umbrellas sail in long flotillas
    through streets you can't cross twice.

The old home town looks just the same
    when you step down off the Sixty-Three.
The jukebox music takes you back
    to the green, green grass of Polmadie.

drizzle

Everything swarms and eddies in smirr.
    Wine flows out from the Saracen's Head.
Mascara runs, like soot from a guttering.
    Day-glo signs glow green on red.

Something for Everyone. Nothing for Nothing.
    Social Security Estimates Free.
It's Scotland's Friendliest Market-Place.
    Watch Your Handbags, Ladies, Please.

Watch the Do-nuts fry in grease,
    the tailgate-auctioneers compete
with the broken-winded squeezebox player,
    wheezing through his leaking pleats.

Or under Clyde Street's railway arches,
    see the stubbled dossers soak
like debris snagged in shallows, blowing
    old Virginia up in smoke.

Down where the fishwives trade in rags,
    they curl like snails in paper shells:
lips of sponge, skins of mould,
    eyes like cinders doused in hell.

They're watching concrete fill the docks,
    the bollards rust on the graving-quays.
The green green grass grows overhead,
    on gantries still as gallows-trees.

Where Gorbals faces Broomielaw,
    the river's black and still as ice.

When the ferryman takes the fare, he says
You can cross this river twice,

Nights in Black Valley

Hours when nothing but the rumours
of the mountain fill your ears:
the vixen wailing, or the whisper of rain
as a cloud caresses the roof.

Hours when nothing moves in the house
but the spider and its thread,
the candle spilling its tallow
when the draught disturbs it,

or the grubs worming from the log,
shrivelling into the flame.
The eye of the dog is entranced,
and his shadow is a behemoth.

In the morning when the light breaks up
the conspiracy of mists,
and the flock flows down to the water
like a liquid finding its level,

the time comes round to choose
what to leave and what to take
back to the electricity.
And I memorise the silence:

the moon sliding on the lough,
as the stars endure their space.
And the hawk stropping his beak,
like an axe dreaming of wood.

ANDREW GREIG (b. 1951)

In the Tool-shed

'Hummingbirds' he said, and spat. Winged tongues
hovered in the half-light of their names;
cat, cobra, cockatoo rose hissing from the juice.
Piece-time in Africa, amid the terrapins
and jerrycans! Steam swirled above the Congo
of his cup, mangrove-rooted fingers plugged the air –
'Baboons? Make sure you look them in eyes.' Birds
of paradise! Parrots, paraffin, parakeets
flashed blue and raucous through
thickets of swoe, scythe, riddle, adze.
He sat bow-backed and slack in the dark
heart of his kingdom – creator, guide
in that jungle of sounds, boxes, cloches, canes,
twine, twill, galoshes, jumbled all
across, over, through and into one another
from floor to roof, prowled by fabled carnivores,
the jaguar! the secateurs! Words poke
wet muzzles through reeds of sound
grown enormous overnight. Twin depths
of pitch and pitcher! Elephants lean
patiently upon their ponderous names.
They come in clutches: azaleas, zebras, zambesi.
Orchids, oranges, oran-utangs hang
from their common mouth. Lemming, gorilla, lynx
slink nose to tail through mango groves,
drenched in this sibilant monsoon: moonstone,
                                        machetes,
peacocks, paw-paws, lepers, leopards – the walls
are creaking but hold them all, swaying, sweating,
in that dark continent between the ears.
Easy, easy genesis! Old witchdoctor, gardener,
deity of the shed, I grew that garden
from his words, caught the fever
pitch of his Niagara; I follow still
the Orinoco of his blue forearm veins

that beat among the talking drums
of all my childhood afternoons.

The Winter Climbing

(For Marj)

It is late January and at last the snow.
I lie back dreaming about Glencoe
as fluent, hungry, dressed in red,
you climb up and over me. That passion
claimed the darkest, useless months
for risk and play. You rise
up on me, I rise through you . . .

The shadowed face of Aonach Dubh
where Mal first took me climbing
and as we clanked exhausted, happy,
downwards through the dark, I asked
'What route was that?' 'Call it
what you want – it's new.'

You reach the top and exit out;
from way above, your cry comes down.
The rope pulls tight. What shall we call
this new thing we're about?
These days we live in taking
care and chances. Why name it?
My heart is in my mouth as I shout *Climbing* . . .

The Maid & I

'At this stage, I work most closely with the Maid.'
New York composer of film scores

It's nothing personal when she slips in
at half-dawn, half-dusk, any drifting
time of day, to make mere solitude complete.
That's how come we get on
so well, so long. You smile, you picture

black seamed stockings, white muslin crown
on hair that's poised to be let down? No,
she is not Naughty Lola –
nor Mrs Mopp! With us it is
importunate to talk or stare;
touch is right out. This fortunate
proximity is all we share.

She has arrived.
You are in the backroom,
by the Steinway, fiddling with the Blues.
You hear her humming as she moves
among the papers and abandoned meals, clearing up
the ashtrays, scripts and coffee cups,
the litter of aloneness. Redeeming fingers touch
your old scores lightly, as if it were yourself
she dusts and settles on the shelf. Praise the maid
who sets out flowers and white clouds
where you might see them and be glad!
The shambles would be total were it not for her.

Now she is singing an old refrain
you can't quite . . . The sky
is pale, washed clean by rain,
hung up against the evening.
As you attend, a melody floats
through apartment walls so intimately
it is as though you quote yourself –
debris is sorted, order
is invented or restored.
Now she is done. You will work on alone
but that's all right. Grace must have its means.
She flicks the light on as she leaves.

FRANK KUPPNER (b. 1951)

Passing Through Doorways

I

i

I can no longer remain in this building,
Not after this latest turn of events;
After I have shut the door, my watch says 9.26;
I walk down those few stairs again, determined,
                          above all, to pass time.

ii

Having spent all my life not merely in one city,
But in a tightly circumscribed part of one city,
I find that most of the significant doors in my life
Opened and shut within a few minutes of each other.

iii

A leisurely evening walk could unite the four of
                          them;
Have I really never gone on such a walk before?
It is autumn, and again the sky is completely dark;
It is the wrong time of the evening to have crowds on
                          the streets.

II

iv

After twenty minutes, and hardly more than four
                          roads,
I am once again in the street where I was born;
Closer with every footstep to the very house;
I hurry guiltily up the steps into the tenement close.

v

I climbed those steps countless times in the 1950s;
I descended those steps countless times in the 1960s;
In the 1970s I visited the place, I think, once;
And this is my first visit of the 1980s.

vi

The names on the doors were mostly those they had
                                              always been;
I crept by them, hand caressing the banister,
Unhappy at the apparent shortage of steps,
By their narrowness, by how deeply worn they were.

vii

For, in all the many times I climbed those stairs,
Hundred upon differentiated hundred,
Perhaps still warehoused within the memory,
Sufficient to erode from it the width of a skin,

viii

From my first, stumbling, partly aided steps,
Wearing small spectacles and a very round face,
Followed by a mother, or preceded by a larger sister,
Who now has two effortlessly walking sons in a
                                              house on the coast

ix

To the routine exhaustion of yet another evening,
Dragging my way round the corners of the banister,
Sunlight through the windows upon me and a grimy
                                              football,
As I climbed towards my mother's call, and cold
                                              water gulped too quickly,

x

And the insecure rushing of an adolescent,
Propelled by the moment's enthusiasm to a record
shop,
Now obliterated, to a park, to a tv programme,
To an illustrated dictionary of medical terms,

xi

I doubt if it ever once occurred to me,
That 50, 70 and 30 years before,
Equivalent breath was expelled from roughly equal
lungs,
In other people's passages of the same stairway.

xii

Now, I am fascinated by such, as it were, pauses in
life,
As being closer to what life normally is
Than the supreme events which documents tend to
fill with,
As if only spectacular oceans are deep.

xiii

My door has changed beyond recognition;
The least recognisable part of an unrecognisable
place;
Reinforced blocks of wood over the lock
Show where some people have tried to force their
way in.

xiv

When, in my dreams I pass through that door so
often,
Why does seeing it with real eyes not seem like a
homecoming?
What door is it then that I pass through in my
dreams?

I return down the dark stairway, too tall for that
                                        building.

xv

And down even to the stairway to the back-court;
Ill-lit, a place of fear to me as a child;
When, carrying down ashes at an untimely hour,
The sight of such a man as I am now,

xvi

Standing, for obscure purposes, at the entrance to the
                                        back garden,
Feeling the high wall of a garage too oppressively
                                                near,
Puzzled by the widespread, moonlit vegetation,
Would have terrified me into immediate retreat;

xvii

The enormously heavy bucket resting against my leg,
As I half-carried, half-levered it along,
The heat of a dead fire still burning at its sides;
Stopping in silence at the turns, to rest my hands.

xviii

So I walked up, from that implausible moonlight,
Into the implausible lamplight of the stairs;
For a second or two, in the turn at the top of the
                                                flight,
Being in the same time in my dreams and in my
                                        childhood;

xix

And continued down a shrunken corridor,
Onto a street abandoned for at most five minutes,
Which would take me off to other destinations,
Unsuspected through the previous 4,001 such exits.

III

xx

As I walk, some minutes later, into the other
                                          building,
It seems even less probable that I have done so
                                          before;
How often was it? A dozen? Two dozen times?
I have made so little impression on this stonework.

xxi

And yet, it is exactly the correct size;
The windows still retain their appropriate views;
I simply did not visit it often enough,
During the years she used to live here with him.

xxii

On what stair did I stop her from the back,
Lean forward over her newly-washed hair,
And inhale its unparalleled perfume, while she stood,
Motionless, in unusual docility?

xxiii

It seems to me I did not really live through those
                                          days;
As it seemed, at the time, so utterly improbable
That, at the top of those curving ordinary stairs,
I could knock at a door and have her answer it.

xxiv

I did not understand then, and do not understand
                                          now,
How such a banal building could contain her;
How her tears could be deadened by such walls;
How these same graceless stairs could daily accept
                                          her feet.

xxv

I do not yet know into what fragments
That particular star exploded when it did explode;
But that some sort of displacement has occurred
At some time during my consecutive years of absence

xxvi

Became obvious as soon as I reached the point
At the very top, when the door became visible:
A heavy chair was propped against its exterior;
The well-remembered nameplate had been removed;

xxvii

And so, knowing that such things were happening
                                        beyond me,
Whether they involved me in the slightest or not,
I picked my way hurriedly back down the stairway,
Hoping, above all else, to meet no-one quite yet.

IV

xxviii

In less than three minutes, another building received
                                        me,
Where she had lived when first I got to know her;
A wider, more spacious stairway than the others,
Leading to a door that opened for me scarcely ten
                                        times.

xxix

As I stood here, looking at a list of names,
On which, for some reason, her own did not appear,
A vague suggestion of noise behind it unnerved me,
And I hurried away before I had intended to.

xxx

Before I had had time to remember such moments
As her padding barefoot behind me to the door,
Asking me to tell her what was wrong:
Something is wrong, isn't it, something is wrong?

xxxi

And I said to her, no, nothing is wrong;
And hurried down the stairway as quickly as this;
Hearing her close the door above me after a longish
                                                    pause,
And reaching the street, in acute misery.

V

xxxii

Half an hour later, I reach the fourth doorway,
The one I am most recently aware of,
Utterly unconnected with the others,
Behind which, I now feel, lies future happiness.

xxxiii

Like the doorway I started out from, it too is on the
                                            ground floor;
And so far, the only unhappiness I have known there
Is the unhappiness of having to leave too early;
No doubt other unhappinesses will arrive in time.

xxxiv

But ah, what hopes I have of the fair occupant!
There will come an evening of stunning buoyancy,
When our nerves and our cautiousness will cancel
                                            each other out,
And love will turn that surprised air to liquid gold.

xxxv

But, at the moment, I am still a semi-stranger,
And must behave as such an oddity should;
Carefully stopping to listen outside her door,
Trying to hear her words, or the silence that is hers.

xxxvi

And then, leaning forward to the nameplate,
Delighted at the precision with which the lettering
Makes an unequivocal public reference to her,
Perhaps (surely not) the only such reference in the
                                                       city,

xxxvii

Delicately placing a lingering kiss on the nameplate,
And, even as I did so, feeling oddly proud
At being the author of that sublimated gesture,
Ridiculously immature for a man of my age.

xxxviii

There is still enough time, I hope, for the mature
                                             gesture;
I have wasted almost an hour and half, all told,
And require from here scarcely ten minutes for home.
Still there are very few people in the streets.

xxxix

And, although the city lies open to the public,
Can anyone else, in the course of a single day,
Have strung precisely those four buildings together?
A doctor, perhaps; or policemen; or only myself.

xl

Surely, even in the complexity of autobiography,
Those four doors have not opened on anyone else's
                                             life?

And those wandering restlessly along the streets
Are going to different places, in different orders.

xli

I open and shut the door of my own house;
I hurry across the common corridor,
Trying not to hear voices in other rooms,
Reach my own room, and close the door behind me.

ANGUS MARTIN (b. 1952)

Malcolm MacKerral

MacKerral, that was one hard winter.
Your father died on the moor road,
his bag of meal buried under snows.
Death relieved him of his load.

Raking wilks with freezing fingers,
your little sisters crawled the shore,
scourged by gusting showers
until their knees were raw and sore.

Your few black cattle, thin and famished,
lay and died at the far end
of the draughty common dwelling.
There was little else you owned.

In the factor's oaken-panelled room
that the shafting sunlight glossed
you looked for your reflection:
you had become a ghost.

That month a stranger entered
the green cleft of the glen.
You watched him coming, from a hill,
and stabbed the earth again.

When he returned he brought the sheep.
At the house where you were born
you closed a door behind you.
Two hundred years had gone.

There was no end to the known land.
You looked, and there were names
on every shape around you.
The language had its homes.

Words had their lives in rivers;
they coursed them to the sea.
Words were great birds on mountains,
crying down on history.

Words were stones that waited
in the silence of the fields
for the voices of the people
whose tenures there had failed.

You knew those names, MacKerral;
your father placed them in your mouth
when language had no tragic power
and you ran in your youth.

You ran in the house of the word
and pressed your face upon the glass
and watched the mute processions
of your grave ancestors pass.

Look back on what you cannot alter.
Not a stone of it is yours to turn.
All that you leave with now:
lost words for the unborn.

Forest

For Sid Gallagher

Since I lately came to live
in an old house with a fire in it,
wood has got into my vision.

I put my saw to wood
and glance a nick, and then I cut
wood into bits that please me.

Weight and form may please me,
and I am pleased to own
what at last I have to burn.

I am a Scottish wood-collector;
I belong to a great tradition
of bleeding hands and thick coats.

Wood accumulates about me;
I build it into piles,
I bag it and I lug it.

I love the look of wood:
its surfaces are maps and pictures,
and staring eyes and voiceless mouths.

Wood to the end is unresisting:
it lets me lift and drag it
far from the place that it lay down.

Wood will never fight
the blade's truncating stroke
or scream when fire consumes it.

But I had dreams of wood.
I was alone in a high forest,
sun and seasons banished.

The trees bent down their silent heads
and closed their branches round about
and I was gathered into air.

I burn in my dreams of wood,
a melting torch suspended
in the dark heart of a silent forest.

JOHN GLENDAY (b. 1952)

The Apple Ghost

A musty smell of dampness filled the room
Where wrinkled green and yellow apples lay
On folded pages from an August newspaper.

She said:
'*My husband brought them in, you understand,*
Only a week or two before he died.
He never had much truck with waste, and
I can't bring myself to throw them out.
He passed away so soon . . .'

I understood then how the wonky kitchen door,
And the old Austin, settling upon its
Softened tyres in the wooden shed,
Were paying homage to the absence of his quiet
                                                                      hands.

In the late afternoon, I opened
Shallow cupboards where the sunlight leaned on
Shelf over shelf of apples, weightless with decay.
Beneath them, sheets of faded wallpaper
Showed ponies prancing through a summer field.
This must have been the only daughter's room
Before she left for good.

I did not sleep well.

The old woman told me over breakfast
How the boards were sprung in that upper hall;
But I knew I had heard his footsteps in the night,
As he dragged his wasted body to the attic room
Where the angles of the roof slide through the walls,
And the fruit lay blighted by his helpless gaze.

I knew besides that, had I crossed to the window
On the rug of moonlight,
I would have seem him down in the frosted garden,
Trying to hang the fruit back on the tree.

DILYS ROSE (b. 1954)

Figurehead

The fog thickens.
I see no ships.
The gulls left days ago

Ebbing into the wake
Like friends grown tired
Of chasing failure.

I miss their uncouth snatch and grab
Their loud insatiable hunger.
I see nothing but fog.

Before my ever-open eyes
The horizon has closed in
The world's end dissolved.

I lumber on, grudging my status –
I'm purpose-built to dip and toss
My cleavage, crudely carved

To split waves
My hair caked with salt
My face flaking off.

Fetish

Whisper if you must
But the walls absorb all confession
    – I've run through this ritual so often
    If he insists, I make a confession
    Kid on his demand has me truly enthralled
    If that's not sufficient try *deeply appalled*.

Your wish, for the moment, is my command
I'm mistress of every disguise
Is it rubber fur leather or silk I've to use
To pull the wool over your eyes?
Watch me concoct your burning obsession
Spell out your lust, own up to your passion.

So that's all it was that you wanted
A secret so paltry – I'd never have guessed
It could send a man scouring the town.
A scrap of mock silk – I'm no longer impressed.
You looked like the type who'd know I don't tout
My quality goods. See yourself out.

JOHN BURNSIDE (b. 1955)

Out of Exile

When we are driving through the border towns
we talk of houses, empty after years
of tea and conversation;
of afternoons marooned against a clock
and silences elected out of fear,
of lives endured for what we disbelieved.

We recognise the shop fronts and the names,
the rushing trees and streets into the dark;
we recognise a pattern in the sky:
blackness flapping like a broken tent,
shadow foxes running in the stars.
But what we recognise is what we bring.

Driving, early, through the border towns,
the dark stone houses clanging at our wheels,
and we invent things as they might have been:
a light switched on, some night, against the cold,
and children at the door, with bags and coats,
telling stories, laughing, coming home.

Vallejo

Me moriré en París con aguacero

I dreamed of you in Paris:

you opened a door and stepped in from the rain
and you were standing in the hallway of
the eternal Thursday where all the dead
wait in their rented rooms;

you smelled the wax and burning vegetables
and the stale rain in your winter coat

as you climbed the stairs of
the eternal Thursday; ten francs

paid in advance to lie down
in your cold suit of hunger
beside mother and brothers and tortured bulls
in the long bed of the eternal Thursday

in the Paris of dreams where bleeding angels
hover like flies in the drapery of rain.

CAROL ANN DUFFY (b. 1955)

Politico

Corner of Thistle Street, two slack shillings jangled
in his pocket. Wee Frank. Politico. A word in the
                                        right ear
got things moving. *A free beer for they dockers
and the guns will come through in the morning. No
                                         bother.*

Bread rolls and Heavy came up the rope to the
                                       window
where he and McShane were making a stand.
                                    *Someone
sent up a megaphone, for Christ's sake.* Occupation.
Aye. And the soldiers below just biding their time.

loathesome person   Blacklisted. Bar L.* *That scunner, Churchill.* The
                                       Clyde
where men cheered theirselves out of work as
                                  champagne
butted a new ship. Spikes at the back of the toilet
                                      seat.
Alls I'm doing is fighting for wur dignity. Away.

*Smoke-filled rooms? Wait till I tell you . . . Listen,
I'm ten years dead and turning in my urn. Socialism?
These days?* There's the tree that never grew. *Och,
a shower of shites.* There's the bird that never flew.

Plainsong

Stop. Along this path, in phrases of light,
trees sing their leaves. No Midas touch
has turned the wood to gold, late in the year

* *Bar L.* Barlinnie Prison

when you pass by, suddenly sad, straining
to remember something you're sure you knew.

Listening. The words you have for things die
in your heart, but grasses are plainsong,
patiently chanting the circles-you cannot repeat
or understand. This is your homeland,
Lost One, Stranger who speaks with tears.

It is almost impossible to be here and yet
you kneel, no one's child, absolved by late sun
through the branches of a wood, distantly
the evening bell reminding you, *Home, Home,
Home*, and the stone in your palm telling the time.

In Your Mind

The other country, is it anticipated or half-
                          remembered?
Its language is muffled by the rain which falls all
                          afternoon
one autumn in England, and in your mind
you put aside your work and head for the airport
with a credit card and a warm coat you will leave
on the plane. The past fades like newsprint in the
                          sun.

You know people there. Their faces are photographs
on the wrong side of your eyes. A beautiful boy
in the bar on the harbour serves you a drink –
                          what? –
asks you if men could possibly land on the moon.
A moon like an orange drawn by a child. No.
Never. You watch it peel itself into the sea.

Sleep. The rasp of carpentry wakes you. On the wall,
a painting lost for thirty years renders the room
                          yours.

Of course. You go to your job, right at the old hotel,
                                                                    left,
then left again. You love this job. Apt sounds
mark the passing of the hours. Seagulls. Bells. A flute
practising scales. You swap a coin for a fish on the
                                                            way home.

Then suddenly you are lost but not lost, dawdling
on the blue bridge, watching six swans vanish
under your feet. The certainty of place turns on the
                                                                    lights
all over town, turns up the scent on the air. For a
                                                                    moment
you are there, in the other country, knowing its
                                                                    name.
And then a desk. A newspaper. A window. English
                                                                    rain.

MICK IMLAH (b. 1956)

Goldilocks

This is a story about the possession of beds.
It begins at the foot of a staircase in Oxford, one
                                        midnight,
When (since my flat in the suburbs of London
                                        entailed
A fiancée whose claims I did not have the nerve to
                                        evict)

I found myself grateful for climbing alone on a spiral
To sleep I could call with assurance exclusively mine,
For there was the name on the oak that the Lodge
                                        had assigned
Till the morning to me (how everything tends to its
                                        place!)

And flushed with the pleasing (if not unexpected)
                                        success
Of the paper on 'Systems of Adult-to-Infant
                                        Regression'
With which the Young Fireball had earlier baffled his
                                        betters
At the Annual Excuse for Genetics to let down its
                                        ringlets,

I'd just sniggered slightly (pushing the unlocked door
Of the room where I thought there was nothing of
                                        mine to protect)
To observe that my theory, so impudent in its
                                        address
To the Masters of Foetal Design and their perfect
                                        disciples,

Was rubbish – and leant to unfasten the window a
                                        notch, –

When I suddenly grasped with aversion before I
                                                    could see it
The fact that the bed in the corner directly behind me
Had somebody in it. A little ginger chap,

Of the sort anthropologists group in the genus of
                                                    tramp,
Was swaddled, as though with an eye to the state of
                                                    the sheets,
With half of his horrible self in the pouch of the
                                                    bedspread
And half (both his raggled and poisonous trouser-
                                                    legs) out;

Whose snore, like the rattle of bronchial stones in a
                                                    bucket,
Resounded the length and the depth and the breadth
                                                    of the problem
Of how to establish in safety a climate conducive
To kicking him out – till at last I could suffer no
                                                    longer

.The sight of his bundle of curls on my pillow, the
                                                    proof
That even the worst of us look in our sleep like the
                                                    angels
Except for a few. I closed to within a yard
And woke him, with a curt hurrahing sound.

And he reared in horror, like somebody late for work
Or a debutante subtly apprised of a welcome
                                                    outstayed,
To demand (not of me, but more of the dreary
                                                    familiar
Who exercised in its different styles the world's

Habit of persecution, and prodded him now)
Phit time is it? – so you'd think that it made any
                                                    difference –

So you'd think after all that the berth had a rota
                                        attached
And Ginger was wise to some cynical act of
                                        encroachment;

But when, with a plausible echo of fatherly firmness,
I answered, 'It's bedtime' – he popped out and stood
                                        in a shiver,
And the released smell of his timid existence swirled
Like bracing coffee between our dissimilar stances.

Was there a dim recollection of tenement stairways
And jam and the Rangers possessed him, and
                                        sounded a moment
In creaks of remorse? 'Ah'm sorry, son – Ah
                                        couldnae tell
They'd hae a wee boy sleepin here – ye know?'

(And I saw what a file of degradations queued
In his brown past, to explain how Jocky there
Could make me out to be innocent and wee:
As if to be wee was not to be dying of drink;

As if to be innocent meant that you still belonged
Where beds were made for one in particular.)
Still, the lifespan of sociable feelings is shortest of all
In the breast of the migrant Clydesider; and soon he
                                        relapsed

Into patterns of favourite self-pitying sentiments.
                                        'Son –
Ah'm warse than – Ah cannae, ye know? Ah'm off
                                        tae ma dandy!
Ah've done a wee josie – aye, wheesh! – it's warse
                                        what Ah'm gettin –
Aye – warse!' And again the appeal to heredity –
                                        'Son.'

(In the course of his speech, the impostor had
                                        gradually settled

Back on the bed, and extended as visual aids
His knocked-about knuckles; tattooed with indelible
                                              foresight
On one set of these was the purple imperative SAVE.)

Now I'm keen for us all to be just as much worse as
                                              we want,
In our own time and space – but not, after midnight,
                                              in my bed;
And to keep his inertia at bay, I went for the parasite,
Scuttling him off with a shout and the push of a boot

That reminded his ribs I suppose of a Maryhill
                                              barman's,
Until I had driven him out of the door and his cough
Could be heard to deteriorate under a clock in the
                                              landing.
(Och, if he'd known *I* was Scottish! Then I'd have
                                              got it.)

                              ✻

But of course he came back in the night, when I
                              dreamed I was coughing
And he stood by the door in the composite guise of a
                                              woman –
A mother, a doting landlady, a shadowy wife –
Sleepless as always, relieved nonetheless to have
                                              found me,

Or half-relieved – given what I had become;
Saying – 'It's just from the coughing and so on I
                                              wondered
If maybe a tramp had got into your bedroom' – and
                                              then,
Disappointedly: 'Couldn't you spare a wee thought
                                              for your dad?'

(I thought I was dreaming again on the train in the
                                        morning
To hear at my shoùlder, before I had properly settled,
'Excuse me – is this seat taken?' spastically spoken;
But it wasn't our friend that I humoured through
                                        Didcot, and Reading,

No, but an anoracked spotter of diesels from
                                        Sheffield
Whose mind was apparently out in the sidings at
                                        Crewe:
Only one more in a world of unwanted connexions,
Who waved like a child when I fled for the toilet at
                                        Ealing.)

                              *

This is my gloss on the story of Goldilocks. Note:
It uncovers a naked and difficult thought about beds,
Namely, that seldom again will there ever be one
With only you in it; take that however you will.

ELIZABETH BURNS (b. 1957)

The Oddity

She is a crooked planet: does not fit
in the thin universe of this house
that peoples itself with gentlefolk
who blink as though they do not see her
when she asks to use the library.

There is a clanking housekeeper
whose spiked mouth, licked, would give off poison,
and a cluster of maidservants
who, in the mothballed linen cupboard,
will gossip on the newcomer.

It's whispered that she's delicate
is delivered of bowls of sopped bread
bland milk puddings
but Cook sees her, the little witch,
sneaking herbs from the kitchen garden.

This household's under the thumb
of the chimes of the grandfather clock
Nothing here is tainted by imagination's kiss
and nothing queer-eyed or peculiarly skinned
gets out to roam the corridors

so that she, with her silences and pencils
her barefoot tiptoeing over the flagstones
in her old grey muslin dress
that billows out in draughty stairwells
feels freak: hears laughter

frothing in the steamy kitchen
whispers bubbling under doors,
is trailed by soft footsteps, rustling silks,
but reaches the room: a fastness:
turns the brass key in the lock behind her.

Soon there will be apron-smothered giggles
outside her door: she will rise
stuff the keyhole with a handkerchief
to block the peering eyes
then draw the shades against the lilac sky

and in thin dusk-light, take ink,
begin, in copperplate,
though hot tears plop, and blot the page,
and voices batter at her head
like scatty moths, to write.

ROBERT CRAWFORD (b. 1959)

Scotland in the 1890s

'I came across these facts which, mixed with
                                    others. . .'
Thinking of Helensburgh, J. G. Frazer
Revises flayings and human sacrifice;
Abo of the Celtic Twilight, St Andrew Lang
Posts him a ten-page note on totemism
And a coloured fairy book – an Oxford man
From Selkirk, he translates Homer in his sleep.

'When you've lived here, even for a short time,
Samoa's a bit like Scotland – there's the sea . . .
Back in Auld Reekie with a pen that sputtered
I wrote my ballad, "Ticonderoga" or
"A Legend of the West Highlands", then returned
To King Kalakaua's beach and torches –
You know my grandfather lit Lismore's south end?'

Mr Carnegie has bought Skibo Castle.
His Union Jack's sewn to the stars and stripes.
James Murray combs the dialect from his beard
And files slips for his massive *Dictionary*.
Closing a fine biography of mother,
Remembering Dumfries, and liking boys,
James Barrie, caught in pregnant London silence,
Begins to conceive the Never Never Land.

Rain

A motorbike breaks down near Sanna in torrential
                                    rain,
Pouring loud enough to perforate limousines, long
                                    enough
To wash us to Belize. Partick's

Fish-scaled with wetness. Drips shower from foliage,
                                cobbles, tourists
From New York and Dusseldorf at the tideline
smeared with mud   Shoes lost in bogs, soaked in potholes, clarted with
                                glaur.
An old woman is splashed by a bus. A gash
In cloud. Indians
Arrived this week to join their families and who do
                                not feel
Scottish one inch push onwards into a drizzle
That gets heavy and vertical. Golf umbrellas
Come up like orchids on fast-forward film; exotic
Cagoules fluoresce nowhere, speckling a hillside, and
                                plump.

Off dykes and gutters, overflowing
Ditches, a granary of water drenches the shoulders
Of Goatfell and Schiehallion. Maps under perspex go
                                bleary,
Spectacles clog, Strathclyde, Tayside, Dundee
Catch it, fingers spilling with water, oil-stained
As it comes down in sheets, blows
Where there are no trees, snow-wet, without thought
                                of the morrow.
Weddings, prunes, abattoirs, strippers, Glen Nevis,
                                snails
Blur in its democracy, down your back, on your
                                breasts.
In Kilmarnock a child walks naked. A woman laughs.
In cars, in Tiree bedrooms, in caravans and
                                tenements,
Couples sleeved in love, the gibbous Govan rain.

The Herr-Knit Bunnet

Ah glaum lik a clood amang Munros, turnin thi
                                dwang
O Scoatlan: gramlochness, thrawnness, granate
                                plotcocks, saving-trees

Ar jist scaffie tae Goad, but it's noo we need
Yon pronyeand scuddin-stanes tae shak us free
An hair butter a naishun. 'Proochie, baist, proochie!'
Ah'd scraich tae thi future – an nae tae a moartcloath
Fur haigs an snibbed haingles tae mak tairensie
owre –
But a kinna hainch tae rase thi laun oot
O bein swiffed in midsimmer an tae tak it doon
Laughin thru thi snaa wi a sairin sae yi'd ken aa its
nocks
Vieve again, thi cunt o thi yird.

Ah tell yi Ah huv seen thi herr-knit bunnet,
Nae Scoatlan's powcap o Orkneys an Arctic
But a het teuchter's bunnet purled fae human herr
Dour lik thi greek o stanes. Yon punk's
Mohican flambé, cockendy-bill-bricht, an yon
Jillet's blak strand ur menkit thegither. Ae jink
Micht skerr it awa. It's plattit oot
O thi scalps o this laun, an Ah've seen it lie
Tiree-naikit–Ah've seen ye, Scoatlan!
If yince yi wur tint Ah'd plowter owre
Yon glumshy Atlantic rubbit wi trais o gowd.
But (Goad!) lik yi ar, yir skerrs aye tappit
Wi locks o thi deid an thi manky blawn herr o thi
vivual,
Ah am in luve wi yir skaab-dark bunnet,
Douce Aranda clood-tip, moosewob atwen thi bens'
shanks
Electric wi threids o herr.

Ah've tuik tae masel thi herr-knit bunnet
Lik a poaridge spune drapt intae cream.

Author's Translation

*I grope in the dark like a cloud among high mountains,
attempting the trial of strength in trying to raise the
heavy caber of Scotland: utter worldliness, stubborn-
ness, ingrained devils, abortionists' plants that kill the
foetus in the womb are just severe passing showers as
far as God is concerned, but it's now we need those
piercing stones skimming the surface of the water to
shake us free and cleanse a nation of impurities.
'Approach, beast, approach!' I'd cry out to the future –
and not to a coffin-drape for tale-telling women and
gelded louts to make evil fury over – but a kind of
sudden throw to pluck the land out of being blown over
by sad winds in midsummer, and to take it down
laughing through the snow with a knowledge of satisfaction so that you would see its beautiful small hills
clear again, the vagina of the earth.*

*I tell you I have seen the hair-knit beret, not Scotland's
cap of Orkneys and Arctic but a hot unsophisticated
Highlander's beret stocking-stiched from human hair
grimly stubborn as the grain of stones. That punk's
Mohican flambé, bright as a puffin's bill, and that
pubertal girl's black strand are mixed together. One
elusive turn might scare it away. It is pleated out of the
scalps of this land, and I have seen it lie naked as Tiree –
I've seen you, Scotland! If once you were lost I would
wade as in a bog over the almost weeping Atlantic
rubbed with gold lace. But (God!) as you are, your bare
precipices always topped with locks of the dead and the
disgusting, woolly blown hair of the living, I am in love
with your beret dark as the bottom of the sea, gently
respectable Aranda cloud-tip, spiderweb between the
legs of the mountains electric with threads of hair.*

*I have taken to myself the hair-knit beret like a porridge
spoon dropped into cream.*

W. N. HERBERT (b. 1961)

Coco-de-Mer

don't bother with the age and unsteadiness of our loins surfeit Dinna bathir wi thi braiggil o wir lends
that maks a cothaman o gravy

cowering hearts i thi cot, but famine in wir crullit herts –

sea-swell* let gae oan thi dumbswaul, be

dolled up/float brankie i thi breakirs, an flocht,
flocht lyk thi crospunk* intae Lewis –

hands/moor thi lucky-bean tae thi haunds o thi misk.

The Derelict Birth

what/childbirth Fit barnie fur yir bairnie-haein?
– Therr's nane
i thi Inane
    wi thi mune fur a midwife,
    bricks fur a crib.

portent* Nae meddum kent o frankincense.
Th'Immense

gentle* maun hud thi mense,
    but thi mune's yir midwife,
    ash his bib

Cormundum

confession

Create in me a clean heart, O God; and renew
a right spirit within me. Psalms LI, 10

unendingly releasing, only to lose the drift of it
I confess my fault Onendanly leasin, tae anely loss
thi lease o ut, Eh creh cormundum, Eh lat

---

* *dumbswaul* a long, noiseless sea-swell in calm, windless weather (W.N.H.); *crospunk* the Molucca bean, drifted to the shores of some of the Western Islands (W.N.H.); *meddum* tickle in the nose, portending a visitor (W.N.H.); *mense* usually means common sense

a rivir gae, as tho

drain ma nostrils werr a cundie, but

sae relucktantly, aa thi Carse* Eh gee awa,

Sidlaw Hills Seedlies lyk snot, Balmarino's solitude o wreckage,

all a decoration* I'm drawn to aa a graith Eh'm draan tae, but

must leave maun laive; aa thi *grana creshentia** o
ma birthin-lands, thi verra stanes
emergin fae thir wintir snoods,
Pictland's buttirflehs o ridirs, z-rods, tunan
foarks an fans o Abernethy.* Eh gee thum up lyk

my guts
abdomen [Japanese]
in the mist ma thairms flang i thi air
ma hara i thi haar an
becumman clood —
Eh tell a leh;
Eh widna gee a smell o ut awa,

layer* of beer thi cotonar o beer that lines thi Seagate,

[seaweed]
Hilltown's
all the edible seaweed's dulse an whulks aa clingan til
thi Hulltoon's shitey pipe; aa thi tangil's reek o ut,

fish-bright/face thi fush-bricht ignorance oan ivry fiss,
thi Cox's Stack* o hung Dundee, game fur
ivry cheap hate o thi urbin, thi wurkir turnin oan
thi wurkir lyk
a cannibal turbine, let alane merry Inglan (aye —
lat well alane) —
Eh cudna gee

crab's shell a cartie o ut awa, a

crab's mussil's shell, a partin's fart: this

is Scoatlan's braith draggin lyk a serpint owre

cobblestoned road thi causie o ma spine: exhale thi haill

---

*Carse low-lying river-lands, e.g. Carse of Gowrie, etc.; *graith* appropriate tools or decorations for a task or ceremony (W.N.H.); *grana creshentia* a rent in corn, here metaphorically a birth-right (W.N.H.); *ridirs, z-rods, tunan foarks an fans o Abernethy* all representations, shapes or symbols on Pictish carved stones; *cotonar* a piece of some small fur, used for lining (W.N.H.); *Cox's Stack* was Dundee's highest jute chimney, in Lochee (W.N.H.)

collection*   bagdalin oot, inhale
whirlpools   thi bullirs o'ut,

                                                            this Disnaeland, this
                                            Brokendoon, Eh breath ut,
breath   aynd withoot end, Eh am
                                            thi coontircheck* that cuts thi groove
on which our severed head and   oan whilk oor severt heid an erse o gless
glass arse
of nothing, the stars   sall open til thir celsitudes o noth, thi stern.

* *bagdalin* anything used to line the hold of a ship before putting the cargo in (w.n.h.); *coontircheck* tool for cutting
the groove that unites two sashes of a window (w.n.h)

JACKIE KAY (b. 1961)

Dance of the Cherry Blossom

Both of us are getting worse
Neither knows who had it first

He thinks I gave it to him
I think he gave it to me

Nights chasing clues where
One memory runs into another like dye.

Both of us are getting worse
I know I'm wasting precious time

But who did he meet between
May 87 and March 89.

I feel his breath on my back
A slow climb into himself then out.

In the morning it all seems different
Neither knows who had it first

We eat breakfast together – newspapers
And silence except for the slow slurp of tea

This companionship is better than anything
He thinks I gave it to him.

By lunchtime we're fighting over some petty thing
He tells me I've lost my sense of humour

I tell him I'm not Glaswegian
You all think death is a joke

It's not funny. I'm dying for fuck's sake
I think he gave it to me.

Just think he says it's every couple's dream
I won't have to wait for you up there

I'll have you night after night – your glorious legs
Your strong hard belly, your kissable cheeks

I cry when he says things like that
My shoulders cave in, my breathing trapped

Do you think you have a corner on dying
You self-pitying wretch, pathetic queen.

He pushes me; we roll on the floor like whirlwind;
When we are done in, our lips find each other

We touch soft as breeze, caress the small parts
Rocking back and forth, his arms become mine

There's nothing outside but the noise of the wind
The cherry blossom's dance through the night.

KATHLEEN JAMIE (b. 1962)

Black Spiders

He looked up to the convent
she'd gone to. She answered no questions
but he knew by the way she'd turned away
that morning.
He felt like swimming to the caves.

*

The nuns have retreated. The eldest still
peals the bell in glee, although no one comes
from the ruins. All their praying was done
when they first saw the ships and the Turks'
swords reflecting the sun.

In the convent the cistern is dry,
the collection boxes empty – cleft skulls
severed and bleached,
are kept in a shrine, and stare to the East.

*

She caught sight of him later, below, brushing salt
from the hair of his nipples. She wanted them
to tickle; black spiders on her lips.

Aunt Janet's Museum

What can be gained by rushing these things?
Huddle in from the rain, compose ourselves, let
a forefinger rest on the bell button which
requests kindly 'p   s'. We wait, listening
to bus tyres on rain say 'hush' and 'west'.
People hurry behind us, we wait,
for shuffling inside the door,
tumbling locks, and admission to dark.

One after the other we make up the stair.
No one looks back, we know what's there,
fear what lies ahead may disappear. Could we
forget these ritual sounds, or alter their order?
Scuffle of feet on the narrow stair,
the alcove, the turn where
pallid light faints through the glass of the doors.

Let it be right. She takes the handle, still
softly exclaiming over our height, and lets her weight
drop it. The click of the latch. She pushes the door
till the shop bell above gives a delicate ting.
Sounds of inside step forward. The faraway drill
of bells warning the kitchen, and the fallible clock.

The Way We Live

Pass the tambourine, let me bash out praises
to the Lord God of movement, to Absolute
non-friction, flight, and the scary side:
death by avalanche, birth by failed contraception.
Of chicken tandoori and reggae, loud, from

                                              tenements,
commitment, driving fast and unswerving
friendship. Of tee-shirts on pulleys, giros and

                                              Bombay,
barmen, dreaming waitresses with many fake-gold
bangles. Of airports, impulse, and waking to

                                              uncertainty,
to strip-lights, motorways, or that pantheon –
the mountains. To overdrafts and grafting

and the fit slow pulse of wipers as you're
creeping over Rannoch, while the God of moorland
walks abroad with his entourage of freezing fog,
his bodyguard of snow.
Of endless gloaming in the North, of Asiatic swelter,
to launderettes, anecdotes, passions and exhaustion,
Final Demands and dead men, the skeletal grip

of government. To misery and elation; mixed,
the sod and caprice of landlords.
To the way it fits, the way it is, the way it seems
to be: let me bash out praises – pass the tambourine.

DON PATERSON (b. 1963)

Nil Nil

Just as any truly accurate representation of a particular geography can only exist on a scale of 1:1 (imagine the vast, rustling map of Burgundy, say, settling over it like a freshly starched sheet!) so it is with all our abandoned histories, those ignoble lines of succession that end in neither triumph nor disaster, but merely plunge on into deeper and deeper obscurity; only in the infinite ghost-libraries of the imagination – their only possible analogue – can their ends be pursued, the dull and terrible facts finally authenticated.

François Aussemain, *Pensées*

From the top, then, the zenith, the silent footage:
McGrandle, majestic in ankle-length shorts,
his golden hair shorn to an open book, sprinting
the length of the park for the long hoick forward,
his balletic toe-poke nearly bursting the roof
of the net; a shaky pan to the Erskine St End
where a plague of grey bonnets falls out of the
           clouds.
But ours is a game of two halves, and this game
the semi they went on to lose; from here
it's all down, from the First to the foot of the Second,
McGrandle, Visocchi and Spankie detaching
like bubbles to speed the descent into pitch-sharing,
pay-cuts, pawned silver, the Highland Division,
the absolute sitters ballooned over open goals,
the dismal nutmegs, the scores so obscene
no respectable journal will print them; though one
           day
Farquhar's spectacular bicycle-kick
will earn him a name-check in Monday's obituaries.

Besides the one setback – the spell of giant-killing
in the Cup (Lochee Violet, then Aberdeen Bon Accord,
the deadlock with Lochee Harp finally broken
by Farquhar's own-goal in the replay)
nothing inhibits the fifty-year slide
into Sunday League, big tartan flasks,
open hatchbacks parked squint behind goal-nets,
the half-time satsuma, the dog on the pitch,
then the Boy's Club, sponsored by Skelly Assurance,
then Skelly Dry Cleaners, then nobody;
stud-harrowed pitches with one-in-five inclines,
grim fathers and perverts with Old English Sheepdogs
lining the touch, moaning softly.
Now the unrefereed thirty-a-sides,
terrified fat boys with calipers minding
four jackets on infinite, notional fields;
ten years of dwindling, half-hearted kickabouts
leaves two little boys – Alastair Watt,   •
who answers to 'Forty', and wee Horace Madden,
so smelly the air seems to quiver above him –
playing desperate two-touch with a bald tennis ball
in the hour before lighting-up time.
Alastair cheats, and goes off with the ball
leaving wee Horace to hack up a stone
and dribble it home in the rain;
past the stopped swings, the dead shanty-town
of allotments, the black shell of Skelly Dry Cleaners
and into his cul-de-sac, where, accidentally,
he neatly back-heels it straight into the gutter
then tries to swank off like he meant it.

Unknown to him, it is all that remains
of a lone fighter-pilot, who, returning at dawn
to find Leuchars was not where he'd left it,
took time out to watch the Sidlaws unsheathed
from their great black tarpaulin, the haar burn off
                                        Tayport
and Venus melt into Carnoustie, igniting
the shoreline; no wind, not a cloud in the sky

and no one around to admire the discretion
of his unscheduled exit: the engine plopped out
and would not re-engage, sending him silently
twirling away like an ash-key,
his attempt to bail out only partly successful,
yesterday having been April the 1st –
the ripcord unleashing a flurry of socks
like a sackful of doves rendered up to the heavens
in private irenicon. He caught up with the plane
on the ground, just at the instant the tank blew
and made nothing of him, save for his fillings,
his tackets, his lucky half-crown and his gallstone,
now anchored between the steel bars of a stank
that looks to be biting the bullet on this one.

In short, this is where you get off, reader;
I'll continue alone, on foot, in the failing light,
following the trail as it steadily fades
into road-repairs, birdsong, the weather, nirvana,
the plot thinning down to a point so refined
not even the angels could dance on it. Goodbye.

ANGELA MCSEVENEY (b. 1964)

Night Shift

I would wake up when I heard Dad
coming in at the front door.

The others slept through his early morning noises:
a toilet flush, one cup of tea boiling.

There seemed no place for him
at home all day Saturday
and most of Sunday.

His skin paled
apart from one weather-beaten patch
at his throat.

'It's no life for a man,' he sometimes grumbled
'this living like a mole.'

During school holidays I made
no noise at home.

Mum went to parents' nights alone,
She was sick of darning where industrial acid
ate away his clothes.

At five o'clock I'd be sent
to waken Dad for tea.

The curtains in my parents' room
were almost always closed.

The Lump

Rolling over in a hot June night
I cradled my breasts in my arms
and felt a hard knot of tissue.

I was fifteen.
My life rose up in my throat
and threatened to stifle me.

It took three attempts to tell my mother.
She promised that my appointment would be
with a woman doctor.

A nurse called my name.
I didn't have cancer.

The stitches in my skin reminded me
of a chicken trussed for the oven.

I felt ashamed
that the first man to see me
had only been doing his job.

Acknowledgements

For permission to reprint copyright material the publishers gratefully acknowledge the following:

IAN ABBOT: 'The Mechanisms of the Gin' and 'A Body of Work' from *Avoiding the Gods* (Chapman, 1988) by permission of Chapman

MARION ANGUS: 'Alas! Poor Queen' from *Selected Poems* (Serif Books, 1950) by permission of Faber and Faber Limited

D. M. BLACK: 'From the Privy Council' and 'Kew Gardens' from *Collected Poems 1964–87* (Polygon, 1991) by permission of Polygon

ALAN BOLD: 'June 1967 at Buchenwald', 'Grass', 'A Special Theory of Relativity', 'Love-Lowe' and 'The Auld Symie' by permission of the author

GEORGE MACKAY BROWN: 'The Funeral of Ally Flett' and 'Hamnavoe Market' from *Poems New and Selected* (The Hogarth Press, 1971), 'Island School' from *The Wreck of the Archangel* (John Murray, 1989), and 'Old Fisherman with Guitar', 'Trout Fisher', 'The Five Voyages of Arnor', 'Kirkyard', 'Taxman' *from* 'Runes from a Holy Island', and 'Beachcomber' from *Selected Poems 1954–1983* (John Murray, 1991) by permission of John Murray (Publishers) Ltd

ELIZABETH BURNS: 'The Oddity' from *Ophelia and Other Poems* (Polygon, 1991) by permission of Polygon

JOHN BURNSIDE: 'Out of Exile' and 'Vallejo' from *The Hoop* (Carcanet Press, 1988) by permission of Carcanet Press Limited

RON BUTLIN: 'This Evening', 'Night-life', 'Inheritance' and 'Claiming My Inheritance' from *Ragtime in Unfamiliar Bars* (Secker & Warburg, 1985) © Ron Butlin, 1985, by permission of Martin Secker and Warburg Limited

NORMAN CAMERON: 'She and I', 'Forgive Me, Sire', 'A Visit to the Dead' and 'Green, Green, is El Aghir' from *Collected Poems*, edited by W. Hope and J. Barker (Anvil Press, 1989) by permission of Anvil Press Poetry Ltd

STEWART CONN: 'Todd', 'On Craigie Hill', 'The Yard', 'Summer Afternoon', 'To My Father' and 'Under the Ice' from *In the Kibble Palace: New and Selected Poems* (Bloodaxe Books, 1987) by permission of Bloodaxe Books Ltd

ROBERT CRAWFORD: 'Scotland in the 1890s' and 'Rain' from *A Scottish Assembly* (Chatto & Windus, 1990) by permission of Random Century Group, and 'The Herr-Knit Bunnet' from *Sharawaggi* (Polygon, 1990) by permission of Polygon

HELEN B. CRUICKSHANK: 'The Ponnage Pool' from *Collected Poems* (Reprographia, 1971) by permission of A. C. Hunter

IVOR CUTLER: 'The Purposeful Culinary Instruments' from *Many Flies Have Feathers* (Trigram Press, 1973), and 'The Darkness' and 'The Railway Sleepers' from *A Flat Man* (Trigram Press, 1977) by permission of the author

JOHN DAVIDSON: 'Snow' from *The Poems of John Davidson*, edited by Andrew

Turnbull, 2 vols. (Scottish Academic Press, 1973) by permission of Scottish Academic Press Limited

JOHN DIXON: 'The Secret Garden' from *Scots Baronial* (Polygon, 1991) by permission of Polygon

CAROL ANN DUFFY: 'Politico' and 'Plainsong' from *Selling Manhattan* (Anvil Press, 1987), and 'In Your Mind' from *The Other Country* (Anvil Press, 1990) by permission of Anvil Press Poetry Ltd

G. F. DUTTON: 'street' and 'clach eanchainn' from *Squaring the Waves* (Bloodaxe Books, 1986) by permission of Bloodaxe Books Ltd

ALISON FELL: 'Desire' and 'Pushing Forty' from *Kisses for Mayakovsky* (Virago Press, 1984) by permission of Peake Associates, and 'Freeze-frame' from *The Crystal Owl* (Methuen, 1988) © 1988 by Alison Fell, by permission of Methuen, London and Peake Associates

VERONICA FORREST-THOMSON: 'Strike' from *Collected Poems and Translations* (London, Lewes, Berkeley: Allardyce, Barnett, Publishers, 1990) Copyright © Jonathan Culler and The Estate of Veronica Forrest-Thomson 1990. Editorial matter Copyright © Anthony Barnett 1990. First printed in Veronica Forrest-Thomson, *Cordelia: or 'A Poem Should Not Mean, but Be'*. Copyright © Veronica Forrest-Thomson 1974; reprinted in Veronica Forrest-Thomson, *On the Periphery*. Copyright © Jonathan Culler 1976, by permission of Allardyce, Barnett, Publishers

ALASTAIR FOWLER: 'Catacomb Suburb' from *Catacomb Suburb* (Edinburgh University Press, 1976) by permission of Edinburgh University Press, and 'Relative' from *From the Domain of Arnheim* (Secker & Warburg, 1982). © Alastair Fowler, 1982, by permission of Martin Secker and Warburg Limited

ROBIN FULTON: 'Remembering an Island' and 'Travelling Alone' from *Selected Poems 1963–1978* (Macdonald Publishers, 1980) by permission of the author, and 'Museums and Journeys', 'Stopping by Shadows', 'Resolutions' and 'Remembering Walls' from *Fields of Focus* (Anvil Press, 1982) by permission of Anvil Press Poetry Ltd

ROBERT GARIOCH: 'Embro to the Ploy', 'To Robert Fergusson', 'The Wire', 'Property', 'Glisk of the Great', 'Heard in the Cougate', 'At Robert Fergusson's Grave', 'Elegy', 'In Princes Street Gairdens' and 'Merulius Lacrymans' from *Complete Poetical Works* (Macdonald Publishers, 1983) by permission of The Saltire Society

VALERIE GILLIES: 'Fellow Passenger' and 'The Piano-tuner' from *Each Bright Eye* (Canongate, 1977), and 'Young Harper' and 'The Ericstane Brooch' from *The Chanter's Tune* (Canongate, 1990) by permission of Canongate Press Plc

JOHN GLENDAY: 'The Apple Ghost' from *The Apple Ghost* (Peterloo Poets, 1989) by permission of Peterloo Poets

W. S. GRAHAM: 'The Children of Greenock', *from* 'Seven Letters – II and VI', 'Baldy Bane', 'Malcolm Mooney's Land', 'The Lying Dear', 'The Night City', 'Johann Joachim Quantz's Five Lessons' and 'The Stepping Stones' from *Collected Poems 1942–1977* (Faber, 1979) by permission of Mrs W. S. Graham

ALASDAIR GRAY: 'Awakening' from *Old Negatives* (Jonathan Cape, 1989) by permission of Random Century Group

SIR ALEXANDER GRAY: 'Scotland' from *Selected Poems* (William MacLellan, n.d.) by permission of Stuart Titles Ltd

ANDREW GREIG: 'In the Tool-shed' from *Surviving Passages* (Canongate, 1982) by permission of the author, and 'The Winter Climbing' and 'The Maid & I' from *The Order of the Day* (Bloodaxe Books, 1990) by permission of Bloodaxe Books Ltd

CHRISTOPHER MURRAY GRIEVE — see HUGH MacDIARMID

GEORGE CAMPBELL HAY: 'Bisearta'/'Bizerta' and 'Atman'/'Atman' from *Modern Scottish Gaelic Poems*, edited by D. Macaulay (Southside, 1976) by permission of Canongate Press Plc

HAMISH HENDERSON: 'Seven Good Germans' from *Elegies for the Dead in Cyrenaica* (Polygon, 1990) by permission of Polygon

W. N. HERBERT: 'Coco-de-Mer', 'The Derelict Birth' and 'Cormundum' from *Sharawaggi* (Polygon, 1990) by permission of Polygon

MICK IMLAH: 'Goldilocks' from *Birthmarks* (Chatto & Windus, 1988) by permission of Random Century Group

KATHLEEN JAMIE: 'Black Spiders', 'Aunt Janet's Museum' and 'The Way We Live' from *The Way We Live* (Bloodaxe Books, 1987) by permission of Bloodaxe Books Ltd

JACKIE KAY: 'Dance of the Cherry Blossom' from *The Adoption Papers* (Bloodaxe Books, 1991) by permission of Bloodaxe Books Ltd

FRANK KUPPNER: 'Passing Through Doorways' from *The Intelligent Observation of Naked Women* (Carcanet Press, 1987) by permission of Carcanet Press Limited

TOM LEONARD: 'Six Glasgow Poems', 'Poetry', 'Jist ti Let Yi No', 'Paroakial', 'Feed Ma Lamz', *from* 'Unrelated Incidents', *from* 'Ghostie Men' and 'Fathers and Sons' from *Intimate Voices: Selected Work 1965–1983* (Galloping Dog Press, 1984) by permission of the author

LIZ LOCHHEAD: 'Dreaming Frankenstein', 'Heartbreak Hotel', 'Mirror's Song', 'The Grim Sisters', *from* 'The Furies' and 'My Mother's Suitors' from *Dreaming Frankenstein and Collected Poems* (Polygon, 1984) by permission of Polygon

GEORGE MACBETH: 'An Ode to English Food', 'The Renewal' and 'Draft for an Ancestor' from *Collected Poems 1958–1982* (Hutchinson, 1989) Copyright © George MacBeth, 1989, by permission of Sheil Land Associates Ltd

BRIAN MCCABE: 'Spring's Witch' from *Spring's Witch* (Mariscat, 1984) by permission of Mariscat Publishers, and 'The Blind' and 'This is Thursday' from *One Atom to Another* (Polygon, 1987) by permission of Polygon

NORMAN MACCAIG: 'Summer Farm', 'Drifter', 'Crofter's Kitchen, Evening', 'Half-built Boat in a Hayfield', 'Explicit Snow', 'Celtic Cross', 'Feeding Ducks', 'Things in Each Other', 'The Shore Road', 'Byre', 'Loch Sionascaig', 'July Evening', 'Porpoises', 'Looking Down on Glen Canisp', 'Blue Tit on a String of Peanuts', 'Old Edinburgh', 'Basking Shark', 'Intruder in a Set Scene' and 'No Interims in History' from

Collected Poems (Chatto & Windus, 1990) by permission of Random Century Group

HUGH MACDIARMID (Christopher Murray Grieve): 'The Bonnie Broukit Bairn', 'The Watergaw', 'The Eemis Stane', 'Scunner', 'Empty Vessel', *from* 'A Drunk Man Looks at the Thistle', 'First Hymn to Lenin', 'Water Music', 'Ho, My Little Sparrow', 'On a Raised Beach' and 'Harry Semen' from *Selected Poems of Hugh MacDiarmid* (Carcanet Press, 1992) by permission of Carcanet Press Limited

WILLIAM MCILVANNEY: 'Bless This House', 'The Song Mickey Heard at the Bottom of his Pint in the Zodiac Bar' and 'Passing Through Petra' from *In Through the Head* (Mainstream Publishing, 1988) by permission of Mainstream Publishing Co. (Edinburgh) Ltd

ALASTAIR MACKIE: *from* 'Back-Green Odyssey' from *Ingaitherins. Selected Poems* (Aberdeen University Press, 1987) by permission of Aberdeen University Press

SORLEY MACLEAN: 'Gaoir na h-Eòrpa'/'The Cry of Europe', 'Am Bata Dubh'/'The Black Boar', 'Ban-Ghàidheal'/'A Highland Woman', 'Calbharaigh'/'Calvary', 'Clann Ghill-Eain'/'The Clan MacLean', 'Dol an Iar'/'Going Westwards', 'Glac a' Bhàis'/ 'Death Valley', 'Curaidhean'/'Heroes' and 'Hallaig'/'Hallaig' from *From Wood to Ridge: Collected Poems in Gaelic and English* (Carcanet Press, 1989) by permission of Carcanet Press Limited

AONGHAS MACNEACAIL: 'dol dhachaigh – 2'/'going home – 2', 'gleann fademach'/ 'glen remote' and *from* 'an cathadh mor'/*from* 'the great snowbattle' from *an seachnadh agus dain eile. The avoiding and other poems* (Macdonald Publishers, 1986) by permission of The Saltire Society

ANGELA MCSEVENEY: 'Night Shift' and 'The Lump' from *Coming Out with It* (Polygon, 1992) by permission of Polygon

GERALD MANGAN: 'Glasgow 1956', 'Heraclitus at Glasgow Cross' and 'Nights in Black Valley' from *Waiting for the Storm* (Bloodaxe Books, 1990) by permission of Bloodaxe Books Ltd

ANGUS MARTIN: 'Malcolm MacKerral' and 'Forest' from *The Larch Plantation* (Macdonald Publishers, 1990) by permission of The Saltire Society

ELMA MITCHELL: 'Thoughts after Ruskin' from *People Etcetera: Poems New & Selected* (Peterloo Poets, 1987) by permission of Peterloo Poets

WILLIAM MONTGOMERIE: 'The Edge of the War' from *From Time to Time* (Canongate, 1985) by permission of Canongate Press Plc

EDWIN MORGAN: 'The Starlings in George Square', 'The Second Life', 'Glasgow Sonnets', 'The First Men on Mercury', 'Cinquevalli', 'The Dowser' and *from* 'Sonnets from Scotland: "Pilate at Fortingall", "De Quincey in Glasgow", "Post-Referendum", "After a Death" and "The Coin" ' from *Collected Poems* (Carcanet Press, 1990) by permission of Carcanet Press Limited

EDWIN MUIR: 'Childhood', 'The Town Betrayed', 'Scotland 1941', 'The Ring', 'The Castle', 'The Labyrinth', 'The Combat', 'One Foot in Eden', 'To Franz Kafka', 'The Difficult Land' and 'The Horses' from *Collected Poems* (Faber, 1960) by permission of Faber and Faber Limited

WILLIAM NEILL: 'Map Makers' from *Wild Places* (Luath Press, 1985), and 'De A Thug Ort Sgriobhadh Ghaidhlig?'/'What Compelled You to Write in Gaelic?' from *Making Tracks* (Gordon Wright Publishing Ltd, 1988) by permission of the author

DON PATERSON: 'Nil Nil' from *Nil Nil* (Faber, 1993) by permission of Faber and Faber Limited

TOM POW: 'Saint Medan' from *The Moth Trap* (Canongate, 1990) by permission of Canongate Press Plc

ALASTAIR REID: 'A Lesson for Beautiful Women', 'Scotland', 'Isle of Arran' and 'James Bottle's Year' from *Weathering* (Canongate, 1978) by permission of Canongate Press Plc

DILYS ROSE: 'Figurehead' and 'Fetish' from *Madame Doubtfire's Dilemma* (Chapman, 1989) by permission of Chapman

CHRISTOPHER SALVESEN: 'Ninian Winyet', 'History of Strathclyde' and 'Among the Goths' from *Among the Goths* (Mariscat, 1986) by permission of Mariscat Publishers

TOM SCOTT: 'The Mankind Toun' from *The Ship, and Ither Poems* (OUP, 1963) by permission of the author

BURNS SINGER: 'A Sort of Language', 'Peterhead in May', 'For Josef Herman' and 'SOS Lifescene' from *Selected Poems*, edited by A. Cluysenaar (Carcanet Press, 1977) by permission of Carcanet Press Limited

IAN CRICHTON SMITH: 'Highlanders' and 'Poem in March' from *The Law and the Grace* (Eyre & Spottiswoode, 1965) © 1965 by Ian Crichton Smith, by permission of the author, extracts from 'By the Sea' from *Selected Poems* (Gollancz, 1970) by permission of Victor Gollancz Ltd, 'The Clearances' and 'Gaelic Stories' from *Selected Poems 1955–1980* (Macdonald Publishers, 1981) by permission of The Saltire Society, 'The Law and the Grace', *from* 'The White Air of March', 'Shall Gaelic Die?', 'Gaelic Songs', 'Christmas 1971', 'The Glass of Water', 'How Often I Feel Like You' and 'Chinese Poem' from *Selected Poems* (Carcanet Press, 1985), three extracts from *A Life* (Carcanet Press, 1986), and 'Listen' from *The Village* (Carcanet Press, 1989) by permission of Carcanet Press Limited

SYDNEY GOODSIR SMITH: *from* 'Armageddon in Albyn', 'The Grace of God and the Meth-Drinker', 'Time Be Brief', 'Omens', 'As My Life' and *from* 'Under The Eidon Tree – V: Slugabed' from *Collected Poems* (John Calder, 1975) Copyright © John Calder (Publishers) Ltd 1975. By permission of Calder Publications Ltd

WILLIAM SOUTAR: 'The Tryst', 'The Guns', 'The Hungry Mauchs', 'Song' and 'The Makar' from *The Poems of William Soutar* edited by W. R. Aitken (Scottish Academic Press, 1988) by permission of The Trustees of The National Library of Scotland

MURIEL SPARK: 'Going up to Sotheby's', 'Against the Transcendentalists', 'Elegy in a Kensington Churchyard' and 'Litany of Time Past' from *Going Up to Sotheby's, and Other Poems* (Granada Publishing, 1982) by permission of David Higham Associates Limited

DERICK THOMSON: 'Dà Thaibhse'/'Two Ghosts', 'An Tobar'/'The Well', 'Srath

Nabhair'/'Strathnaver', 'Eilean Chaluim Chille, an Loch Eiriosort, Leòdhas'/'St Columba's Isle, Loch Erisort, Lewis', 'Clann-Nighean an Sgadain'/'The Herring Girls', 'Dùn Nan Gall'/'Donegal', 'Cisteachan-Laighe'/'Coffins' and 'An Dàrna Eilean'/'The Second Island' from *Creachadh na clarsaich . . . : Plundering the Harp. Collected Poems 1940–1980* (Macdonald Publishers, 1982) by permission of The Saltire Society

RUTHVEN TODD: 'Trout Flies' and 'Of Moulds and Mushrooms' from *Garland for the Winter Solstice* (Dent, 1961) by permission of David Higham Associates Limited

SYDNEY TREMAYNE: 'Legend', 'A Burial' and 'Wanting News' from *Selected and New Poems* (Chatto & Windus, 1973) Copyright © Sydney Tremayne, 1973, by permission of Sheil Land Associates Ltd

RAYMOND VETESSE: 'Prologue', 'My Carrion Words' and 'The Vieve Cry' from *The Richt Noise* (Macdonald Publishers, 1988) by permission of The Saltire Society

KENNETH WHITE: 'The House at the Head of the Tide', and *from* 'Late August on the Coast' from *The Bird Path: Collected Longer Poems* (Mainstream Publishing, 1989) by permission of Mainstream Publishing Co. (Edinburgh) Ltd

ANDREW YOUNG: 'On the Pilgrim's Road', 'The Stockdoves', 'A Heap of Faggots', 'A Prehistoric Camp', 'Passing the Graveyard', 'Sudden Thaw' and 'The Shepherd's Hut' from *The Poetical Works* (Secker & Warburg, 1985) by permission of The Estate of Andrew Young

DOUGLAS YOUNG: 'For a Wife in Jizzen', 'Sainless' and 'The Shepherd's Dochter' from *A Clear Voice: Douglas Young, Poet and Polymath*, edited by C. Young and D. Murison (Macdonald Publishers, 1976) by permission of The Saltire Society

Faber and Faber Limited apologize for any errors or omissions in the above list and would be grateful to be notified of any corrections that should be incorporated in the next edition or reprint of this volume.

Index of Poets

Index of Titles